Life and Letters in France

Life and Letters in France
General Editor
Austin Gill CBE, MA
Marshall Professor of French,
University of Glasgow

Other volumes

The Seventeenth Century
W D Howarth MA

The Eighteenth Century
R Fargher B Lit, MA, D Phil

Life and Letters in France

in France

The Nineteenth Century

A W Raitt, MA, DPhil
Fellow of Magdalen College, Oxford

Charles Scribner's Sons New York

A - 8.71 (I)

Printed in Great Britain by Fletcher & Son, Ltd, Norwich
Library of Congress Catalog Card Number 74-166299
SBN 684-12619-2 (college paper)
SBN 684-12618-4 (trade cloth)

Preface

The type of commentary presented in this series is not meant to serve as an alternative to, and still less to compete with, the close analytical study known as *l'explication de textes*. It is intended rather as a complement, fulfilling a need which teachers of French literature in this country are acutely aware of, and which *la lecture expliquée* on the normal lines cannot conveniently satisfy. Our pupils are not equipped, like those brought up in French schools, with the knowledge of French history, political, social, economic and cultural, which should be brought to the understanding and appreciation of French authors. On that side of their study they need help which a method devised for teaching French literature in France does not afford. It is to the familiar problem of how best to give this help that the *Life and Letters in France* series suggests an answer. How good the answer may be, experience must decide, but *a priori* the method has some promising advantages. It places the historical facts not in an historian's arrangement, but in perspectives directly relevant to the study of literature. Also, since the historical commentary is always directed to the explanation of particular passages, the literary usefulness of a knowledge of history (about which students are often sceptical) is constantly illustrated.

The extent to which our understanding of literature is thus sharpened and deepened by systematic attention to what is conveniently called historical background depends a good deal on the nature of the works studied, and the choice of passages for commentary naturally reflects that fact. The passages are varied enough to show that the method is appropriate to many different kinds of work, but it is not claimed that they represent adequately the variety of French literature at any period in its history. Nor, on the other hand, do the commentaries in any of the volumes attempt to cover, taken together, all the main aspects of background for the century concerned. It was desirable to aim at diversity, but it would have been foolish to try to be complete.

Such, in rather bare outline, is what we have attempted. The authors of the different volumes, and I, are all tutors in French in Oxford colleges. That is a fair guarantee, I hope, that we have kept firmly in view the practical aim of teaching our compatriots to read French literature with profit and enjoyment. It is as tutors also that we particularly wish to guard against two possible misunderstandings. First, what we are proposing is a technique for teaching and learning; it has nothing to do with examining. Secondly, our concern here for historical aspects of the study of literature does not mean that those are the aspects which all or any of us are most interested in, or as teachers would stress most. The commentaries themselves make it quite clear, I believe, that their authors are alive to the strictly literary qualities of the passages they are discussing.

A.G.

Contents

List of Plates

Acknowledgments

For permission to reproduce photographs, the author makes grateful acknowledgment to the Académie de Paris (Plate VI: photo H. Roger-Viollet, Paris); the Assemblée Nationale (Plate III: photo B. J. Harris, Oxford); the Bibliothèque Nationale (Plates I, II, IV, V and VIII); and the Musée de l'Armée (Plate VII: photo J.-E. Bulloz, Paris).

Introduction

ONE'S first impression on comparing the literary history of nine-teenth-century France with that of other centuries is of a dramatic foreshortening of perspective. Classicism, Romanticism, *l'art pour l'art*, Parnassianism, Realism, Naturalism, Symbolism—all these schools, to say nothing of innumerable independent writers, follow one another so rapidly within the space of less than a hundred years that it would be as legitimate to speak of simultaneity as of succession.[1] The longevity of Victor Hugo shows up the speed and extent of the changes which swept over literature. Born in 1802, when the classical aesthetic still held sway, he took the leading part in mobilising the Romantic revolution of 1830; from then until 1885, he continued to write what remained essentially Romantic poetry, and with such success that his figure seemed to dwarf all his competitors. But in the meantime, the Parnasse had come and gone again, at least as a living force; realism had had its heyday; Baudel-aire was long since dead; Mallarmé and Verlaine had produced the bulk of their best work; Moréas was on the point of issuing the mani-festo of Symbolism; and Naturalism had become so much an accepted part of the literary scene that only six years later one of Zola's disciples was moved to telegraph to an inquiring journalist: 'Naturalisme pas mort. Lettre suit'. The constant evolution from one conception of literature to another and the regular clash of opposing opinions make the period singularly rich, varied and exciting. They also give it a character hitherto unknown in the progress of French literature, since it is the first time that so many widely differing views on the nature and function of art had confronted each other simultaneously.

Not that the changes are always as drastic as they at first appear. The vilification of pseudo-Classicism by the Romantics did not exclude the persistence of Classical habits of thought and style in their own writings, which meant that French Romanticism, seen in the context of European literature, remained a relatively moderate, even timorous movement.

[1] That is why the passages in this book are not arranged in the order in which they were written, but in the approximate order of appearance of the preoccupations which lie behind them.

Equally, the development of Realism, if it led to a radical criticism of the Romantic use of imagination, was itself set in motion by the Romantic insistence on *couleur locale*. Certain features of the Romantic temperament—reliance on the irrational forces of the human personality, longing for an impossible ideal, love of the flamboyant in style and invention—continue to mark new authors long after the official demise of the movement. Neither Flaubert nor Baudelaire could shake off their Romantic heredity; whatever disguises he imposed on them, Zola's lurid and incredible visions were fundamentally Romantic; and the Symbolists made no secret of their affiliation to Romanticism. Sometimes differences were artificially magnified by the natural exaggeration of polemics. For instance, the supporters of the ideal of *l'art pour l'art* were undoubtedly tempted into overstating their indifference to contemporary problems by the zealous didacticism of their utilitarian colleagues, and when one divests Zola's novels of the specious theoretical jargon in which he was wont to pronounce on them, it becomes clear that his use of symbols is almost as consistent as Mallarmé's. These factors of unconscious assimilation and over-stimulated reaction modify somewhat the original picture of dozens of warring sects: the fact nevertheless remains that the rate of change in literary taste accelerated in the nineteenth century as never before, and that real and basic divergences of opinion were continually coming to light.

The reasons for this acceleration are various. Perhaps the most important of them is, paradoxically, the conservatism of French literature until the early nineteenth century. The strength and antiquity of the classical tradition in France, unequalled elsewhere in Europe, had as its consequence a deeply entrenched resistance to change which delayed the advent of Romanticism there for some twenty or thirty years after it had established itself, in one form or another, in England and Germany. If one takes 1830 as the high-water mark of French Romanticism, one notices that the first generation of Romantics in other countries was already passing away. The *Lyrical Ballads* of Wordsworth were published in 1798, the same year as some of Coleridge's most characteristic poems; Keats died in 1821, Shelley in 1822, Byron in 1824. Likewise, in Germany, the *Sturm und Drang*, which partially prefigures Romanticism, flourished in the 1770s; by 1830, Wackenroder, Novalis, Kleist and Hoffmann were all dead. In other words, French Romanticism was a belated arrival on the international scene and got into its stride only when its fellow movements elsewhere were already declining. The evolution of post-Romantic literature in France is thus compressed into a briefer space of time and so gives a much stronger impression of precipitancy.

Almost as important was the stagnation in literature caused by the events of the Revolution and the Empire. For twenty-five years, the energies of the rising generations were absorbed by political and military activities of compelling urgency and passionate interest. The normal process of taste changing from fathers to sons was largely suspended because the sons had little leisure for artistic pursuits. Moreover, the considerable weight of Napoleon's police state was thrown into the scales on the side of Classicism, and the fortuitous circumstances of the disappearance of Chénier's manuscripts until 1819 meant that the example of a great poet's originality was lost until long after his death. Again, the effect of these external factors was to retard what might otherwise have been a natural development.

Once the movement did get under way, it gained momentum with extraordinary rapidity, not only because of its previous compression, but also because it was pushed along by a host of new forces. Some of these were of a social nature, and to them we shall return later. But the most vigorous of them was certainly the integration of French intellectual life into a European community. More than at any time since the sixteenth century, French writers became conscious that their contemporaries in other countries, notably England and Germany, were doing new and exciting things that they themselves had not yet learnt. Once the substantial initial difficulties of acclimatisation and adjustment had been overcome, the impetus received from these outside impulses never slackened. At first, the French learnt from the English— from Scott how to write historical novels, from Byron how to strike defiant attitudes in lyrical poetry. Then it was Germany: Goethe and Schiller provided new models for tragedy, Heine showed how folk-song could transform cultivated poetry, Hoffmann popularised the fantastic tale, Wagner opened the way to a vivification of literature by music. Later, with Poe and Whitman, American influences made themselves felt, and the discovery of the Russian novelists at the end of the century put a new face on Realism. At the same time, the revelation of the writings of the East and of the poetry of the European Middle Ages provided yet more sources of inspiration. The relative isolation in which French literature had lived since pre-classical times (with scattered exceptions like the penetration of the Italian *commedia dell'arte*,

Richardson's novels and the English philosophers of the eighteenth century) came to an end, and the climate of the times was exposed to winds of change from every direction.

Another reason for the constant shifts in literary interest must be sought in the instability of institutions and the pressure of historical events during the period. In the course of less than a hundred years, France changed from a dictatorial empire to a reactionary monarchy, then to a limited *bourgeois* monarchy, from there to a democratic republic, back to a dictatorial empire and finally, after a brief interlude of communism, to a relatively conservative republic. Each of these *régimes* had its effect on literature. Napoleon, anxious to restore a semblance of stability in art as in other fields, tried to impose a classical straitjacket on literature, but the example of his feats of arms ultimately worked towards a mood of exaltation. The Restoration monarchy with its clericalism encouraged writers to sing the praises of the throne and the altar and reduced others to impotent fury. The July Monarchy saw the dominance of the philistine but prosperous middle classes and the aggravation of social and political dissension. The approach of 1848 was heralded by a surge of social idealism; the Second Empire on the other hand stifled political discussion and induced in writers a mood either of frivolity or of inner emigration into art. The loss of the Franco-Prussian War and the upheaval of the Commune led to a disillusioned pessimism and a critical re-examination of long-cherished assumptions, which continued throughout the Third Republic. Add to this three successful revolutions, any number of abortive insurrections and two foreign invasions, and it will be seen that the situation in which thinking men formulated their conception of art rarely remained constant for more than a few years at a time.

Similarly, the conditions of life and thought were transformed completely between 1800 and 1900. The world was no longer the same after the invention of railways, the utilisation of gas and electricity, the vast progress of knowledge in science and medicine, the advance of industrialisation and the sudden spread of urban civilisation. Hastened in its course by these changes in the relationship between man and his habitat, French philosophy saw the rise and fall of several different systems, each of which in its turn altered the general intellectual climate of the time. The *idéologues*, who helped to form Stendhal's special mentality, were succeeded by Victor Cousin's eclecticism, which included a partial revelation of German idealism, favourable to the development of Romantic ideas. In the middle of the century, the scene was dominated by positivists or pseudo-positivists—Comte, Littré, Taine, Renan—whose opinions, whether one accepted or rejected them, could not be ignored by anyone concerned with man's situation in the universe. At the end of the period, a re-interpretation of thinkers like Hegel and Schopenhauer, and the rehabilitation of intuition by Bergson, again produced a new conception of human nature and of its contacts with the world around it. The average educated men of 1900 were probably more different from their grandfathers than any generation had been since the Renaissance.

Yet all these factors conducing to change should not blind one to the continued existence of certain traditions. We have already mentioned that the disappearance of the idea of Classicism in literature as it had been understood for perhaps two hundred years did not imply the sudden cessation of all classical influence, and, apart from the solid classical culture of writers like Chateaubriand or Anatole France, there were after 1830 several concerted attempts to re-establish the classical basis of French literature: Ponsard's tragedies, the Hellenism of Leconte de Lisle, Ménard and Bouilhet, the *école romane* of Moréas, Maurras and their followers in the 1890s. A rationalist tradition emanating from the eighteenth century also persisted throughout the period. We have noted Stendhal's debt to the *idéologues*, but one could further instance Mérimée's anti-clericalism, the Goncourts' predilection for eighteenth-century art and humanitarianism, the positivists' respect for the immutable order of nature and the Voltairean attitudes of Anatole France. Even Gérard de Nerval, the most truly Romantic of the French Romantics, emphasises again and again that he is indelibly marked by the scepticism of the *philosophes*—'fils d'un siècle déshérité d'illusions', 'fils d'un siècle douteur', 'un Parisien nourri d'idées philosophiques, un fils de Voltaire, un impie', he calls himself in his *Voyage en Orient*. On the other side, a strong Catholic presence maintains a certain continuity from beginning to end of the century. The list of Catholic writers is a long and impressive one, even if their orthodoxy is frequently suspect. All these persistent strands in the literary fabric of the time help to give a pattern which may not at first be apparent but which, even if it never amounts to a restoration of a common heritage, ensures that, beneath the changing surface, the connections with the past have not been totally obliterated.

＊　　＊　　＊　　＊

One of the most profound alterations in the relationship between life and literature in the nineteenth century is the changed attitude of the writer towards his public. Hitherto, there had always been a community of interest and culture between men of letters and their readers, partly due to the existence of common assumptions about the nature of literature (notably its debt to classical antiquity) and partly due to the fact that authors and public both came from a relatively narrow section of the population—an educated *élite* who shared a certain social and cultural background which meant that, whatever their disagreements, they were at least always talking a mutually comprehensible language. There had of course been disputes in plenty—between Malherbe and the successors of the sixteenth-century poets, between the *Anciens* and the *Modernes*, between the *philosophes* and their opponents—but at least each side understood the other's position and knew why it had been adopted. Sometimes, as at the height of seventeenth-century Classicism, the audience was so restricted and so closely-knit that a writer could sense immediately if his works had any chance of success or not. Until Rousseau's time, it is probably true to say that no author would deliberately have flown in the face of the taste of the public—writers were in a very real sense spokesmen of the public.

Towards the end of the eighteenth century, the situation began to change. The middle classes, becoming ever more numerous and ever more wealthy, began to supplant the aristocracy as the arbiters of taste, and once the Revolution had abolished the Court as a centre of refinement, the nobles never regained their former power in literary and artistic matters. Neither Louis XVIII, Charles X, Louis-Philippe nor Napoleon III ever really tried to make the Court the centre of cultural activity, perhaps because they saw that it was a hopeless task. But the middle classes lacked the tradition of aristocratic patronage of the arts; they worked hard for their money and had little time left for non-essentials; and they tended to see life exclusively in terms of the material factors on which their own position was based. The result was that artists and writers no longer felt themselves in sympathy with the class which was economically most powerful and which they had to please if they were not to starve. As we shall see in more detail later, Vigny's *Chatterton* affords a particularly dramatic illustration of this situation, which grew steadily worse throughout the century.

A further complication was the growth of a new reading public which had not previously impinged on the problem of literary supply and demand: this was the lower classes, the urban and rural proletariat. The spread of literacy among the peasantry, for instance, is not unfairly characterised by George Sand when she describes the family of the young miller in *Le Meunier d'Angibault* (1845): the old grandmother can neither read nor write, the mother can just read but cannot write, the miller himself can do both. In 1833, a law was passed establishing a primary school in every commune; by the end of the century, primary education had become both free and compulsory. A vast and formerly inarticulate majority had at last attained a state when it too wanted its supply of literature, in however rudimentary a form. Parallel to this developing need for a new kind of mass culture was the growth of the press. In the 1820s, no newspaper had a circulation of more than 20,000; by 1900, *L'Écho de Paris* alone had over a million readers. Some of the consequences of this tremendous expansion will become apparent when we examine the extract from Balzac's *Illusions perdues;* the figures already make it clear that the type of publication accessible to a tiny *élite* will be quite inappropriate for a vast and incalculably mixed readership. There was thus a literate but wholly uncultivated audience for a certain kind of undemanding literature, and authors had consciously to decide whether or not they were going to try to appeal to this potentially omnipotent but unartistic public.

The fact is that the widening of the public meant at the same time a fragmentation of the public, indeed a multiplicity of publics. The basis of a common culture and status which the writer and his readers had once enjoyed having now largely vanished, the problem arose of what readers an author hoped to reach. At one extreme, it was still conceivable to address oneself to humanity at large and to use a language which would be understood by anyone who could read. Hugo managed to do this, but he was the last great poet to succeed in that way; to some extent, Zola's popularity at the end of the century was of the same nature. On the other hand, one could restrict one's appeal more to the classes who still retained a certain intellectual background, who were aware of moral and social problems, who read regularly, who could follow at least some allusions to things outside their daily ken. It is to these readers, essentially middle-class, that the bulk of the writing of the time is directed—most novels are written for them, most Romantic and Parnassian poetry, almost all plays, some historical works. But there is also a new phenomenon and a very significant one: literature for specialists, for limited sectional audiences of one sort or another.

The most obvious category of specialists in this sense is that of other men of letters. The workmanship, immaculate to the point of fanaticism, of Baudelaire, Flaubert or Leconte de Lisle really implies an effort of appreciation on the part of the reader which it would be reasonable to expect only from another technician of literature. The practice of writing for *cénacles* conduces to the same tendency: the *petit cénacle* around Petrus Borel in 1830, for instance, certainly shows signs of clannishness in its modes of thought and expression, and the numerous groups and sects of Symbolism make no secret of their indifference to comprehension by the general public. But there are also the categories of intellectual specialists, who tend in the course of the century to confine themselves more and more within their own branch of erudition. The sum of human knowledge, especially in the sciences, had grown by such leaps and bounds since the eighteenth century that it had become extremely difficult for anyone to acquire a thorough understanding of more than one or two subjects. The time when amateur scientists like Voltaire and Goethe could hope to make sensational discoveries was gone beyond recall; indeed, Goethe was perhaps the last 'universal man' in the old sense of the term. Instead, the nineteenth century saw the growth of generations of eminent scientists whose competence scarcely extended outside their own subjects and who found it increasingly hard to explain their activities to laymen (and when a layman like Zola tried to understand a specialist like Claude Bernard, the results were liable to be disastrous). As far as literature was concerned, this meant the decay of the concept of the *honnête homme* who was capable of discoursing without pedantry on any topic, and it meant that philosophers tended to write for other philosophers, scientists for other scientists, historians for other historians. It is true that French men of erudition, on the whole, shunned the excessive technicality in which their German counterparts liked to enshroud their ideas, but the immense respect which German intellectual methods acquired in mid-nineteenth-century France weakened even that tradition.

The logical conclusion (or, as the case may be, *reductio ad absurdum*) of this splitting-up of the public is that, ultimately, the artist should cease to bother about communicating with others and write for himself alone. This is a position towards which, either by accident or by design, more than one writer tended in the latter part of the century. The obscurity of Nerval's sonnets *Les Chimères* can probably never be dispelled; Nerval himself said of them: 'Ils perdraient de leur charme à être expliqués, si la chose était possible.' It is very doubtful whether Mallarmé really intended his later poetry to be understood by anyone except himself, whatever he may have pretended to the contrary. Rimbaud, too, when he exclaims at the end of one of his *Illuminations*: 'J'ai seul la clef de cette parade sauvage', is laying claim to exclusive possession of a secret he has himself created. To some extent, this kind of attitude springs from a mode of literary creation which plunges deeper into the unconscious and irrational than artists had hitherto thought feasible or desirable (of this, more later), but it is also the product of their doubts about the existence of any public able or worthy to comprehend them. The general reader, if he chances to open their works, is liable to find himself deliberately repulsed (as by Mallarmé) or deceived and confused (as by Villiers de l'Isle-Adam). The bonds which once linked a writer and the public have been severed.

Elements of this kind play a large part in overturning what had until then been the customary hierarchy of *genres*. In the nineteenth century, plays with literary pretensions tended for the first time to be unactable. In that respect, the title of Musset's *Un Spectacle dans un fauteuil* is symptomatic, and though the Symbolists wrote innumerable plays, the majority of them were neither staged nor meant to be. Just as the theatre lost some of the character of a communal artistic celebration and became instead the imaginary location of a solitary entertainment, so poetry moved away from being the lyrical consecration of universal human emotions to being a private cult of individual experiences. Under the circumstances, it is not surprising that the theatre lost the primacy it had held in the seventeenth and eighteenth centuries, or that poetry failed to retain the prestige it had momentarily acquired through the Romantics. In their place, the novel assumed the leadership of the hierarchy of the *genres*, and there were few writers who did not at one time or another try their hand at it. This was because the novel, the most versatile of forms, could be adapted either to the needs of the largest possible public (as happened with Hugo, George Sand, Daudet and Zola) or to the more refined desires of a single ideal reader (as, one may assume, with Stendhal and his 'happy few', with Flaubert, who regarded misunderstandings as the inevitable lot of an artist, or with Villiers de l'Isle-Adam and Léon Bloy, who well knew that what they wrote would be practically incomprehensible to the average consumer of fiction). The novel moreover satisfied the eternal human craving for hearing stories; it did not demand that one should live in a city or have special social habits as theatre-going does; it could even, in the form of the *roman-feuilleton*, be exploited by the press. So, by the end of the nineteenth century, the novel, which for so long had been scarcely a respectable form at all, had become the most commonly practised *genre* and the one for which a great many artists reserved their highest ambitions.

However, even in the novel, the gap between artist and public remains noticeable. A list of the best-sellers of the nineteenth century would be far from the same thing as a list of the greatest novels—it would admittedly include works by Balzac, Flaubert and Zola, but it would certainly omit Stendhal and the Goncourts, and it might well be headed by names like Eugène Sue, Paul de Kock, Alexandre Dumas and Jules Verne. It is true that, in a sense, a similar phenomenon occurred with works like *L'Astrée* and *Clélie* in the seventeenth century, but the parallel is in fact misleading, since the readers of d'Urfé and Mlle de Scudéry were the same people who applauded Racine and dissected La Rochefoucauld's maxims, whereas those who devoured the works of Paul de Kock probably read nothing much apart from that. There tended to be one kind of reader for artistic literature and another for what Sainte-Beuve called 'la littérature industrielle', and it was largely accidental if the two happened to coincide. The same is true of the theatre—the Romantics briefly won general acclaim, but the other great successes of the century—Ponsard's *Lucrèce*, the massive output of Scribe and Sardou, the dramas of Augier and Dumas *fils*, Rostand's *Cyrano de Bergerac*—nowadays seem to possess few literary virtues apart from impeccable technical stagecraft. In poetry, after the Romantics had exhausted their vogue, the three writers best known to the man in the street were neither Leconte de Lisle, Baudelaire, Mallarmé nor even Verlaine, but Béranger, François Coppée and Albert Samain. It would probably not be unjust to speak of the formation in the nineteenth century of a sort of literary *demi-monde*—works which enjoyed huge success and masqueraded as something much grander than they were, while often hiding humble, not to say disreputable origins.

From all this it follows that the writer in the nineteenth century found himself in a position of growing isolation, either the deliberate seclusion of a Vigny or a Flaubert or the baffled failure to make contact of a Villiers or a Barbey d'Aurevilly. The public was indifferent to or suspicious of many of the country's finest artists; for their part, the artists were often scornful of or hostile to their potential readers.

*   *   *   *

It is scarcely surprising that, in these circumstances, the conditions of literary creation should have changed completely (though it is often hard to tell whether circumstances were responsible for altered processes of creation, or whether the latter themselves produced a new sort of relationship between author and public). At one time, the pre-existing harmony between the artist and the people for whom he was writing meant that the act of invention and composition derived in large part from a common fund of ideas, attitudes, feelings, and tastes: the Classicism of Louis XIV's reign is the outstanding example of such community of aesthetic opinion. But once writers and readers had started to separate into two distinct and sometimes antagonistic groups, the kind of creation in which a whole civilisation was tacitly associated with the individual's artistic activities became almost impossible, at least in the realm of serious art. The writer was thus more and more driven back on the private resources of his own class, his own group or his own personality. The process was accelerated by the Romantic cult of the individual and of his personal and emotional life. Once it was granted that a writer's most intimate feelings were an object of legitimate interest to the world at large, it became more and more common for artists to see art as a form of confession, as something composed from the substance of their own inmost being—Musset's image of the pelican tearing its own breast, though theatrical, is a just summary of the new concept of literary creation adopted by (or perhaps unwillingly forced on) a generation which no longer had access to a corporate fund of productive material.

The case is obvious for the Romantics themselves—openly or obliquely, Lamartine tells us about Mme Charles, Musset about George Sand, Hugo about Juliette Drouet, Vigny about Marie Dorval, Balzac about Mme de Berny, Nerval about Jenny Colon, to name only the clearest examples of the most straightforward sort of autobiographical romancing. However much facts may be altered, irrelevances suppressed or emotions ennobled in the interests of aesthetic effect, the technique is basically the same: art is produced by moulding violent personal experience into literary form. However, it should not be thought that subsequent schools have eliminated this procedure, simply because they are so vocal in condemning it. Flaubert indignantly repudiates the idea of literature as confession, yet he can rightly say: 'Madame Bovary, c'est moi', and transmute his adoration of Mme Schlesinger into *L'Éducation sentimentale*. Leconte de Lisle may vituperate 'les montreurs' of Romanticism, yet his pessimism can be shown to be personal and temperamental. Zola's canons of scientific impersonality do not prevent his using the pretext of filling out a fictitious character in *Le Docteur Pascal* for hymning his mistress. In the case of poets like Rimbaud or Lautréamont, the anecdotal side of Romantic inspiration from the self has been excised, but at deeper level, it is still the individual preoccupations and urges which supply the material out of which his art is formed. With other authors like the Goncourts, Daudet, Verlaine, Loti or Huysmans, the utilisation of autobiography may not be so declamatory as it is with the Romantics; it is none the less direct. Sainte-Beuve's interest in 'l'homme et l'œuvre' as a method of literary criticism is only the recognition of what had in his time become a commonplace of artistic creation, after having been, in previous centuries, the exception rather than the rule.

The combined effect of this reliance on one's personality for inspiration and of the isolation of the artist in society is to produce, in some writers, a new view of their position in relation to their times: what Sainte-Beuve called the 'ivory tower'. The artist takes refuge in his own works, which he creates for their own sake and which he declines to relate to the issues of the day. Art becomes its own justification: social relevance, public demand, moral improvement, the conveying of information are all discarded as impure and intrusive. Seventeeth-century preoccupations with ethical training, eighteenth-century concern with enlightenment are banned: the sole aim of art is beauty. It is an attitude defended successively, and with great vigour, by Gautier, Baudelaire, Leconte de Lisle, Flaubert and Mallarmé, and by the end of the century it had been carried to such extremes that art is often regarded as the sole value in life. Although protestations of moral or didactic intent in previous centuries are not always to be taken at their face value, never before had art been held to exist autonomously and without reference to the life which surrounded it.

Yet at the same time another impulse came into being which helped to counteract the solitude of the inhabitants of ivory towers. That was the desire to reflect the life of the times and to provide a continuous record of it in art, the ambition to be, as Hugo put it in *Les Feuilles d'automne*, 'un écho sonore'. Perhaps the main reason for this tendency was the feeling, very marked in the dissatisfaction with pseudo-Classicism at the beginning of the century, that a timeless aesthetic was false and illusory, that each age had to find its own form of art, that art, in a word, had to be modern. That, as we shall see, is one of the main arguments in Mme de Staël's *De l'Allemagne*, and if it was temporarily sidetracked by the Romantic fascination with the Middle Ages, it was not long before it made its full impact on men of letters and convinced them that modernity necessarily involved the depiction, in one way or another, of what was happening around them. From then on, there were even more writers looking at their times and reproducing what they saw than there were those locking themselves up in ivory towers: Balzac, Stendhal (who defined the novel as 'un miroir qu'on promène le long d'un chemin'), the Flaubert of *Madame Bovary* and *L'Éducation sentimentale*), the Second Empire dramatists, the Goncourts, Zola, Daudet, Maupassant—the catalogue could be extended almost indefinitely. Previous ages had of course had their commentators—La Bruyère for the declining years of Louis XIV, Montesquieu with his *Lettres persanes* for the Regency, Chamfort for the reign of Louis XVI— but it had not previously been the ambition of so many authors to become what Balzac in the preface to the *Comédie humaine* called the 'secretary' of the times in which they lived.

Nor was this desire for modernity confined to writers of what one might broadly term the realist stream. Baudelaire, for instance, laid great stress on the idea that an artist must, unless he is to be convicted of dishonesty, take the elements of the beauty he seeks to attain from the society which surrounds him—'tu m'as donné ta boue et j'en ai fait de l'or', he tells Paris in an unfinished preface to *Les Fleurs du mal*. Musset, too, in *La Confession d'un enfant du siècle* and *Rolla* sought to arrive at a diagnosis of the spiritual malaise from which he and his contemporaries were suffering. The settings of Laforgue's poems, though their effect is to translate his melancholy into concrete terms, are largely taken from the banal, everyday objects which surround him. The trend towards contemporaneity of subject, style and psychology is so strong in the second half of the century, that deviations from it—*Poèmes antiques*, *Salammbô*, the pseudo-archaic poetry of the *école romane*—cannot avoid an air of conscious artifice.

Not unnaturally, the desire to record events frequently merges into a desire to influence them. Again, 'committed' literature is no novelty. A vast amount of what was written in the eighteenth century is deeply 'committed' for or against the teaching of the *philosophes*. What is new about the nineteenth-century idea of commitment is that it is not necessarily thought incompatible with the highest kind of artistic achievement. Whereas Voltaire would doubtless have distinguished between works like *Candide* intended above all as propaganda and works like *Zaïre* composed primarily for aesthetic reasons, Balzac or Zola saw no reason why their novels should not be at one and the same time channels of pressure on public opinion and imaginative creations in their own right. The result is something in which the argumentative element is much more obliquely presented and of much less central significance than in eighteenth-century 'littérature de combat'. Church and monarchy in Balzac, anti-capitalist principles in Zola are there to influence readers in their views on current affairs, but they by no means inform the whole of the work. So one finds constantly that works by nineteenth-century authors contain controversial references to topical problems without necessarily degenerating into ephemeral pamphleteering (not that everything written as a contribution to a passing debate fades as the issue itself ceases to occupy men's minds, as witness the perennial appeal of the *Satyre Ménippée*, Pascal's *Lettres à un provincial*, or *Candide* itself —but it is usually an accident if such works survive, whereas Balzac and Zola wrote for posterity as well as for their contemporaries).

One could thus trace the course of all manner of current problems in the nineteenth century simply through the imaginative literature of the time. Balzac preaches legitimist politics; Stendhal satirises the Restoration and the July Monarchy; Hugo in *Les Châtiments* denounces Napoleon III and all he stands for; Zola analyses the causes for the defeat of 1870 and proposes remedies; Anatole France unmasks the secret motives behind the Dreyfus case; Barrès expounds his nationalism and the cult of 'la terre et les morts'. The history of the times is written directly into its fiction in a way which had never happened in the past. The same is true of social questions. The place of the workers in an industrial society is probably the biggest single unsolved problem which the nineteenth century left to the twentieth, and it preoccupies Sand, Hugo, the Goncourts, Zola and dozens of less distinguished writers. Other subjects of investigation or protest include the emancipation of women (Mme de Staël and George Sand); the status of illegitimate children (Dumas *père* and *fils*); the changing class-structure (Balzac, Stendhal, Dumas *fils*, Augier); the social responsibility of the philosopher (Bourget). Religion too is a constant theme of argument and discussion, as well as of private heart-searching. Chateaubriand, Lamartine, Balzac, Villiers de l'Isle-Adam, Huysmans, Claudel, Bloy, seek to keep the old traditions alive by re-interpreting them for their own times. Anti-clericalism and scepticism characterise the works of Mérimée, Stendhal, the Goncourts, Maupassant and Anatole France. Unorthodox solutions attract Nerval, Hugo, Nodier, George Sand and Baudelaire, as well as affecting some of those who declare themselves Catholics, Balzac and Villiers among them. Others, regretfully or triumphantly, dissect religion as a phenomenon which has had its time and has disappeared without replacement—Renan, Leconte de Lisle, Flaubert, Zola. The sensitivity with which literature reacts to new developments in all these fields and the alacrity with which artists—as artists—propose their own solutions is one of the most characteristic features of the period.

This penetration of literature by the events and preoccupations of the time extended even to those authors who most resolutely set their faces against any form of didacticism or utilitarianism. No ivory tower, however strenuously it was defended, remained proof against the invasion of the life around it. Vigny himself, who inspired the ivory tower image, found himself drawn to socialist thought, and there are unmistakable echoes of his concern with the social problems of his time in *Chatterton* and *Servitude et grandeur militaires*. Flaubert, too, who used to say that a novelist had no right in his novels to express his opinion on anything whatever, was caught up in the political turmoil of the age, and, as he watched the Tuileries burning down when the Commune was crushed in 1871, was unable to resist saying: 'Dire que cela ne serait pas arrivé si on avait compris *L'Éducation sentimentale*!' Even Mallarmé, the most remote and reticent of poets, spent years meditating on the problem of how to associate the rest of the world with the great work which he was preparing—and which would have been incomprehensible to it. Between the writer and the intellectual climate of the age, there is a constant chain of action and reaction from which no one is exempt. It is one of the typical signs of the period that inner and outer sources of inspiration, individualism and involvement, are permanently commingled.

*   *   *   *

What has been said so far has been intended to show in what ways the conditions of literary creation in the nineteenth century differ from those in preceding periods. It must be added that they also differ considerably from those which obtain today. Because the nineteenth century is still close to us and because we still experience so many of its problems, its fears, its hopes, it is easy to fall into the trap of supposing that nothing essential separates us from it. The relations between the working classes and the rest of society, the place of science in modern civilisation, the difficulties of life in great cities, the status of the Church in politics, commitment in literature, uncertainty over the true nature of the human personality—all these themes of nineteenth-century thought are familiar to us nowadays as everyday topics of discussion. Most of the modes of nineteenth-century artistic endeavour still persist in at least some plays and novels—historical romances, sordid slices of life, escapist exoticism, faithful reflections of the activities of average people, all of them characteristically nineteenth-century forms, are perpetuated in books, plays, films and television programmes. It is possible to read *Les Fleurs du mal* as though the poems had been written yesterday; no obvious effort of comprehension or imagination seems to be needed to make Baudelaire into our contemporary, whereas with Racine or Voltaire, difficulties of accessibility are immediately apparent. All this, and much more, undoubtedly constitutes a living legacy from the last century, and it would be foolish to deny the community of feeling which links the two periods.

But one must not forget how many apparently simple and stable notions have acquired a wholly different resonance in the last fifty or a hundred years. To take a key example, the word 'science', for a contemporary of Taine and Renan, evoked the idea of a mechanistically determined universe, the sense of an immense power for good which, harnessed to man's needs, would make him master of his environment, the image of men who had in their hands an infallible instrument of knowledge. Some of these associations naturally still survive. In the meantime, however, the transformation of scientific theory into something much less rigidly deterministic, the recognition of the fact that scientists were not in the end going to solve philosophical problems unaided, the fear that scientific developments like the atomic bomb might destroy the world, the gradual invasion of human activities by machines, have given the word quite different and much more disturbing overtones. Other factors like the shift of world dominance away from Europe, the rise and fall of colonialism, the emergence of scores of new nations, the establishment of whole new branches of study such as experimental psychology, the rise of the working classes to relative prosperity, the multiplication of State interference with the individual have made the world of today quite unlike the world of the 1860s. The apparent facility with which most nineteenth-century literature can be approached is deceptive:

nineteenth-century man and twentieth-century man are by no means identical creatures.

That is perhaps why, retrospectively, the end of the nineteenth century looks so much like the end of an epoch—the nostalgic phrase 'la belle époque' betrays how irrevocably it has flown. Naturalism and Symbolism, the two movements which had dominated literature for twenty or more years were both visibly in recession; many of the great figures of the last decades of the century were disappearing. Maupassant died in 1893, Verlaine and Edmond de Goncourt in 1896, Daudet in 1897, Mallarmé in 1898, Zola in 1902. The young writers who were coming to the fore in the 1890s and early 1900s were mostly men whom one would unhesitatingly assign to a new era, imbued with a new spirit—authors like Gide, Claudel, Valéry, Proust, Giraudoux. Those of the old guard who were still alive after the first World War look, on the other hand, like survivals from some past civilisation; Anatole France, Maurice Barrès, Paul Bourget scarcely seem to belong to the post-1918 world at all. If it was 1914 which definitively marked the passage from one period to another, one would be inclined to say that, in literature, it is around 1900 that there is a visible substitution of one generation for another. That is the reason why this volume includes nothing written after 1900; arbitrary as such divisions must always be, that is approximately where the break appears to be situated.

* * * *

Complex and contradictory, the nineteenth century lives on paradoxes and conflicts. Certain that some final synthesis was about to provide the solution to all human problems, darkened by near-nihilistic pessimism; proud that revealed religion had been relegated to the past, profoundly tormented by metaphysical questionings; eager for innovation, disorientated by the lack of an agreed tradition; hopeful of constructing vast associations of humanity, tremulously conscious of the solitude of the individual—the writers of the nineteenth century seem to be in discord not only with each other but even with themselves. If the present volume throws some light on the hidden reasons for these contrasts and demonstrates something of the multiplicity of the elements from which the literature of the period draws its life-blood, it will have done its work.

Bibliography

A complete bibliography of general background reading for nine-teenth-century literature would be beyond the scope of this work. The following suggestions may serve as a basis for further investigations. More detailed references for particular topics will be found at the end of each commentary.

Albert Thibaudet, *Histoire de la littérature française de 1789 à nos jours* (Paris, Stock; 1936). The best guide to the literary history of the period, in which the literature is continually related to the general trends of the time.

Pierre Barrière, *La Vie intellectuelle en France du XVIe siècle à l'époque contemporaine* (Paris, Albin Michel; 1961). The only full-scale attempt to provide a general analysis of the intellectual life of France from the sixteenth century to the present day, especially as it has affected literature. Pp. 439–540 provide an admirable introduction to the study of nineteenth-century literature from this point of view.

Jacques Robichez, *Panorama illustré du XIXe siècle français* (Paris, Seghers; 1962). A brief but lively account of the literary, artistic and historical events of the nineteenth century, with excellent illustrations.

Hans Kohn, *The Making of the Modern French Mind* (Princeton, Van Nostrand; 1955). A useful little book with an introductory essay and selected passages (in English) from French historians, philosophers and sociologists since the eighteenth century.

P. E. Charvet, *A Literary History of France*, vol. IV: *The Nineteenth Century 1789–1870*; vol. V: *The Nineteenth and Twentieth Centuries 1870–1940* (London, Ernest Benn; New York, Barnes & Noble; 1967). This survey sets literature firmly in its historical, social and intellectual context.

Raymond Pouilliart, *Le Romantisme*, III: 1869–1896 (Collection 'Littérature Française', 14. Paris, Arthand; 1968). Contains a great deal of valuable background information. The other nineteenth-century volumes in this series have not yet appeared.

John Cruikshank (ed.), *French Literature and its Background*, 4: *The Early Nineteenth Century*; 5: *The Late Nineteenth Century* (London, Oxford University Press; 1969). Essays by diverse hands on major authors and on the background to literature.

Alfred Cobban, *A History of Modern France* (London, Penguin Books; 1961). The second volume is a sound and interesting survey of the history of the period. It has a good bibliography which may be consulted for further reading on historical matters.

Valuable studies of French literary *milieux* at different times in the nineteenth century will be found in the following volumes of the collection *La Vie littéraire*:

Jules Bertaut, *L'Époque romantique* (Paris, Tallandier; 1947)

René Dumesnil, *L'Époque réaliste et naturaliste* (Paris, Tallandier; 1945)

André Billy, *L'Époque 1900* (Paris, Tallandier; 1951).

Another series which provides revealing information on what life was like in the nineteenth century is that of *La Vie quotidienne*:

J. Robiquet, *La Vie quotidienne au temps de Napoléon* (Paris, Hachette; 1942)

R. Burnand, *La Vie quotidienne en 1830* (Paris, Hachette; 1943)

Maurice Allem, *La Vie quotidienne sous le Second Empire* (Paris, Hachette; 1948)

R. Burnand, *La Vie quotidienne en France de 1870 à 1900* (Paris, Hachette; 1947).

Neither this general bibliography nor the reading list at the end of each commentary attempts to deal with purely literary history. The most up-to-date and accessible reference work for books of that kind is:

Pierre Langlois and André Mareuil, *Guide bibliographique des études littéraires* (5th ed., Paris, Hachette; 1968).

I

Mme de Staël

(1766–1817)

<small>FROM</small> *De l'Allemagne*

Si de nos jours les beaux-arts étaient astreints à la simplicité des anciens, nous n'atteindrions pas à la force primitive qui les distingue, et nous perdrions les émotions intimes et multipliées dont notre âme est susceptible. La simplicité de l'art, chez les modernes, tournerait facilement à la froideur et à l'abstraction, tandis que celle des anciens était pleine de vie. L'honneur et l'amour, la bravoure et la pitié sont les sentiments qui signalent le christianisme chevaleresque; et ces dispositions de l'âme ne peuvent se faire voir que par les dangers, les exploits, les amours, les malheurs, l'intérêt romantique enfin, qui varie sans cesse les tableaux. Les sources des effets de l'art sont donc différentes à beaucoup d'égards dans la poésie classique et dans la poésie romantique : dans l'une, c'est le sort qui règne; dans l'autre, c'est la Providence; le sort ne compte pour rien les sentiments des hommes, la Providence ne juge les actions que d'après les sentiments. Comment la poésie ne créerait-elle pas un monde d'une tout autre nature, quand il faut peindre l'œuvre d'un destin aveugle et sourd, toujours en lutte avec les mortels, ou cet ordre intelligent auquel préside un Être suprême, que notre cœur interroge, et qui répond à notre cœur?

La poésie païenne doit être simple et saillante comme les objets extérieurs; la poésie chrétienne a besoin des mille couleurs de l'arc-en-ciel pour ne pas se perdre dans les nuages. La poésie des anciens est plus pure comme art, celle des modernes fait verser plus de larmes; mais la question pour nous n'est pas entre l'imitation de l'une et l'inspiration de l'autre. La littérature des anciens est chez les modernes une littérature transplantée : la littérature romantique ou chevaleresque est chez nous indigène, et c'est notre religion et nos institutions qui l'ont fait éclore. Les écrivains imitateurs des anciens se sont soumis aux règles du goût les plus sévères; car, ne pouvant consulter ni leur propre nature, ni leurs propres souvenirs, il a fallu qu'ils se conformassent aux lois d'après lesquelles les chefs-d'œuvre des anciens peuvent être adaptés à notre goût, bien que toutes les circonstances politiques et religieuses qui ont donné le jour à ces chefs-d'œuvre soient changées. Mais ces poésies d'après l'antique, quelque parfaites qu'elles soient, sont rarement populaires, parce qu'elles ne tiennent, dans le temps actuel, à rien de national.

MME DE STAËL, *De l'Allemagne*, pt. II, ch. II,
ed. Mme de Pange (Paris, Hachette; 1958–9), vol. II, pp. 133–5

Mme de Staël's *De l'Allemagne*, completed in 1810 but not published in France until 1814, was one of the most important contributions to the violent debate on the state and the future of French literature which raged during the first thirty years of the nineteenth century. The significance of her views can be gauged from the number of issues raised in the present passage, which occurs in the second part of the book, in a chapter entitled *De la poésie classique et de la poésie romantique*.

The main argument which Mme de Staël develops here is one which had been gaining currency for some time past: that imitation of the Ancients, whether in subject-matter or form, had long since ceased to be appropriate to the social and psychological conditions of modern France. Ever since Du Bellay's *Défense et illustration de la langue française* in 1549, the majority of French writers and critics had been agreed that, at least in the most elevated literary *genres*, the pre-eminence of the Greek and Latin models could not be disputed and that modern literature could not do better than take them as its basis if it was to equal them in quality. Not even the quarrel of the *Anciens* and the *Modernes* a hundred years earlier had altered this fundamental assumption. But dissentient voices had been heard in rapidly increasing numbers since the late eighteenth century. The theatre was admitted to be stagnating, the public was tired of the conventions of the endless series of pseudo-classical plays, knowledge and appreciation of the very different dramaturgy of English and German playwrights were spreading, and the whole principle of French Classicism was subjected to much more radical scrutiny and criticism than it ever had been before. On all hands, there were echoes of the famous line by Berchoux:

'Qui nous délivrera des Grecs et des Romains?'

Mme de Staël and her friends emphasised above all the fact that man and society in the nineteenth century had become so complex and so diverse that the artificial simplicity of classical literature, especially in the theatre, was an insuperable obstacle to meaningful artistic expression. 'La simplicité des Anciens' is unsuitable for the presentation of 'l'intérêt romantique' required by contemporary audiences. Already in 1813 the same idea had been propounded by her colleague and adviser August Wilhelm Schlegel in his *Cours de littérature dramatique*, the French translation of which fluttered a good many academic dovecots. There, he had argued along exactly the same lines as Mme de Staël:

> L'inspiration des Anciens était simple, claire et semblable à la nature, dans ses œuvres les plus parfaites. Le génie romantique, dans son désordre même, est cependant plus près du secret de l'univers, car l'intelligence ne peut jamais saisir qu'une partie de la vérité, tandis que le sentiment embrasse tout, pénètre seul le mystère de la nature.[1]

Mme de Staël, more sensitive to the classical tradition than Schlegel, is less aggressively categorical (and thereby more accessible to French readers brought up to revere that tradition), but her attitude is basically the same. Another of her associates, Benjamin Constant, had likewise proclaimed the urgency of breaking away from the restrictions of pseudo-Classicism and of adopting some dramatic system which would permit a fuller and more natural representation of reality. In 1809, in the preface to *Wallstein*, his shortened version of Schiller's *Wallenstein* trilogy, he had distinguished between tragedy of passion and tragedy of character, the latter being more suitable to modern conceptions because of its looser framework:

> Les Français, même dans celles de leurs tragédies qui sont fondées sur la tradition et l'histoire, ne peignent qu'un fait ou qu'une passion. Les Allemands, dans les leurs, peignent une vie et un caractère entiers.... Ils nous présentent leurs personnages avec leurs faiblesses, leurs inconséquences et cette mobilité ondoyante qui appartient à la nature humaine, et qui forme les êtres réels.[2]

So for Mme de Staël and for many of her contemporaries the imitation of the forms of Greek and Latin literature and the repeated adaptation of subjects from it no longer constituted a viable mode of literary creation.

This necessitated a drastic reconsideration of the idea that 'le goût' was constant, unchanging and absolute. Seventeenth- and eighteenth-century aesthetics had been largely dominated by the assumption that

---

[1] (Paris, 1813), III, p. 285.
[2] *Wallstein* (Paris, 1809), p. xxxvi.

good taste in art consisted in recognising beauty which was essentially the same in whatever age or country it appeared. But Mme de Staël and her followers, mindful of the theories current since Montesquieu's time concerning the influence of climate and geography on human institutions, set out to prove that good taste was relative to a particular set of historical, social and cultural conditions, and that each epoch had to find its own form of beauty. So she is able to declare with perfect sincerity that 'la question pour nous n'est pas entre la poésie classique et la poésie romantique' but between a transplanted literature and an indigenous one. Unlike some of the more intemperate critics of the day, she sees no need to denigrate classical literature—so long as it is admitted to be the product of its own time rather than the unique embodiment of ideal beauty. At about the same time, Stendhal was giving a more impertinent formulation to the same idea:

> Le *romanticisme* est l'art de présenter aux peuples les œuvres littéraires qui, dans l'état actuel de leurs habitudes et de leurs croyances, sont susceptibles de leur donner le plus de plaisir possible. Le *classicisme*, au contraire, leur présente la littérature qui donnait le plus grand plaisir à leurs arrière-grands-pères.[1]

Or, as he put it in 1818:

> Voici la théorie romantique : il faut que chaque peuple ait une littérature particulière et modelée sur son caractère particulier, comme chacun de nous porte un habit modelé pour sa taille particulière.[2]

So it was no use claiming that a single set of immutable standards culled from the art of a long-dead civilisation could be used to determine the value of art-forms produced by a quite different society. As Hugo insisted in the preface to his play *Cromwell* in 1827:

> Voilà donc une nouvelle religion, une société nouvelle; sur cette double base, il faut que nous voyions grandir une nouvelle poésie.[3]

This in its turn meant that the art of each country must be built on national foundations. The relativity of taste implied much more attention to local and national differences; according to Mme de Staël, it is

[1] *Racine et Shakespeare* (Paris, Le Divan; 1928), p. 43.
[2] ibid., p. 195.
[3] *Théâtre* (Paris, Imprimerie Nationale; 1912), vol. I, p. 14.

impossible for works written on classical subjects and in classical forms to strike deep roots in a modern country, 'parce qu'elles ne tiennent, dans le temps actuel, à rien de national'. So begins a search for a national literary heritage other than that of Classicism. What has hitherto been extolled for its universal validity is now dismissed as irrelevant because it takes no account of the divergences between the different European nations. England and Germany are praised because they have evolved national literary traditions appropriate to their own circumstances, and the great movement of interest for contemporary foreign literature which surged through France in the first thirty years of the century is concerned less with proposing new models for imitation than with inciting French writers to discover a truly national style of their own.

But where is this untilled field of French resources to be found? Mme de Staël, like many of her friends, is clear about the answer. The Greek and Latin tradition is pagan; France is Christian and has its own national history. So it is to 'le christianisme chevaleresque' that modern French writers must turn for their inspiration. In other words, Mme de Staël recommends that the French Middle Ages should replace antique myth and legend as a source for themes and subjects. That indeed is the primary meaning she attaches to the word *romantique*, as she explains at the beginning of the chapter:

> Le nom de *romantique* a été introduit nouvellement en Allemagne pour désigner la poésie dont les chants des troubadours ont été l'origine, celle qui est née de la chevalerie et du christianisme.[1]

This new direction of curiosity in French literature heralds a whole series of plays, novels and poems which exploit either the Middle Ages —notably Hugo's *Notre-Dame de Paris*, Balzac's *Contes drolatiques* and Aloysius Bertrand's *Gaspard de la nuit*, or later periods of French history —Vigny's *Cinq-Mars* and *La Maréchale d'Ancre*, Mérimée's *Chronique du règne de Charles IX*, Dumas's *Henri III et sa cour* and his numerous historical romances, even Balzac's *Les Chouans*. In all this vast awakening of consciousness of French history as an inexhaustible repository of subjects and local colour, the example of Sir Walter Scott did much

---

[1] *De l'Allemagne*, vol. II, pp. 127–8. Mme de Staël's use of the word is influenced by Schlegel. In the late eighteenth century, it had been applied to landscapes especially, in the sense of 'picturesque, wild, productive of strong emotion'. The Staël-Schlegel use of it to designate a great sector of modern non-classical art is gradually narrowed down in the next twenty years until it refers only to a relatively small and well-defined group of writers.

to reinforce the counsels of theorists like Mme de Staël. It is also true that the vogue for historical plays and novels did not prove very durable. The Middle Ages were soon recognised for what they were even in Mme de Staël's argument—a half-way house on the road to complete contemporaneity of subject-matter.[1] In the meantime, however, the medievalism of the French Romantics not only served as a necessary transitional stage after the desiccation of the classical tradition but also gave rise to some impressive works in its own right.

Inherent in Mme de Staël's line of thought are some difficulties which soon came to hamper the progress of Romantic literature. For example, her insistence on the Christian basis of modern literature became a fertile source of misunderstanding in the 1820s. The young Romantics of that decade clung as she had done, and as Chateaubriand did, to the idea of a specifically Christian tradition in art; but in the France of Louis XVIII and Charles X, attachment to the Church nearly always went hand in hand with support for the monarchy. The paradoxical result of this situation was that the revolutionaries in literature tended to be conservatives in politics. Leading Romantics like Hugo, Lamartine and Vigny were at that time Royalists; many of their classical opponents were liberals. At the same time, there formed a liberal wing of the Romantic camp—anti-clerical atheists like Stendhal and Mérimée, and anarchic freethinkers like Petrus Borel and Gérard de Nerval—some of whom were at least as hostile to the Catholic Romantics as they were to the liberal Classics. These cross-currents between religion, politics and literature obscured the real drift of the stream and prevented the unification of the Romantic movement until close on 1830, when the Revolution finally swept them all off in the direction of liberalism in politics as well as literature.

Equally fraught with unexpected consequences is Mme de Staël's emphasis on the differences in outlook implied by the change from a belief in blind fatality to a belief in a beneficent providence. She asks: 'Comment la poésie ne créerait-elle pas un monde d'une tout autre nature, quand il faut peindre l'œuvre d'un destin aveugle et sourd, toujours en lutte avec les mortels, ou cet ordre intelligent auquel préside un Être suprême, que notre cœur interroge, et qui répond à notre cœur?' She does not appear to notice that, by urging the establishment of a specifically Christian art, she is hastening the end of tragedy

[1] cf. commentary v on *Antony*.

as a living literary *genre*. Her friend Schlegel, who shared her opinions on the gulf separating art based on fatality from art based on providence, had already in 1807 voiced some misgivings about the viability of tragedy in the context of an essentially consoling philosophy:

La fatalité est directement opposée à notre croyance religieuse; le christianisme lui a substitué l'idée de la providence. Il pourrait donc être mis en doute si un poète chrétien, en voulant faire passer dans ses ouvrages la manière de voir qui est en rapport avec sa religion, ne se trouverait dans l'impossibilité de composer une véritable tragédie, et si la poésie tragique, création de l'homme abandonné à ses propres forces, ne disparaît pas, comme les autres fantômes nocturnes d'une imagination superstitieuse, devant l'aurore de la révélation.[1]

Although Schlegel himself then concludes that this need not happen, since Christianity does not promise to everyone happiness on earth or salvation hereafter, the fact remains that the turning away from the classical modes of thought and expression which both he and Mme de Staël desire is one of the factors which brought about a sudden decline in the prestige and practice of tragedy. The *genre* which for more than two centuries had occupied the supreme position in the hierarchy of literary values (despite its visible sickness in the latter part of the eighteenth century) appealed from now on to fewer and fewer writers and ceased to be regarded as the natural medium for high genius. The transfer of pre-eminence from tragedy to the novel is one of the most remarkable features of the evolution of literary *genres* after 1800.

The circumspectness with which Mme de Staël refers to classical literature—it is said to be 'pleine de vie', 'simple et saillante', 'plus pure comme art' and to be capable of producing masterpieces—should make one wary of concluding that her desire to abandon imitation of the Ancients as an artistic principle betokens the cessation of all classical influence in the literature of the time. Though she criticises writers who persist in adapting Greek and Roman models to French taste, she does something very similar in her own presentation of German works—except that, in her case, the adaptation is governed by a lingering Classicism. Her translations soften asperities of style, her summaries ennoble trivialities of incident or character, her choice of texts ignores the most typical products of German Romanticism, and she reproves

---

[1] *Comparaison entre la Phèdre de Racine et celle d'Euripide* (Paris, Tourneisen; 1807), p. 83.

the Germans sternly when they transgress the rules of good taste. Plainly, her Romanticism, like that of many Frenchmen, is tempered by her classical education, her love of classical art and her inability to divest herself of classical habits of literary appreciation. Chateaubriand, Lamartine, Vigny and Gautier show notable traces of the same tendency—it is symptomatic of the hybrid nature of French Romanticism that even someone like Musset can cry:

> Grèce, ô mère des arts, terre d'idolâtrie,
> De mes vœux insensés éternelle patrie,
> J'étais né pour ces temps où les fleurs de ton front
> Couronnaient dans les mers l'azur de l'Hellespont.
> Je suis un citoyen de tes siècles antiques.[1]

Later in the century, once Classicism has lost its air of being a retrograde tyranny, there are repeated instances of nostalgia for a lost tradition. 'L'école du bon sens', with Ponsard's *Lucrèce* as its rallying-point, 'l'école païenne', with its return to hellenistic values in the works of Louis Ménard, the 'païen mystique', the Parnasse, with Leconte de Lisle's glorification of Greece, the 'école romane' which attempted to draw French poetry away from Symbolism and back to its Greco-Roman heritage, the neo-classical style and method of Henri de Régnier and Paul Valéry—all these reappearances of the classical idea in the midst of modernism show the extent to which Classicism persisted throughout the century, no longer as the dominant force in art, but as a strong subterranean current continually forcing its way to the surface. Dislike for the decadence of modern life, rehabilitation of physical form, hostility to Christianity, cult of an ideal, unchanging beauty were factors which encouraged the continuance of what in Mme de Staël's time had seemed an outworn habit.

Notwithstanding these implicit ambiguities, this passage marks one of the vital turning-points in modern French literature. It signals the disintegration of a cultural background common to the whole of the cultivated public. It indicates the necessity for a drastic revision of the severe rules imposed by the narrowness of pseudo-classical taste. It proclaims the end of the idea that canons of beauty are everywhere and at every time applicable in the same way and substitutes for it the belief that each age and each country must elaborate its own art-forms.

---

[1] Alfred de Musset, *Les Vœux stériles* (1831), in *Poésies* (Paris, Pléiade; 1951) pp. 114–15.

It opens the way to the utilisation of specifically national themes in literature, to the enthusiasm for history as a live, relevant, picturesque source of new material. It foreshadows the rediscovery of the pre-classical French literary heritage. It tacitly admits the imminent demise of the *genre* which, so long as classical aesthetics prevailed, appeared to epitomise sublimity. It anticipates the extent to which Romantic literature will tend towards emotionalism ('les émotions intimes et multi-pliées') and violent action ('les dangers, les exploits, les amours, les malheurs'). By its hesitations it indicates that Classicism will never entirely vanish from the literary scene in France. It could even be said to symbolise the moment at which it is recognised that not only ephemeral journalism but also great literature must draw its life-blood from the age in which it is written. For though the needs, the prejudices and the conventions of Mme de Staël's time cause writers to turn to the Middle Ages instead of to the contemporary world, the whole of her argument constitutes a resolute call for modernity in art, and that was indeed the direction in which literature was to evolve for the next half-century.

FURTHER READING

Edmond EGGLI and Pierre MARTINO, *Le Débat romantique en France* (Paris, Les Belles Lettres; 1933).
I. A. HENNING, *L'Allemagne de Mme de Staël et la polémique romantique* (Paris, Champion; 1929).
Guy MICHAUD and Philippe VAN TIEGHEM, *Le Romantisme* (Paris, Hachette; 1952).
Pierre MOREAU, *Le Classicisme des Romantiques* (Paris, Plon; 1932).
Louis REYNAUD, *Le Romantisme. Ses origines anglo-germaniques* (Paris, Armand Colin; 1926).
Paul VAN TIEGHEM, *Le Mouvement romantique* (Paris, Vuibert; 1923).

II

François-René de Chateaubriand

(1768–1848)

Je ne suis rien; je ne suis qu'un simple solitaire; j'ai souvent entendu les savants disputer sur le premier Être, et je ne les ai point compris : mais j'ai toujours remarqué que c'est à la vue des grandes scènes de la nature que cet Être inconnu se manifeste au cœur de l'homme. Un soir (il faisait un profond calme) nous nous trouvions dans ces belles mers qui baignent les rivages de la Virginie; toutes les voiles étaient pliées; j'étais occupé sous le pont, lorsque j'entendis la cloche qui appelait l'équipage à la prière : je me hâtai d'aller mêler mes vœux à ceux de mes compagnons de voyage. Les officiers étaient sur le château de poupe avec les passagers; l'aumônier, un livre à la main, se tenait un peu en avant d'eux; les matelots étaient répandus pêle-mêle sur le tillac : nous étions tous debout, le visage tourné vers la proue du vaisseau, qui regardait l'occident.

Le globe du soleil, prêt à se plonger dans les flots, apparaissait entre les cordages du navire au milieu des espaces sans bornes. On eût dit, par les balancements de la poupe, que l'astre radieux changeait à chaque instant d'horizon. Quelques nuages étaient jetés sans ordre dans l'orient, où la lune montait avec lenteur; le reste du ciel était pur : vers le nord, formant un glorieux triangle avec l'astre du jour et celui de la nuit, une trombe, brillante des couleurs du prisme, s'élevait de la mer comme un pilier de cristal supportant la voûte du ciel.

Il eût été bien à plaindre, celui qui, dans ce spectacle, n'eût point reconnu la beauté de Dieu. Des larmes coulèrent malgré moi de mes paupières, lorsque mes compagnons, ôtant leurs chapeaux goudronnés, vinrent à entonner d'une voix rauque leur simple cantique à *Notre-Dame-de-Bon-Secours*, patronne des mariniers. Qu'elle était touchante, la prière de ces hommes qui, sur une planche fragile, au milieu de l'Océan, contemplaient le soleil couchant sur les flots! Comme elle allait à l'âme, cette invocation du pauvre matelot à la Mère de Douleur! La conscience de notre petitesse à la vue de l'infini, nos chants s'étendant au loin sur les vagues, la nuit s'approchant avec ses embûches, la merveille de notre vaisseau au milieu de tant de merveilles, un équipage religieux saisi d'admiration et de crainte, un prêtre auguste en prières, Dieu penché sur l'abîme, d'une main retenant le soleil aux portes de l'occident, de l'autre élevant la lune dans l'orient, et prêtant, à travers l'immensité, une oreille attentive à la voix de sa créature : voilà ce qu'on ne saurait peindre, et ce que tout le cœur de l'homme suffit à peine pour sentir.

FRANÇOIS-RENÉ DE CHATEAUBRIAND, *Le Génie du christianisme*, pt. i, bk. v, ch. 12 (Paris, Didot; 1868–70), vol. i, pp. 139–40

In the controversy over religion which raged throughout the eighteenth century, Christianity had much the worst of the argument with its rationalist opponents. The intellectual discredit into which the Church had fallen among thinking people was aggravated by its association with a tyrannical, corrupt and inefficient *régime*, so that when the Revolution broke out, numerous anti-clerical measures were instituted to diminish its influence and cripple its efficacy. These included the reduction of its temporal power, the closure of monasteries and convents, and the imposition on the clergy of an oath of fidelity to the 1791 Constitution. As a result, the Church at the turn of the century was in a state of disarray, its unity lost, its doctrines in disrepute, its ministers harried and browbeaten. But the decline of Christianity had left an unfilled gap in the moral life of the nation. Attempts to establish a deistic cult of the *Être suprême* foundered miserably and the excesses of revolutionary persecutions had reawakened sympathy for the priesthood. When Napoleon came to power, he realised that only the conclusion of a *modus vivendi* with the Church could give his government the support of tradition and authority; the moment was ripe for a new approach to the whole problem of religion.

So, only a few months after Napoleon signed his Concordat with the Pope in 1801, restoring to the Church in France some of its former rights, Chateaubriand published his *Génie du christianisme*, from which this passage is taken. Rarely can a book of such importance have appeared at such an opportune moment, and rarely can a book on religion have been so exactly adjusted to what the public wanted to hear. People were tired of the interminable wrangle about the abstractions of doctrine and theology, and were emotionally disposed to accept a rehabilitation of religion. All they needed was a convincing exposition of the irrational attractions of belief, and this is what Chateaubriand gave them. The stress in *Le Génie du christianisme* is laid on the beauty and the consolations of religion, with reasoning relegated to a subordinate position and logic replaced by the most personal and emotional kind of rhetoric.

This passage is a typical example of the attitude which Chateaubriand adopted and which became typical of almost all the Romantic generation. The philosophic disputes of the eighteenth century are dismissed as arid technicalities, of interest only to 'les savants', and instead 'le cœur' is extolled as the sole arbiter. Religion is recognised to be true, not by the exercise of the intellect nor even by an effort of will, but through an instinct or an emotion—'voilà... ce que tout le cœur de l'homme suffit à peine pour sentir'. Reason is accounted of so little significance that Chateaubriand disdains to trace any logical connection between the beauty of nature and the existence of God, substituting for it a peremptory emotional certitude which brooks neither argument nor discussion: 'Il eût été bien à plaindre, celui qui, dans ce spectacle, n'eût point reconnu la beauté de Dieu'. Following the example of Rousseau, the writers of the early nineteenth century almost all display the same transfer from reason to emotion as the touchstone for what is valuable in life, in every domain—personal, social and political as well as religious.

A consequence of this insistence on the dominance of subjective emotion is that the individual, rather than the community or an abstract notion of truth, becomes himself the centre of his world, detached from his fellow-men and often opposed to them. This tendency (of which we shall see further instances in the commentary on *Chatterton*) is exemplified here by Chateaubriand's resounding introduction to the scene he is about to describe: 'Je ne suis rien; je ne suis qu'un simple solitaire... mais j'ai toujours remarqué...' Nominally, Chateaubriand is minimising his own importance, but in practice the effect of the fivefold repetition of *je* is to place him fairly and squarely in the centre of the picture, the more so as the incident he relates, like so much Romantic literature, is autobiographical. The *moi* has usurped the place which Man in general held in classical literature as the primary reality and the proper object of literary activity. If Chateaubriand still retains a sense of aristocratic restraint in revealing only as much of his inmost personality as he deems it fit for the public to see, his Romantic successors often discard any such scruple (which, in the later years of his life, was one of the main grounds for his quarrel with them). The private affairs of the poets of the 1830s come close to forming the staple diet of literature. In literary as well as in religious affairs, it is easy to see what prompted Renan's ironic question: 'Que serait-il arrivé si M. de Chateaubriand avait été modeste?' [1]

But the fact that Chateaubriand here deliberately draws the reader's attention to himself as an individual is as much the result of artistic calculation as of the spontaneous overflow of strong emotion. Just as Lamartine modified the facts about the death of Mme Charles so as to heighten the pathos of Le Crucifix, just as Musset and George Sand consciously stimulated each other's wildest feelings in order to provide more fertile matter for literary creation, just as Hugo alters the dates of the poems in Les Contemplations to correspond to the image of himself which he wishes to project, so Chateaubriand too filters his experience to make it fit a literary intention. There is no reason to doubt that he saw what he describes here—he mentions it too often elsewhere for one to suppose that it was sheer invention, as were some of his supposed experiences in the New World—but he himself admits in the Mémoires d'outre-tombe, written many years afterwards, that his reactions to the scene were far from the religious fervour which he attributes to himself in Le Génie du christianisme. This is his later comment:

Quand je peignis ce tableau dont vous pouvez revoir l'ensemble dans le Génie du christianisme, mes sentiments religieux s'harmonisaient avec la scène; mais, hélas! quand j'y assistai en personne, le vieil homme était vivant en moi : ce n'était pas Dieu seul que je contemplais sur les flots dans la magnificence de ses œuvres. Je voyais une femme inconnue et les miracles de son sourire; les beautés du ciel me semblaient écloses de son souffle; j'aurais vendu l'éternité pour une de ses caresses. Je me figurais qu'elle palpitait derrière ce voile de l'univers qui la cachait à mes yeux. Oh! que n'était-il en ma puissance de déchirer le rideau pour presser la femme idéalisée contre mon cœur, pour me consumer sur son sein dans cet amour, source de mes inspirations, de mon désespoir et de ma vie! [2]

Indeed, at the time of his voyage to America in 1791, to which this description refers, Chateaubriand was anything but a convinced Christian, and though he had moments of ardent quasi-religious

[1] Souvenirs d'enfance et de jeunesse (Paris, Calmann-Lévy; 1897), p. 219.
[2] Mémoires d'outre-tombe (Paris, Pléiade; 1951), vol. I, p. 215.

inspiration, surprising his fellow-passengers with soulful readings and sermons, he also spent much time and effort trying to 'deconvert' a young English Catholic named Tulloch.

This discrepancy between the untroubled faith by which he later claimed to have been filled at the sight of the majesty of the scene and the very mixed feelings which he really had at the time leads one to two conclusions. The first is that the Romantic belief in direct confessional inspiration in art is less simple than it seems. Almost always, an element of conscious arrangement intervenes so as to invest the original experience with higher significance and to purify it of accidental accretions. Even more than sincerity in everyday affairs, sincerity in literature is a complex phenomenon. It is unwise to use it too readily as a criterion of artistic excellence, even if that is what the Romantics themselves would have us do, and it is unwise to assume that the mechanism of creation can really work with the spontaneity and the facility that they claim.

The second conclusion is that the emotion aroused by the beauty of nature is a poor guide to religious truth. If the same experience, viewed at different times, can be attributed with equal plausibility to a vaguely erotic ideal and to a sense of the presence of God, then it is not good evidence about the meaning of the universe.

Chateaubriand himself, in a strange and revealing passage of *Le Génie du christianisme*, involuntarily betrays the precariousness of the link with any God except the deification of one's own heart when he writes:

> Lorsqu'on n'a point de religion, le cœur est insensible et il n'y a pas de beauté, car la beauté n'est point un être existant hors de nous : c'est dans le cœur de l'homme que sont les grâces de la nature.[1]

In other words, the whole process is entirely subjective; the argument begins and ends with human emotions.

It is this gap between the exalted feelings which the Romantics cultivated and the external stimuli supposed to provide them, which is in a large measure responsible for the bitter criticism both of the cult of emotion and of the inadequacy of the real world to supply it, that one finds in the works of Flaubert and Baudelaire. Both are aware that overexcited emotional raptures may be remote from the realities of the outside world: Emma Bovary (and Flaubert said that there were dozens

---

[1] *Le Génie du christianisme*, pt. III, bk. II, ch. 2, vol. II, p. 382.

of her kind throughout France) counts on all manner of ecstasy from her affairs with men who are either nonentities, brutes or weaklings, and inevitably succumbs to the bitterness of disillusionment; just as Baudelaire, in works like *La Chambre double* and *Un Voyage à Cythère*, brings out the depressing contrast between inner ideals and the degrading facts of our physical existence. The excessive reliance which the Romantics placed on extreme emotion as the only way to a happy and meaningful life carried within it the seeds of its own destruction, and the dangers of their attitude are already implicit in the ambiguity of Chateaubriand's reactions to the beauty of nature. The mid-century mistrust of emotion is a natural product of the Romantics' exaggerated cult of it.

At the same time, whatever one may think of Chateaubriand's motives in advancing arguments in favour of Christianity when he must have known them to be extremely fragile, his position typifies that of many nineteenth-century writers. Unable to justify fidelity to religion by logical means, they tend increasingly either to turn to irrational supports for their religious attitudes, or to divert their religious fervour to profane objects. Vigny's long search for moral certitude, Hugo's table-turning, Nerval's anguished interrogation of his visions are all instances of attempts to find a way of preserving beliefs which do not seem to be defensible on purely intellectual grounds. On the other hand, the quasi-mystical ardour with which Michelet, Quinet and even Auguste Comte attach themselves to social, political or philosophic creeds seems to provide a substitute for normal forms of religious activity. Later in the century, when men of Renan's generation find themselves forced into a categorical rejection of revealed religion, faith in the ideal is often reintroduced into their scheme of things by some devious and unexpected detour, as we shall see in commentaries XII and XIII. Chateaubriand's emotionalism in fact provides only a temporary postponement of the despair over the death of religion which affects so many of his successors.

Of more immediate consequence in the evolution of literature is the changing attitude to the evocation of nature for its own sake which this passage exemplifies. Nature figures only marginally in seventeenth-century literature and even La Fontaine normally confines his description of it to brief if suggestive settings for his fables. Nor has the eighteenth-century literature of ideas much use for it save as an object of philosophic curiosity, and it is only with Rousseau and his disciples, notably Bernardin de Saint-Pierre, that it comes to be regarded as a major literary theme in its own right. Chateaubriand follows firmly in this tradition, and his brilliant landscapes owe much to the works of Bernardin de Saint-Pierre—to *Paul et Virginie* for their brilliant and exotic colouring and to the *Études de la nature* for the religious conclusions which he draws from them. One sees in the present instance how skilfully Chateaubriand unfurls the full splendour of his prose to make the scene vivid and persuasive—the relatively sober details at the beginning, the hints of something more striking to come, the slow crescendo, the dramatic pause at the end of the first paragraph, then at last the sustained and majestic description of the sun, the moon and the waterspout. After that, conscious of the spell which he has cast, Chateaubriand launches into a sonorous declaration of faith which carries the reader along without resistance. The motive power of this rhetorical technique is provided both by the importance assigned to the human and emotional experience of nature, now considered worthy of the most sumptuous treatment in its own right, and the pomp of the stylistic resources lavished on it. It is indeed difficult to say whether one is more impressed by the splendour of nature or by the magnificence of Chateaubriand's style.

A less obvious means of reinforcing the emotive impact of the passage lies in Chateaubriand's introduction of the hymn to *Notre-Dame-de-Bon-Secours*, which is a genuine Breton folk-song. Chateaubriand was one of the first French writers to take a serious interest in folk-song, and in this he differed from the vast majority of his contemporaries, who tended to be too attached to a tradition of highly organised and refined forms of poetry and music to see much value in the rough simplicity of popular art. As we shall see in commentary XIX, this absence of interest in popular material meant that French Romantic poetry, unlike that of either the English or the German Romantics, tended to remain formal, rhetorical and declamatory, thereby retaining a closer link with the Classicism it reviled than is often realised. Even in the present case, although the memories of his native Brittany move Chateaubriand when he hears the hymn, the music is no more than an adjunct to what is primarily a visual experience: it is an accompaniment more than anything else. Like most of his French contemporaries, Chateaubriand is more susceptible to visual impressions than to auditory ones, and

French Romanticism as a whole, under the aegis of that great visionary
Victor Hugo, is, like the Parnassianism which criticised it, a movement
in which visual themes and inspiration predominate to a surprising
degree.

The outstanding success which Chateaubriand attains in the description of natural scenery leads to an immense increase in emotive
nature description in Romantic writing. It may well be that the French
Romantics are less interested than, say, the English Romantics in the
simpler aspects of nature unaffected by human preoccupations; they
seek above all, as does Chateaubriand, to associate nature with human
joys and woes and to find in it a friend, a solace and a dispenser of
mystical experiences. It is for instance common to find poets repeating
Chateaubriand's assertions about the connection between nature and
God, often in terms which come close to pantheism. Hugo too affirms
that God is manifest in the beauties of nature:

> Ces nuages de plomb, d'or, de cuivre, de fer,
> Où l'ouragan, la trombe, et la foudre et l'enfer
>   Dorment avec de sourds murmures,
> C'est Dieu qui les suspend en foule aux cieux profonds
> Comme un guerrier qui pend aux poutres des plafonds
>   Ses retentissantes armures![1]

Sometimes the emphasis is on God acting through nature to console
man, as in Lamartine's *Le Vallon*:

> Mais la nature est là qui t'invite et qui t'aime;
> Plonge-toi dans son sein qu'elle t'ouvre toujours :
> Quand tout change pour toi, la nature est la même,
> Et le même soleil se lève tous les jours.
>
> De lumière et d'ombrage elle t'entoure encore;
> Détache ton amour des faux biens que tu perds :
> Adore ici l'écho qu'adorait Pythagore,
> Prête avec lui l'oreille aux célestes concerts.[2]

On other occasions, there is simply a poetic re-statement of the line of
argument adopted in *Le Génie du christianisme*—Lamartine is very close
to Chateaubriand when he writes in *L'Immortalité*:

---

[1] *Soleils couchants*, in *Les Feuilles d'automne* (Paris, Imprimerie Nationale; 1909), p. 101.
[2] *Méditations poétiques* (Paris, Gosselin; 1847), p. 120.

Dieu caché, disais-tu, la nature est ton temple!
L'esprit te voit partout quand notre œil la contemple;
De tes perfections, qu'il cherche à concevoir,
Ce monde est le reflet, l'image, le miroir;
Le jour est ton regard, la beauté ton sourire.[1]

And of course there is a superabundance in Romantic literature of seductive and sentimental word-pictures of nature. The pathetic fallacy was so widespread in French Romanticism that, despite the protests of Vigny in *La Maison du berger*, it was still possible (and necessary) for Baudelaire to proclaim himself, nearly fifty years after *Le Génie du christianisme*, 'incapable de s'attendrir sur les végétaux'.[2]

FURTHER READING

Gustave CHARLIER, *Le Sentiment de la nature chez les romantiques français* (Paris, Fontemoing; 1912).

Victor GIRAUD, *Le Christianisme de Chateaubriand* (Paris, Hachette; 1925–8).

André JOUSSAIN, *Romantisme et religion* (Paris, Alcan; 1910).

Julien TIERSOT, *Les Écrivains romantiques et la chanson populaire* (Paris, Plon; 1931).

Léon GUICHARD, *La Musique et les lettres au temps du Romantisme* (Paris, Presses Universitaires de France; 1955).

---

[1] *Méditations poétiques*, p. 116.
[2] Quoted by M. Ruff, *L'Esprit du mal et l'esthétique baudelairienne* (Paris, Armand Colin; 1955), p. 268.

III

Alfred de Musset

(1810–57)

FROM *La Confession d'un enfant du siècle*

Pendant les guerres de l'Empire, tandis que les maris et les frères étaient en Allemagne, les mères inquiètes avaient mis au monde une génération ardente, pâle, nerveuse. Conçus entre deux batailles, élevés dans les collèges au roulement des tambours, des milliers d'enfants se regardaient entre eux d'un œil sombre, en essayant leurs muscles chétifs. De temps en temps leurs pères ensanglantés apparaissaient, les soulevaient sur leurs poitrines chamarrées d'or, puis les posaient à terre et remontaient à cheval.

Un seul homme était en vie alors en Europe; le reste des êtres tâchait de se remplir les poumons de l'air qu'il avait respiré. Chaque année, la France faisait présent à cet homme de trois cent mille jeunes gens; c'était l'impôt payé à César, et, s'il n'avait ce troupeau derrière lui, il ne pouvait suivre sa fortune. C'était l'escorte qu'il lui fallait pour qu'il pût traverser le monde, et s'en aller tomber dans une petite vallée d'une île déserte, sous un saule pleureur.

Jamais il n'y eut tant de nuits sans sommeil que du temps de cet homme; jamais on ne vit se pencher sur les remparts des villes un tel peuple de mères désolées; jamais il n'y eut un tel silence autour de ceux qui parlaient de mort. Et pourtant jamais il n'y eut tant de joie, tant de vie, tant de fanfares guerrières, dans tous les cœurs. Jamais il n'y eut de soleils si purs que ceux qui séchèrent tout ce sang. On disait que Dieu les faisait pour cet homme, et on les appelait ses soleils d'Austerlitz. Mais il les faisait bien lui-même avec ses canons toujours tonnants, et qui ne laissaient des nuages qu'aux lendemains de ses batailles.

C'était l'air de ce ciel sans tache, où brillait tant de gloire, où resplendissait tant d'acier, que les enfants respiraient alors. Ils savaient bien qu'ils étaient destinés aux hécatombes; mais ils croyaient Murat invulnérable, et on avait vu passer l'empereur sur un pont où sifflaient tant de balles, qu'on ne savait s'il pouvait mourir. Et, quand même on aurait dû mourir, qu'était-ce que cela? La mort elle-même était si belle alors, si grande, si magnifique dans sa pourpre fumante! Elle ressemblait si bien à l'espérance, elle fauchait de si verts épis, qu'elle en était comme devenue jeune, et qu'on ne croyait plus à la vieillesse. Tous les berceaux de France étaient des boucliers, tous les cercueils en étaient aussi; il n'y avait vraiment plus de vieillards, il n'y avait que des cadavres ou des demi-dieux.

ALFRED DE MUSSET, *La Confession d'un enfant du siècle*,
in *Œuvres en prose*, ed. M. Allem (Paris, Pléiade; 1951), pp. 81–2

Alfred de Musset was born in 1810, and when his autobiographical novel *La Confession d'un enfant du siècle* was published in 1836, Napoleon had been dead for fifteen years. But it is Napoleon who occupies the dominant place in the analysis of the state of mind of his generation with which Musset begins the novel and from which this passage is taken. Napoleon had indeed become a legend even during his lifetime, with his astonishing career first as a brilliant soldier in the Revolutionary armies (when at the battle of Arcole in 1796 he had the near-miraculous escape from death which Musset mentions); as First Consul from 1799 and as Emperor from 1804; as the leader of the French armies which swept victoriously through Europe in the first decade of the century, with Austerlitz—lit by a winter sun so glorious that it became a byword—as his greatest triumph; then as the fallen hero after the disastrous campaign in Russia in 1812; and finally, after the abortive return from Elba in 1815 and the defeat of Waterloo, as the victim of foreign persecution on St Helena—'une île déserte'—until his death in 1821. Thereafter, his name continued to act as a rallying-cry for liberals and other malcontents under the Bourbons and the July Monarchy, his memory being kept alive by such ceremonies as the return of his ashes to Paris in 1840, until eventually the Bonapartist succession was re-established when his nephew Louis-Napoleon seized power and had himself proclaimed Emperor as Napoleon III in 1852. To say that 'un seul homme était en vie alors en Europe' seems scarcely an exaggeration when one realises to what extent the fate not only of France but of the whole Continent hinged on Napoleon.

His shadow fell differently on his contemporaries according to their generation and their temperament. Those who were young men during the Napoleonic wars wrote little. As Renan says in *L'Avenir de la science*:

La Révolution et l'Empire n'ont produit aucun poème qui mérite d'être nommé; ils ont fait bien mieux. Ils nous ont laissé la plus merveilleuse des épopées en action.[1]

[1] *L'Avenir de la science* (Paris, Calmann-Lévy; 1890), p. 195.

A whole generation ('les maris et les frères' of this passage), fascinated by military glory, was too busy fighting to find time for literature—and in any case the pressure of a dictatorial government was being exercised in favour of a return to conservatism and Classicism in art. But after the fall of Napoleon, when France and Europe entered into a period of peace and stability which, to many minds, came close to stagnation, literature was full of the problems left behind by the Napoleonic era. The *demi-solde*, the flotsam and jetsam of the *Grande Armée*, men who had grown up to fight for Napoleon, who had never known any other life and who after Waterloo found themselves pensioned off on half-pay in a civilian existence for which they had neither taste nor aptitude, are legion in the novels of Balzac, eking out a meagre and discontented life with makeshift jobs, chafing at their enforced and unwelcome leisure, conspiring more or less seriously against the Bourbons and frequently finding themselves in trouble with authority. Philippe Bridau and his companions in *La Rabouilleuse* are the best portraits of this type, but one comes across examples elsewhere—Genestas in *Le Médecin de campagne*, for instance, is a more sober and resigned specimen, as is the old army doctor, in Stendhal's *Le Rouge et le Noir*, who inculcates into Julien Sorel his own cult for Napoleon.

The following generation, which was Musset's, came to maturity just too late to share in the exploits of Napoleon and was left with an unrealisable longing for violence, excitement and glory. Musset himself argues that this sense of frustration and boredom was one of the prime causes of *le mal du siècle* in the Romantic youth of 1830, and in *Les Vœux stériles* he sighs:

> Heureux, trois fois heureux, l'homme dont la pensée
> Peut s'écrire au tranchant du sabre et de l'épée![1]

This diagnosis neglects the deeper causes of the emotional pessimism which had afflicted more and more young people since the time of *La Nouvelle Héloïse* and Goethe's *Werther* (though in *Rolla*, written in 1833, Musset had laid more blame on the legacy of eighteenth-century atheism), but there is no doubt that many writers of the same age would have agreed with him. Only a few months before the publication of *La Confession d'un enfant du siècle*, Alfred de Vigny, who was born in 1797, admitted in strikingly similar terms:

[1] *Poésies* (Paris, Pléiade; 1951), p. 128.

J'appartiens à cette génération née avec le siècle, qui, nourrie de bulletins par l'Empereur, avait toujours devant les yeux une épée nue, et vint la prendre au moment même où la France la remettait dans le fourreau des Bourbons... Les événements que je cherchais ne vinrent pas aussi grands qu'il me les eût fallu.[1]

Likewise, Stendhal shows in Julien Sorel in *Le Rouge et le Noir* a young man fired with the ambition to emulate Napoleon and at the same time deprived of the most obvious way to do it through the Napoleonic armies:

— Ah! s'écria-t-il, que Napoléon était bien l'homme envoyé de Dieu pour les jeunes Français! qui le remplacera? que feront sans lui les malheureux, même plus riches que moi, qui ont juste les quelques écus qu'il faut pour se procurer une bonne éducation et pas assez d'argent pour acheter un homme à vingt ans[2] et se pousser dans une carrière! Quoi qu'on fasse, ajouta-t-il avec un profond soupir, ce souvenir fatal nous empêchera à jamais d'être heureux![3]

One result of this obsession with Napoleonic feats of arms and of the rapid rise to fame of his young officers is a desire to attain the same pinnacles of ambition by such means as remained open in the stultifying atmosphere of the Restoration. Here again, Musset and Stendhal coincide in their view of what was possible for the young men of their time. A few pages after the passage we are considering, Musset writes:

Quand les enfants parlaient de gloire, on leur disait : « Faites-vous prêtres » ; quand ils parlaient d'ambition : « Faites-vous prêtres » ; d'espérance, de force, d'amour, de vie : « Faites-vous prêtres ».[4]

To Musset such advice is so inappropriate that it sounds ironical, but for Julien Sorel, it is the logical consequence of a lucid inspection of the social situation:

Quand Bonaparte fit parler de lui, la France avait peur d'être envahie; le mérite militaire était nécessaire et à la mode. Aujourd'hui, on voit des prêtres de quarante ans avoir cent mille francs d'appointements, c'est-à-dire trois fois autant que les fameux généraux de division de Napoléon. Il leur faut des gens qui les secondent.... Il faut être prêtre.[5]

---

[1] *Servitude et grandeur militaires* (Paris, Garnier; 1955), p. 8.
[2] With the system of partial conscription then in force, it was possible for young men of wealth to pay for someone to replace them if they happened to be called up.
[3] *Le Rouge et le Noir* (Paris, Garnier; 1953), p. 93.
[4] op. cit., p. 5.   [5] op. cit., p. 24.

After the Red, the Black. For both Musset and Stendhal, the choice of the priesthood as a career is symbolic of the pious, conventional, unadventurous Restoration monarchy. The social ambition of the young men in Balzac's *Comédie humaine*—Rastignac, Rubempré, Marsay and all the rest—assumes different but no less egoistic forms, and in Rastignac's apostrophe to Paris ('A nous deux, maintenant!') there is certainly a Napoleonic desire to take on the whole world single-handed and emerge victorious.

It is remarkable that while the narrative literature of the 1830s and 1840s is full of the difficulties of the aftermath of Napoleonic times, it makes no real effort to come to grips with the Napoleonic epic itself on a scale comparable with, say, Tolstoy's *War and Peace* or Hardy's *The Dynasts*. The *Scènes de la vie militaire* is one of the most sparsely furnished sections of the *Comédie humaine*, and apart from a horrifying account of the retreat from Moscow in *Adieu!*, the grim story of Chabert's disappearance in *Le Colonel Chabert* and one or two short anecdotes elsewhere, Balzac never attempted to describe the Napoleonic campaigns at any length. The battle of Waterloo figures prominently at the beginning of *La Chartreuse de Parme* (Stendhal was one of the few writers to have seen something of the Napoleonic wars at first hand, and he twice embarked on a biography of Napoleon which he never finished), but it is narrated from a highly personal viewpoint, the ironical levity of which excludes any consideration of the battle as a turning-point in the history of nations. Hugo goes to the opposite extreme of portentousness in his elaborate but melodramatic account of Waterloo in *Les Misérables*, but again, despite the large number of other Napoleonic fragments in which his works abound (especially in *Les Châtiments*), he never treated the subject of Napoleon's rise and fall as a whole (though it is true that he omitted it from *La Légende des siècles* only because he proposed to devote to it part of his vast unfinished poem, *Dieu*). Otherwise the wars of the Empire are represented in French literature by one or two famous but brief set pieces like Hugo's *Le Cimetière d'Eylau* or Mérimée's *L'Enlèvement de la redoute* rather than by the monumental constructions which one might have expected.

The absence of any large-scale literary celebration of the Napoleonic wars comes probably from both political causes and the extreme difficulty of finding a fictional form adequate to the extraordinary nature of the subject. Napoleon's despotism alienated from him some of the more brilliant talents of his own generation; the two outstanding literary figures of the Empire are both implacable opponents of the *régime*—Chateaubriand the Royalist and Mme de Staël the liberal, one a returned *émigré* and the other an exile. But even they cannot escape the fascination of Napoleon. A large part of the *Mémoires d'outre-tombe* is taken up by a biography of Napoleon in a style compounded of severe criticism and grudging admiration, and though *De l'Allemagne* and *Dix Années d'exil* are animated by a spirit of uncompromising opposition to Napoleon, Mme de Staël had at one time conceived ambitions to be his wife. After Napoleon's fall and death, he remained a subject of heated controversy, in which his supporters were embarrassed by his excesses and mistakes, while his opponents could not suppress their envy and wonderment at his undeniable genius. After the accession to power of Napoleon III, attitudes towards him became if anything even more ambivalent—republicans like Michelet saw in him the man who had so demoralised the French people that they meekly accepted an illegal and debilitating *régime*; Hugo on the other hand praised him fervently in *Les Châtiments* in order to make a more humiliating contrast with 'Napoléon le Petit'. At no stage in the nineteenth century was there a sufficiently concerted opinion on Napoleon to make possible anything like a national epic about him.

Almost more important in perpetuating the memory of the Emperor and his victories was popular art—the songs of Béranger, the innumerable cheap reproductions of pictures of incidents from his reign ('images d'Épinal'), the reminiscences of doting old soldiers like the fanatical veteran who gives such a moving and picturesque biography of him in Balzac's *Le Médecin de campagne*. Above all, there was the *Mémorial de Sainte-Hélène*, an account of his last years in exile, his opinions, his reflections on past events, his conversations, collected by one of his acolytes, Las Cases, and published with enormous success from 1822 onwards (it is a book which Julien Sorel, like so many other Bonapartists, treats with the reverence normally reserved for the Bible).

If neither the 'génération ardente, pâle, nerveuse' of Musset nor any subsequent one felt itself equal to the task of producing a fictional record of Napoleon's achievements, he and his contemporaries, robbed of the chance of performing military feats of their own, saw in literature a compensatory means of achieving a glory comparable to that of Napoleon. Even apart from the case of Vigny, who joined the army in the hope of fame, honour and excitement and then turned to writing as an escape from the eternal monotony of garrison duty, there was more than one author whose clear ambition it was to become a Napoleon of letters. Chateaubriand lays such stress in the *Mémoires d'outre-tombe* on the theme of 'Napoléon et moi' only because he sees a real parallel between the greatest captain of the age and the person whom he obviously regards as the greatest author of the age. Similarly, one remembers the motto Balzac inscribed on a bust of Napoleon: 'Ce qu'il a commencé par l'épée, je l'achèverai par la plume', and of course Hugo, hailed almost at once as the poetic leader of his generation, never tired of suggesting comparisons between himself and Napoleon. As early as 1831, one finds him asking pointedly, in the preface to *Marion Delorme*: 'Pourquoi, maintenant, ne viendrait-il pas un poète qui serait à Shakespeare ce que Napoléon a été à Charlemagne?' [1] The cult of genius in Romantic literature is in part an echo of the roars of acclamation which had greeted the triumphal progress of Napoleon, an attempt to lead off into art some of the immense popularity which had attended the heroes of the time, the 'demi-dieux' of whom Musset speaks. That the generation of 1830 flung itself into literature with such enthusiasm and such brilliance is one of the more paradoxical results of the desire for emulation of his exploits which Napoleon awoke in so many hearts.

In the same way, the constant reminders of action, of bloodshed, of great deeds, of mighty passions which recur in French Romanticism, represent a transference into literary terms of some of the violence, the excitement and the variety of the Napoleonic era. The duels, the plots, the murders, the flamboyant deeds in plays like *Hernani, Ruy Blas, Henri III et sa cour, La Maréchale d'Ancre* and *Lorenzaccio*, or novels like *Notre-Dame de Paris* and *Cinq-Mars*, exist to satisfy a craving for those turbulent feelings which their authors, during Napoleon's reign, had come to regard as the freest and fullest expression for youthful vigour and for which there now seemed to be no outlet save in imagination. The remote historical settings imposed by the fashion of the day may obscure the extent to which such a way of life seemed to be only just out of their grasp, but the case of Stendhal reveals how close the Romantics felt to the most hectic periods of history, since *La Chartreuse de Parme* with all its Napoleonic references is a transplantation into a modern setting of an Italian Renaissance tale originally relating to the

[1] *Marion Delorme* (Paris, Imprimerie Nationale; 1908), p. 9.

same epoch as his *Chroniques italiennes*. The Napoleonic wars and the Italian Renaissance in Stendhal's eyes were distinguished by the same reckless fire of passion, and his contemporaries must have felt something of the same parallelism in their predilection for historical settings in the Shakespearian manner, whether in Italy, Spain, Germany or medieval France.

Napoleon's effect on French Romanticism is thus incalculable. Just as Napoleon's reign left profound and permanent marks on French public life—in education, in administration, in law, in politics—so French literature for decades was affected by its contacts with the out-standing personality of the age. Hugo, who so often and so fervently hymned the glory of Napoleon, summarises as accurately as Musset the impression which the Emperor made on the men of his generation when he writes in *Lui*:

> Tu domines notre âge; ange ou démon, qu'importe?
> Ton aigle dans son vol, haletants, nous emporte.
> L'œil même qui te fuit te retrouve partout.
> Toujours dans nos tableaux tu jettes ta grande ombre;
> Toujours Napoléon, éblouissant et sombre,
>   Sur le seuil du siècle est debout.[1]

FURTHER READING

J. LUCAS-DUBRETON, *Le Culte de Napoléon* (Paris, Albin Michel; 1959).

M. DESCOTES, *La Légende de Napoléon et les écrivains français du XIXᵉ siècle* (Paris, Minard; 1967).

[1] *Lui*, in *Les Orientales* (Paris, Imprimerie Nationale; 1912), p. 752.

IV

Alfred de Vigny

(1797–1863)

FROM *Chatterton*

CHATTERTON, *avec chaleur*

Si vous saviez mes travaux!... J'ai fait de ma chambre la cellule d'un cloître; j'ai béni et sanctifié ma vie et ma pensée; j'ai raccourci ma vue, et j'ai éteint devant mes yeux les lumières de notre âge; j'ai fait mon cœur plus simple : je me suis appris le parler enfantin du vieux temps; j'ai écrit, comme le roi Harold au roi Guillaume, en vers à demi saxons et francs; et ensuite, cette muse du dixième siècle, cette muse religieuse, je l'ai placée dans une châsse comme une sainte. — Ils l'auraient brisée s'ils l'avaient crue faite de ma main : ils l'ont adorée comme l'œuvre d'un moine qui n'a jamais existé, et que j'ai nommé Rowley.

LE QUAKER

Oui, ils aiment assez à faire vivre les morts et mourir les vivants.

CHATTERTON

Cependant on a su que ce livre était fait par moi. On ne pouvait plus le détruire, on l'a laissé vivre; mais il ne m'a donné qu'un peu de bruit, et je ne puis faire d'autre métier que celui d'écrire. — J'ai tenté de me ployer à tout, sans y parvenir. — On m'a parlé de travaux exacts; je les ai abordés, sans pouvoir les accomplir. — Puissent les hommes pardonner à Dieu de m'avoir ainsi créé! — Est-ce excès de force, ou n'est-ce que faiblesse honteuse? — Je n'en sais rien, mais jamais je ne pus enchaîner dans des canaux étroits et réguliers les débordements tumultueux de mon esprit, qui toujours inondait ses rives malgré moi. J'étais incapable de suivre les lentes opérations des calculs journaliers, j'y renonçai le premier. J'avouai mon esprit vaincu par le chiffre, et j'eus dessein d'exploiter mon corps. — Hélas! mon ami! autre douleur! autre humiliation! — Ce corps, dévoré dès l'enfance par les ardeurs de mes veilles, est trop faible pour les rudes travaux de la mer ou de l'armée, trop faible même pour la moins fatigante industrie.

Il se lève avec une agitation involontaire.

Et d'ailleurs, eussé-je les forces d'Hercule, je trouverais toujours entre moi et mon ouvrage l'ennemie fatale née avec moi, la fée malfaisante trouvée sans doute dans mon berceau, la Distraction, la Poésie! — Elle se met partout; elle me donne et m'ôte tout; elle charme et détruit toute chose pour moi; elle m'a sauvé... elle m'a perdu!

ALFRED DE VIGNY, *Chatterton*, act I, sc. 5, in *Œuvres complètes*, ed. F. Baldensperger (Paris, Pléiade; 1948), vol. I, pp. 838–9

One of the tendencies of nineteenth-century literature is narcissism. It had not previously been common for writers to appear as the heroes of plays or novels, or for poetry to have itself as its main subject; now, art tends to turn in on itself and investigate the problems of its own genesis and diffusion. The question of the writer and his place in society looms large in the substantial catalogue of works devoted to fictional biographies of artists, from Mme de Staël's *Corinne* to Jules Renard's *L'Écornifleur*, but perhaps nowhere is it so dramatically highlighted as in Alfred de Vigny's *Chatterton* (1834). Vigny had already published *Stello*, a lengthy discussion in semi-fictitious form, of the artist's lot in different types of society; in the play, he again takes the young English poet Chatterton as a typical example of the fate of the poet among people who have no use for his works. The plot is extremely simple: Chatterton is starving because his contemporaries scorn what he writes and because his temperament makes him incapable of anything except composing poetry. Bullied by his brutal landlord and offered only menial jobs, he decides that his situation is hopeless and commits suicide.

Our extract is taken from an exchange between Chatterton and his friend the Quaker in the first act, and it clearly shows that, for Vigny as for Chatterton, the writing of poetry is something akin to a religious vocation, to be regarded with awe and veneration. The mystical and monastic imagery—'la cellule d'un cloître', 'béni', 'sanctifié', 'cette muse religieuse', 'dans une châsse comme une sainte'—is not just decoration, but points to a double truth about poets: that their calling is an irresistible and holy command, and that it is attended with sacrifices and suffering. Both these opinions are widely held in Romantic and post-Romantic literature, and underlie a great deal of the thinking about ways and means of securing the poet's position in society.

That poets are privileged beings, set above and apart from the rest of mankind, is one of the commonplaces of Romanticism, given its most glittering expression in the dithyrambic paeans of praise which Hugo never tires of addressing to poets and poetry.

> Peuples! écoutez le poète!
> Écoutez le rêveur sacré!
> Dans votre nuit, sans lui complète,
> Lui seul a le front éclairé.
> Des temps futurs perçant les ombres,
> Lui seul distingue en leurs flancs sombres
> Le germe qui n'est pas éclos,[1]

he exclaims in *Fonction du poète*, and in *Les Mages*, he returns to the religious metaphor which Vigny employs:

> Pourquoi donc faites-vous des prêtres
> Quand vous en avez parmi vous?
> Les esprits conducteurs des êtres
> Portent un signe sombre et doux.
> Nous naissons tous ce que nous sommes.
> Dieu de ses mains sacre des hommes
> Dans les ténèbres des berceaux;
> Son effrayant doigt invisible
> Écrit sous leur crâne la bible
> Des arbres, des monts et des eaux.
> Ces hommes, ce sont les poètes.[2]

This exaltation of the poet as one of the supreme representatives of humanity (a consequence of the Romantic cult of feeling as the key to life) stands in sharp contrast to the mocking denigrations of the utilitarian eighteenth century (for instance in Montesquieu's *Lettres persanes*) and is characteristic of the Romantic movement not only in France but in the whole of Europe. After 1830, when the Romantics added a sense of social mission to their other attributes (see commentary VII), the tendency is still further accentuated. The poet is a leader, a legislator, a prophet, a saint.

But the poet is also a man marked out for solitude, pain and incomprehension. His art itself is born only through suffering:

---

[1] *Les Rayons et les Ombres* (Paris, Imprimerie Nationale; 1909), p. 546.
[2] *Les Contemplations* (Paris, Imprimerie Nationale; 1905), p. 389.

Les plus désespérés sont les chants les plus beaux,
Et j'en sais d'immortels qui sont de purs sanglots.[1]

For Nerval, the creative processes of a great artist are akin to a descent
into hell, like that accomplished by Adoniram in his *Histoire de la reine
du matin et de Soliman prince des génies*. Even that might be bearable if
the poet's fellow-men accorded him his just reward. Instead, they
revile him, maltreat him, scorn him or ignore him:

Si c'est un poète, il entend
Ce chœur : — Absurde! faux! monstrueux! révoltant!
Lui, cependant, tandis qu'on bave sur sa palme,
Debout, les bras croisés, le front levé, l'œil calme,
Il contemple, serein, l'idéal et le beau.[2]

Poets, 'éducateurs des âmes' according to Leconte de Lisle, are always
'en proie aux dédains instinctifs de la foule comme à l'indifférence des
plus intelligents'.[3] Poets live in an ideal world and are totally unfitted
for a petty, competitive existence among men exclusively preoccupied
with material things:

Frère, voilà pourquoi les poètes, souvent,
Butent à chaque pas sur les chemins du monde;
Les yeux fichés au ciel ils s'en vont en rêvant.[4]

For Baudelaire, in *L'Albatros*, the poet is like some huge bird trapped
and tortured by ignorant sailors:

Ses ailes de géant l'empêchent de marcher.[5]

The poet is in the agonising situation of Vigny's Moïse:

Laissez-moi m'endormir du sommeil de la terre.
— Que vous ai-je donc fait pour être votre élu?...
Sitôt que votre souffle a rempli le berger,
Les hommes se sont dit : « Il nous est étranger ».[6]

---

[1] Alfred de Musset, *Poésies*, p. 316.
[2] Victor Hugo, *Melancholia*, in *Les Contemplations*, p. 122.
[3] *Poèmes antiques*, Preface, in *Derniers Poèmes* (Paris, Lemerre; 1928), p. 207.
[4] Théophile Gautier, *Terza Rima*, *Poésies* (Paris, Charpentier; 1877), vol. 1, p. 307.
[5] *Les Fleurs du mal*, *Œuvres complètes* (Paris, Pléiade; 1951), p. 84.
[6] *Œuvres complètes*, vol. 1, p. 59.

All these concordant complaints arise from a growing conviction that, in the modern world, there is no place for the poet, even though he is in reality the most important member of it. The patronage of the court, of great nobles, even of wealthy commoners, which had once given to a substantial number of writers a position of security, though a subordinate one, virtually came to an end with the Revolution, and as the number of the leisured rich who could take up literature as a pastime gradually diminished, so it became ever more necessary for writers to make a living from their pen if they were to subsist at all. This in turn meant that their works had to appeal to the middle classes if they were to bring in money in any quantity, since the middle classes now formed the great majority of the reading public. But the middle classes had no tradition of interest in the arts; they were composed of busy people whose energies were of necessity fiercely concentrated on their everyday business, which alone guaranteed their own prosperity; and if they wanted to read at all, it was in pursuit of entertainment rather than sublimity. The Romantics, on the other hand, with their elevated ideas of the poet's dignity and their militant individualism, were highly disinclined to cater for such debased and conformist tastes; they insisted on going their own way, even though the public might show no interest in following them. The *bourgeois* is thus identified with the philistine, and a breach between author and public opens up and goes on widening throughout the century.

It is in this context that Vigny presents Chatterton as a martyr to the philistinism and heartlessness of the *bourgeoisie*—'Ils aiment assez à faire... mourir les vivants', says the Quaker. Chatterton's tormentors are led by John Bell, the gross, arrogant, materialistic manufacturer whose indifference to the poet's plight is ultimately responsible for his suicide. John Bell is only one of many such symbolic caricatures in which nineteenth-century artists embodied their hatred of the forces which they thought hostile to them. Flaubert, whose detestation of the *bourgeois* almost attains the proportions of an obsession, returns again and again to the theme of the self-satisfied, stupid, petty-minded middle classes, and successively invents 'le Garçon' of his youthful jokes in Rouen, the chemist Homais of *Madame Bovary*, and finally the two clerks Bouvard and Pécuchet, in order to anatomise more fully the mentality which he loathed. Villiers de l'Isle-Adam raises a similar character to the status of a symbol when he creates Dr Tribulat

Bonhomet, 'le démon-bourgeois, ou Moderne',[1] as Mallarmé calls him, who is the central figure in half a dozen long tales of the murder of artists. In Villiers's view, what distinguishes the *bourgeois* of this world is 'leur natale haine de la Pensée, leur soif, inextinguible, *organique*, foncière, d'abaisser, d'aniaiser, de profaner toute noble et pure tendance'.[2] Remy de Gourmont follows suit by imagining the typical *bourgeois*, M. Amateur, amusing himself by buying fine engravings in order to destroy them: 'M. Amateur avait la haine de l'art'.[3] Even the peaceable Mallarmé once thought of joining the anti-*bourgeois* campaign and had it in mind to write a work which would have had as its title *Esthétique du bourgeois, ou la Théorie universelle de la laideur*.[4]

The particular aspect of this conflict which exercises Vigny in *Chatterton* is the contradiction between the absence of any regular financial rewards for poetry and the poet's incapacity for any other form of activity: 'Je ne puis faire d'autre métier que celui d'écrire', protests the hero. That he should be a poet rather than a novelist or a playwright aggravates the situation, since poetry rarely wins popular success— poets with vast followings like Lamartine and Hugo are exceptional cases. Moreover, it is in part the Romantic conception of the unbridled emotionalism of true poetry which unfits him for more mundane occupations: 'Jamais je ne pus enchaîner dans des canaux étroits et réguliers les débordements tumultueux de mon esprit, qui toujours inondait ses rives malgré moi'. The result is that, faced with an insoluble dilemma, he opts out of life altogether.

Chatterton's problem was a very real one for the artists of the nineteenth century. Should they demean themselves to some trivial breadwinning task and keep literature for their spare time (and thereby run the risk of finding their energies wholly dissipated on what they regard as meaningless and mechanical activities)? Or should they rather devote themselves entirely to their art, regardless of the economic consequences, and face the opposite danger of finding themselves without even the bare means of subsistence? Leconte de Lisle puts it in a

[1] *Œuvres complètes* (Paris, Pléiade; 1945), p. 506.
[2] Villiers de l'Isle-Adam, *Œuvres complètes* (Paris, Mercure de France; 1914–31), vol. III, p. 160. Cf. Flaubert's remarks on p. 81.
[3] *D'un Pays lointain* (Paris, Mercure de France; 1898), p. 119.
[4] Stéphane Mallarmé, *Correspondance 1862–71*, ed. H. Mondor and J.-P. Richard (Paris, Gallimard; 1959), p. 261.

nutshell (and shows how accurately *Chatterton* hits off the mood of the young writers of the time) when he writes to a friend:

> Je dois vivre de mon travail, ce qui me paraît impossible, car je ne suis bon à rien, sinon à réunir des rimes simples ou croisées, lequel travail n'a pas cours sur la place, comme dit Chatterton.[1]

For the great Romantics, the problem, though present, was not usually acute: Lamartine, Hugo, Musset and Vigny came of families which were by no means penniless, and in any case practised a type of literature which was not unsalable. Many of their less fortunate colleagues, on the other hand, could not help but sink into 'la vie de Bohème', celebrated by Mürger for its joyous freedom from constraint, but often in reality disagreeably hard.

As the century wore on, the problem became more pressing, since the reaction against Romantic poetry led to the cultivation of poetic styles which lacked its universal appeal. From the Second Empire onwards, the word 'Bohème' signifies less and less a carefree flaunting of *bourgeois* conventions and carries more and more overtones of real hardship and of Verlaine's idea of 'poètes maudits'. Journalism appealed to more and more young men as a compromise solution (as Balzac had noted—see commentary VIII); others resigned themselves to extra-literary jobs for which they felt little if any enthusiasm—Mallarmé became a schoolmaster, Huysmans a civil servant, Remy de Gourmont a librarian. Others again, like Verlaine, Léon Bloy, Villiers de l'Isle-Adam (who, so Mallarmé said, 'rejetant tout emploi autre que le sien, n'avait voulu être que ce pourquoi il était né',[2]) accepted the most abject poverty in order to be free to write as and when they liked. Seventy years after *Chatterton*, the dilemma of the artist in search of social security was no nearer solution, as witness this letter written by Paul Claudel to a young man contemplating giving up his career as a teacher in order to make a living as a writer:

> Il n'y a pas de pire carrière que celle d'un écrivain qui veut vivre de sa plume. Vous voilà donc astreint à produire avec les yeux sur un patron, et à lui donner non pas ce que vous aimez, mais ce qu'il aime, lui, et Dieu sait

[1] Letter to Rouffer, December 1839, in *Premières Poésies et lettres intimes* (Paris, Charpentier; 1902), pp. 197–8.
[2] *Œuvres complètes*, p. 498.

s'il a le goût élevé et délicat... J'ai toujours dans la mémoire les figures tragiques d'un Villiers de l'Isle-Adam, d'un Verlaine, avec des restes de talent sur eux comme les derniers poils d'une vieille fourrure mangée.[1]

In part, *Chatterton* is a propaganda piece designed to arouse public indignation about what Vigny considered a scandalous state of affairs, and its author was much concerned to find some practical solution for the difficulties of young writers. In *De Mademoiselle Sedaine et de la propriété littéraire*, he put forward an elaborate scheme for a form of State patronage, just as Mallarmé, casting envious glances sixty years later at the comfortable existence of intellectuals in Oxford and Cambridge, was to call for the establishment of a fund for the support of deserving authors, presumably in collegiate institutions. Balzac, too, with his passionate interest in money, not only analysed the plight of writers and thinkers in *L'Illustre Gaudissart*, but took effective steps to help them by participating in the foundation of the Société des Gens de lettres. Edmond de Goncourt tried to alleviate their lot by leaving his considerable fortune to found an academy and an annual prize. Various other measures to protect the livelihood of authors were instituted at different times in the century—formation of mutual assistance societies, stricter copyright laws, regularisation of theatre royalties, banning of pirated editions. The result was that the profession of authorship attained a degree of organisation which it had never previously known, at the same time as it came to form a group more and more outside the norms of society.

Beneath the exaggerations of its style and attitudes, Vigny's picture of the poet hounded to death by a vindictive philistinism thus contains a serious investigation of a problem which was anything but imaginary. It reveals the changed relationship between authors and a public which often seems to be fundamentally different in nature from them and with which they were continually at odds. It helps us to appreciate the justice of this notation from the diary of the Goncourt brothers:

> Il me semble voir une séparation, un abîme de distance entre l'artiste et le public de nos jours. Dans les autres siècles, un homme comme Molière n'était que la pensée de son public. Il était pour ainsi dire de plain-pied avec lui. Aujourd'hui, les grands hommes sont plus haut et le public plus bas.[2]

[1] Paul Claudel and Jacques Rivière, *Correspondance* (Paris, Gallimard; 1926), pp. 195–6.
[2] Edmond and Jules de Goncourt, *Journal* (Paris, Flammarion et Fasquelle; 1935), vol. II, p. 253, 27th November 1865.

FURTHER READING

Maurice Z. SCHRODER, *Icarus. The Image of the Artist in French Romanticism* (Cambridge, Mass., Harvard University Press—London, Oxford University Press; 1962).

Maurice Z. SHRODER, *Icarus. The Image of the Artist in French Romanticism* (Cambridge, Mass., Harvard University Press—London, Oxford University Press; 1962).

C. GRANA, *Bohemian versus Bourgeois French Society and the French Man of Letters in the Nineteenth Century* (New York and London, Basic Books Inc.; 1964).

Joanna RICHARDSON, *The Bohemians* (London, Macmillan; 1969).

V

Alexandre Dumas *père*

(1802–70)

LA VICOMTESSE

Est-ce que vous faites une préface?

LE BARON DE MARSANNE

Les romantiques font tous des préfaces... *Le Constitutionnel* les plaisantait l'autre jour là-dessus avec une grâce...

ADÈLE

Vous le voyez, monsieur, vous avez usé, à vous défendre, un temps qui aurait suffi à développer tout un système.

EUGÈNE

Et vous aussi, madame, faites-y attention... Vous l'exigez, je ne suis plus responsable de l'ennui... Voici mes motifs: la comédie est la peinture des mœurs; le drame, celle des passions. La Révolution, en passant sur notre France, a rendu les hommes égaux, confondu les rangs, généralisé les costumes. Rien n'indique la profession, nul cercle ne renferme telles mœurs ou telles habitudes; tout est fondu ensemble, les nuances ont remplacé les couleurs, et il faut des couleurs et non des nuances au peintre qui veut faire un tableau.

ADÈLE

C'est juste.

LE BARON DE MARSANNE

Cependant, monsieur, *le Constitutionnel*...

EUGÈNE, *sans écouter*

Je disais donc que la comédie de mœurs devenait, de cette manière, sinon impossible, du moins très difficile à exécuter. Reste le drame de passion, et ici une autre difficulté se présente. L'histoire nous lègue des faits, ils nous appartiennent par droit d'héritage, ils sont incontestables, ils sont au poète:

il exhume les hommes d'autrefois, les revêt de leurs costumes, les agite de leurs passions, qu'il augmente ou diminue selon le point où il veut porter le dramatique. Mais, que nous essayions, nous, au milieu de notre société moderne, sous notre frac gauche et écourté, de montrer à nu le cœur de l'homme, on ne le reconnaîtra pas... La ressemblance entre le héros et le parterre sera trop grande, l'analogie trop intime; le spectateur qui suivra chez l'acteur le développement de la passion voudra l'arrêter là où elle se serait arrêtée chez lui; si elle dépasse sa faculté de sentir ou d'exprimer à lui, il ne la comprendra plus, il dira : « C'est faux; moi, je n'éprouve pas ainsi; quand la femme que j'aime me trompe, je souffre sans doute... oui... quelque temps... mais je ne la poignarde ni ne meurs, et la preuve, c'est que me voilà ». Puis les cris à l'exagération, au mélodrame, couvrant les applaudissements de ces quelques hommes qui, plus heureusement ou plus malheureusement organisés que les autres, sentent que les passions sont les mêmes au XVe qu'au XIXe siècle, et que le cœur bat d'un sang aussi chaud sous un frac de drap que sous un corselet d'acier...

ADÈLE

Eh bien, monsieur, l'approbation de ces quelques hommes vous dédommagerait amplement de la froideur des autres.

ALEXANDRE DUMAS *père*, *Antony*, act IV, sc. 6,
in *Théâtre romantique* (Paris, Firmin-Didot; n.d.), pp. 194-5.

Antony, by Alexandre Dumas *père*, was first produced in May 1831, at the height of the great flowering of Romantic drama. On the title page, it is called a *drame*, but Dumas later said of it: '*Antony* est une scène d'amour, de jalousie, de colère, en cinq actes'.[1] Its frantic emotionalism, its theatrical gestures, its exalted volubility make it a typical example of the dramatic literature of the time, with the important exception that, instead of a historical setting, it has a contemporary one. Dumas, no great theorist but well aware of the interest of this innovation, had the ingenious idea of drawing attention to his audacity and at the same time justifying it by inserting this conversation in the fourth act, during a party given by the Vicomtesse de Lacy. Adèle, the heroine, asks Eugène, a dramatist, if he is still writing plays about the Middle Ages, and when he replies that he is, she inquires: 'Mais pourquoi ne pas attaquer un sujet au milieu de notre société moderne?' The Vicomtesse agrees:

C'est ce que je lui répète à chaque instant : « Faites de l'actualité ». N'est-ce pas que l'on s'intéresse bien plus à des personnages de notre époque, habillés comme nous, parlant comme nous?

[1] Alexandre Dumas *père*, *Mes Mémoires* (Paris, Cadot; 1854), vol. XXI, p. 119.

Eugène is persuaded to explain his reasons, after which the discussion moves on and the plot resumes its headlong course.

Dumas was largely right in predicting the decline of the traditional *genres* in the years following 1830, even if the causes he adduces are not entirely convincing. Tragedy was too intimately associated with the classical aesthetic to be revived once that doctrine had been discredited, and the anomalies and artificialities which had been debilitating it since the eighteenth century in any case now effectively discouraged most writers from trying to resuscitate it; Dumas does not even bother to mention it. As for comedy, in one form or another, it persisted on the stage throughout the July Monarchy, but without vigour or distinction; indeed, the dearth of formal comedies with literary pretensions was such that in 1838 the Academy complained that, for five years, it had been trying to award a prize of 10,000 francs for a five-act comedy in verse, without finding a single play worthy of consideration. For the moment, it appeared to be generally agreed that it was not worth trying to write comedies. This was a view which had even seeped through to the unsophisticated provincial hero of Flaubert's first *Éducation sentimentale*:

> On lui avait dit aussi — il l'avait lu dans les revues — que le caractère individuel s'étant considérablement mûri par suite des préoccupations politiques de la nation, les rangs s'étant nivelés et les conditions rapprochées, la comédie était devenue une chose impossible, une forme de l'art entièrement perdue.[1]

On the other hand, the historical drama which the cautious Eugène clings to so stubbornly was a safe bet in 1831—as Mme de Staël had proclaimed in *De l'Allemagne*, 'la tendance naturelle du siècle c'est la tragédie historique',[2] and the triumph of Hugo's *Hernani*, as well as of Dumas's own earlier plays like *Henri III et sa cour*, had fully confirmed that judgment.

But the infatuation with medieval and other historical subjects around 1830 soon gave rise to a set of conventions in the theatre which were at least as remote from contemporary reality as the cardboard Greek and Roman trappings of the pseudo-classical repertoire, and one is conscious of a faint self-irony when Dumas, hitherto a specialist in historical drama, makes Eugène admit that what he writes about is

---

[1] *L'Éducation sentimentale* (first version), *Œuvres de jeunesse* (Paris, Conard; 1910), p. 270.
[2] Vol. II, p. 256.

'toujours du moyen âge'. Dumas seems to have realised sooner than most
of his fellow-playwrights that the logical conclusion of the Romantic
view of art was complete modernity, and that it was something of an
accident that the return to modern times had become bogged down
half-way through past history. And so, with commendable forthright-
ness, he set about writing a play with a wholly contemporary theme and
setting and had the good fortune to see his experiment wildly applauded
by an excited public and not just by 'quelques hommes... plus
heureusement ou plus malheureusement organisés que les autres'.

It is true that Dumas was not the first dramatist to deal with modern
themes, nor even the only one of his time. There was the precedent of
Diderot's *drame bourgeois* in the eighteenth century, and numerous
minor authors were busily scribbling mediocre plays on contemporary
subjects in the 1830s and 1840s. Even the Romantics introduced topics
of the same kind into their plays, albeit in disguised form. *Chatterton*,
though set in eighteenth-century England, contains some pertinent
observations on industrial relations; *Ruy Blas* is, among other things,
an impassioned plea for the emancipation of the lower classes; and
Angélo, another costume drama by Hugo, written in 1835 but set in
1549, incriminates 'le fait social' [1] for the injustices done to women in
society. But Dumas is the only major dramatist among the Romantics
to have faced the problem of the social responsibility of the theatre in
the modern world by bringing the action of his play right up to the time
at which he was writing.

Not that his example in *Antony* was followed by any other playwrights of note, at least for some years. The vogue for exotic and
picturesque historical subjects went on unabated, fed by the inexhaustible imagination of Hugo, and, for the time being, it might have seemed
that Dumas's doubts about the way in which the majority would react
to contemporary settings on the stage were justified. In fact, 'les cris au
mélodrame' which Dumas feared had been heard long before he or anyone else had thought of producing Romantic drama in modern dress, if
only because melodrama—popular plays with music and full of spectacle and action—had for thirty years been a powerful if disreputable
rival to classical tragedy, and held attractions for many of the Romantic
playwrights. When the Romantics, too, attempted to cater for the
public's insatiable appetite for violent events and startling scenic effects,

---

[1] *Angélo*, in *Théâtre* (Paris, Imprimerie Nationale; 1905), vol. III, p. 139.

it was only natural that their critics should accuse them of debasing higher dramatic forms to the level of melodrama—even Shakespeare's plays were frequently accused of being melodramas. That is one reason why the life-span of Romantic drama proved to be so short: by 1843, when *Les Burgraves* crashed to such a resounding failure, people had so tired of its improbabilities, its over-inflated style and its ruthless pillaging of history that Ponsard's *Lucrèce* even briefly tempted them back to pseudo-Classicism.

However, if Dumas did not persuade the other Romantics to take to contemporary settings, he did foresee the course which the drama would be forced to follow, though not in the form which he expected. It was true that the spectator at a 'drame de passion' would soon complain that in real life people behaved more calmly and talked less poetically: 'Le spectateur qui suivra chez l'acteur le développement de la passion voudra l'arrêter là où elle se serait arrêtée chez lui'. Eugène's argument that such an objection could be met if the actors were decked out in medieval costume failed to hold good for long. Ten years after *Antony*, the public was coming to think that at no time had anyone lived as depicted in *Hernani* or *Ruy Blas*, and was beginning to hanker after something closer to its own experience both in setting and in emotion. Even in *Antony*, Dumas has not solved that particular problem. The high-flown tirades jar with the modern costume and contrive to suggest that reality is still several removes away. Instead of people realising, as Dumas had hoped, that 'le cœur bat d'un sang aussi chaud sous un frac de drap que sous un corselet d'acier', they became sceptical about the possibility of its ever having beaten as hectically as the Romantic dramatists would have had them believe.

The result of this change in taste was the formation, by about 1850, of a realistic theatre in France, which depended for its effect on what Dumas aptly terms 'la ressemblance entre le héros et le parterre', and which dominated the stage until the last decade of the century. The leading writers of this school—Dumas *fils*, Augier, Labiche—not only brought their characters and settings up to date, but treated subjects which they knew to be close to the hearts of their audiences, and with a mentality which was also that of their audiences. So one finds the theatre transformed both into a mirror for the spectators and into a debating society where the topical talking-points of the day were aired —money in Dumas's *La Question d'argent* and Augier's *La Ceinture dorée*, difficulties of married life in Dumas's *L'Ami des femmes* and Meilhac and Halévy's *Froufrou*, questions of class prejudice in Augier's *Le Gendre de M. Poirier*, the social relations between the sexes in Dumas's *La Dame aux camélias* and *Monsieur Alphonse*, and so on. In so doing, they were fulfilling the programme sketched out for them in *Antony*, for though Dumas does not say so specifically here, the rest of the play makes it clear that he too envisages modern-dress drama as a suitable place for raising controversial issues. Indeed, the problems on which *Antony* centres—the status of illegitimate children, the position of women in marriage, the social consequences of adultery—are precisely those which were to attract the writers of social plays thirty years later.

This impetus towards modernism which Dumas tried to impart to the theatre in *Antony* was in effect helping the theatre to keep up with the novel, which in the 1830s had no inhibitions about dealing with modern subjects in a modern way. Although the historical novel was still popular, at least in the first half of the decade, the novel which treated of the society of the Restoration or the July Monarchy was rapidly gaining ground, through the works of Balzac, Stendhal and George Sand. The progression from the Romantic view of art, which is reluctant to descend to displaying real life in all its tedious triviality, to the realist one, which insists that that is the only honest function of art, is much more continuous and much more obvious in narrative fiction than it is on the stage, since the novel had always enjoyed greater freedom in its subject-matter. In both *genres*, the movement was speeded up by the fact that, after 1830, authors tended to modify the intransigent individualism which had distinguished the early stages of Romanticism and to show an increasing social conscience in their works (as we shall see in commentary VII). This in its turn encouraged authors to turn towards subjects set firmly in their own times, which alone could enable them to deal cogently with current social issues. If the theatre shows less forcefully than the novel the literary consequences of the hope that society would be regenerated after the 1830 Revolution, that is perhaps because the major authors of the time shared only too fully the misgivings which Dumas here attributes to Eugène.

Dumas himself was well aware of the dangers involved in adopting a combative position on current affairs. *Antony*, for all its contemporary trappings, is scarcely a committed play as we would understand the term nowadays. Yet even the relatively innocuous piece of dialogue we quote had awkward repercussions for the author. The Baron de Marsanne (a very minor figure in the play) is ridiculed by the fact that he never opens his mouth without making some absurdly flattering reference to *Le Constitutionnel*, the newspaper of the liberal middle classes, which, after having at one time lent lukewarm support to the Romantics, had since 1830 been among their sternest critics. But *Le Constitutionnel* took its revenge on Dumas in 1834, when *Antony* was due to be revived. It claimed that the play was immoral and succeeded in blackmailing Thiers, then Minister of the Interior, into banning it. Dumas went to law and won his case, but even this trifling incident illustrates the fact that the more authors take it upon themselves to comment on personalities and events of the day, the more they are liable to find their freedom interfered with. This had been so in the eighteenth century; it had been so in Napoleonic times; it was so again under the Second Empire—to mention only those periods when the State was particularly sensitive to criticism and particularly quick to repress it. But throughout the nineteenth century, the desire of men of letters to make a positive contribution to the study of the affairs of their times constantly led to friction with authority. Mme de Staël, Charles Nodier, Hugo, Jules Vallès and Zola all suffered from official persecution; the Goncourts, Baudelaire, Flaubert and Barbey d'Aurevilly were subjected to legal sanctions on the grounds of alleged immorality in their works.

Dumas *père*, unlike his son, was not cut out to be a polemist, either in politics or in literature, and when the Baron de Marsanne says that 'les romantiques font tous des préfaces', Dumas is one of the few who could plead innocent. But he nevertheless had ideas of his own about the theatre, and what he used to call 'le feuilleton', that is to say, this page of dramatic criticism, 'l'apologie du drame moderne', is 'la vraie préface d'*Antony*'.[1] For all its uncertain arguments, its over-simplifications and its fallacies, it might also be called the real preface to the post-Romantic theatre in France.

FURTHER READING

D. O. EVANS, *Le Drame moderne à l'époque romantique* (Paris, Presses Universitaires de France; 1937).

[1] *Mes Mémoires*, vol. XXI, p. 103.

VI

Stendhal

(1783–1842)

FROM *Lucien Leuwen*

— C'est moi, Messieurs, qui compte avec ma cuisinière; par ce moyen, ma femme n'a que l'embarras des bambins, et moi, en laissant bavarder cette fille, je sais tout ce qui se passe chez moi; ma conversation, Messieurs, est toute dévouée à ma police, et bien m'en prend, car je suis environné d'ennemis. Vous n'avez pas d'idée, Messieurs, des frais que je fais : par exemple, j'ai un perruquier libéral pour moi, et le coiffeur des dames légitimistes pour ma femme. Vous comprenez, Messieurs, que je pourrais fort bien me faire la barbe. J'ai deux petits procès que j'entretiens uniquement pour donner occasion de venir à la préfecture au procureur, M. Clapier, l'un des libéraux les plus matois du pays, et à l'avocat, à M. Le Beau, personnage éloquent, modéré, pieux comme les grands propriétaires qu'il sert. Ma place, Messieurs, ne tient qu'à un fil; si je ne suis pas un peu protégé par son Excellence, je suis le plus malheureux des hommes. J'ai pour ennemi, en première ligne, Mgr. l'évêque; c'est le plus dangereux, il n'est pas sans relations avec quelqu'un qui approche de bien près l'oreille de S.M. la Reine, et les lettres de Mgr. l'évêque ne passent point par la poste. La noblesse dédaigne de venir dans mon salon et me harcèle avec son Henri V et son suffrage universel. J'ai enfin ces malheureux républicains, ils ne sont qu'une poignée et font du bruit comme mille. Le croiriez-vous, Messieurs, les fils des familles les plus riches, à mesure qu'ils arrivent à dix-huit ans, n'ont pas de honte d'être de ce parti. Dernièrement, pour payer l'amende de mille francs à laquelle j'ai fait condamner le journal insolent qui avait semblé approuver le charivari donné à notre digne substitut du procureur général, les jeunes gens nobles ont donné soixante-sept francs, et les jeunes gens riches, non nobles, quatre-vingt-neuf francs. Cela n'est-il pas horrible? nous qui garantissons leurs propriétés de la République!

— Et les ouvriers? dit Coffe.

— Cinquante-trois francs, Monsieur, cela fait horreur, et cinquante-trois francs tout en sous. La plus forte contribution parmi ces gens-là a été

six sous; et, Messieurs, c'est le cordonnier de mes filles qui a eu le front de
donner ces six sous.

— J'espère que vous ne l'employez plus, dit Coffe en fixant son œil
scrutateur sur le pauvre préfet.

Celui-ci eut l'air très embarrassé, car il n'osait mentir, redoutant la
contre-police de ces messieurs.

— Je serai franc, dit-il enfin, la franchise est la base de mon caractère.
Barthélemy est le seul cordonnier pour femmes de la ville. Les autres
chaussent les femmes du peuple... et mes filles n'ont jamais voulu con-
sentir... Mais je lui ai fait une bonne semonce.

STENDHAL, *Lucien Leuwen*
(Paris, Champion; 1927), vol. IV, pp. 41-2

A large part of Stendhal's unfinished novel *Lucien Leuwen*, on which
he was working between 1834 and 1836, consists of a satire on politics
under the July Monarchy, and this extract is a typical example of his
ironic observation of men and manners. The time of the action is 1834,
four years after the July Revolution had made Louis-Philippe 'roi des
Français' (and not 'roi de France'). The two 'messieurs' to whom the
unhappy prefect M. de Riquebourg is addressing himself so queru-
lously are Lucien Leuwen, the hero, and his friend Coffe, who have been
sent by the Minister of the Interior on a mission to Champagnier (a
fictitious town), where an election is about to take place. Their task
there is to ensure that the candidate favourable to the Government is
returned to the Chamber of Deputies. Arriving late at night, they are
received by the nervous and obsequious prefect, who pours out to them
this tale of woe.

The difficulties of the prefect's position are understandable. The job
of a prefect in France since Napoleon's time has been to represent the
authority of the central government in his own *département*, and at
times his functions have been held to include that of influencing voters
so as to ensure the return of Government candidates. This, in Louis-
Philippe's time, was an arduous and delicate undertaking, partly
because the Revolution of 1830 was still too recent for the Orleans
dynasty to feel securely settled on the throne, and partly because so
many dissenting factions were competing for the votes of a very
restricted electorate. (Only men paying more than 200 francs annually
in direct taxation had the vote—a little over 200,000 voters for the
whole of France, at the time of Stendhal's novel, or less than 3 per cent

of the adult male population.) The prefect had thus to keep his finger on the pulse of local opinion, both friendly and hostile, in order to keep the Government in touch with the electoral situation. That is why M. de Riquebourg takes such trouble with his cook, his barber and his lawyer, the more so as the pro-Governmental party in Champagnier is surrounded by enemies.

The Government in office, the prefect, and the minister who has dispatched Lucien and Coffe to Champagnier, belong to the *juste milieu*, that is, to the moderate Orleanist centre group which supports a constitutional monarch governing through a two-chamber parliament, and bound by the *Charte* of 1830, which set out the monarch's responsibilities and severely limited his power. Within that framework, they represent a relatively conservative tendency. Immediately after the Revolution, Stendhal himself, having been violently opposed to the clerical and authoritarian *régime* of Charles X, had welcomed the accession of Louis-Philippe, and indeed in one of the prefaces which he sketched out for *Lucien Leuwen* he declared: 'L'auteur est simplement partisan modéré de la Charte de 1830'.[1] But though Stendhal may have preferred Louis-Philippe to his predecessor, his hankering for a republic (which, paradoxically, his aristocratic temperament prevented from taking the form of out-and-out republicanism) and his contempt for the failings of the Government, especially its manipulation of elections, meant that he judged the King and his ministers with the severity of disillusionment. That is why he depicts the prefect as a cringing, time-serving imbecile, while Lucien is in process of learning by experience that in a corrupt society it is no use being too sensitive if one wishes to succeed. Only the imperturbable Coffe remains indifferent to the moral embarrassments of the situation and aims simply to do his job as efficiently as possible.

The opponents of the Government whose machinations so alarm the prefect form three groups. First come the liberals, the parliamentary opposition who do not seek to depose Louis-Philippe but who wish for some democratisation of his policies—it is their candidate whose election Lucien and Coffe have orders to prevent and with whom Stendhal himself appears to feel most sympathy. Then there are the legitimists, the supporters of the elder Bourbon branch, who regard Louis-Philippe, a scion of the younger Orleans branch, as a usurper

[1] *Lucien Leuwen*, vol. I, p. 2.

with no right to the throne. In their view, the rightful King is the
young comte de Chambord, whom they call Henri V, and in whose
favour Charles X had abdicated at the beginning of August 1830, in a
vain and belated attempt to stem the tide of revolution. As for universal
suffrage, that was the one point on which the legitimists found themselves in surprising agreement with the republicans ('deux partis dont le
triomphe est le renversement de la chose actuelle', as Balzac says[1]), both
groups believing that only the restriction of the vote was keeping the
Orleanist dynasty in power. The legitimists were mainly recruited from
the old aristocracy, hoping for a return to the *ancien régime*, which
explains their disdain for the prefect and their refusal to frequent his
salon. They were usually in alliance with the Church, Charles X's
Government having been very much under clerical influence and having strengthened the position of Catholicism in France by means of a
number of highly controversial laws. The 1830 *Charte* having declared
that Catholicism was not the religion of the State but only of the majority
of Frenchmen, the Bishop is regarded by the prefect as his most
dangerous adversary. He is all the more redoubtable as he is reputed to
have the ear of Louis-Philippe's wife, Queen Marie-Amélie—not that
she ever took any part in politics, but she was involuntarily an object of
interest to the legitimists because she was the aunt of the duchesse de
Berry, who had tried to start a legitimist insurrection in 1832. At the
other extreme stand the republicans, who were disappointed that the
fall of Charles X had not meant the return of the Republic and who,
like the legitimists, had since 1830 been plotting the overthrow of
Louis-Philippe. It was generally thought by the prosperous middle-
class electorate that under a Republic their money, their possessions and
even their lives would be in jeopardy. That is why the prefect is so
indignant that young men of wealthy families should profess republican
opinions against the Government—'nous qui garantissons leurs propriétés contre la République!' The only major political group which
the prefect does not mention are the Bonapartists. They were not
particularly prominent in the 1830s, partly because Louis-Philippe had
some success in designing policies to appeal to them, and partly
because the attempts at invasion and revolution by the current Bonapartist claimant, Napoleon's nephew Louis-Napoleon, were—for the
present—notoriously inefficient. Otherwise the picture is complete,

---

[1] *Z. Marcas*, in *La Comédie humaine* (Paris, Pléiade; 1955), vol. VII, p. 751.

with the legitimists, including M. Le Beau and the Bishop, on the right, the Government's own supporters in the centre, represented by the prefect and his two visitors, then the liberals, with M. Clapier at their head, and finally the anonymous republicans on the left.

It will be noticed that a burning local issue is the fine which the prefect had had imposed on a newspaper for appearing to approve of a demonstration against one of the Crown legal officials. Incidents of this sort gave rise to much dissension under the July Monarchy, since freedom of the press, which had vanished under Charles X, was one of the prime articles of the *Charte* which Louis-Philippe on his accession had sworn to respect. Censorship had indeed been abolished, but that did not mean that the Government was content to sit back and accept the often virulent criticism which newspapers were liable to level at it, and prosecutions of editors and journals were frequent: there were cases within a year or two of 1830 against opposition papers like *La Tribune*, *Le Figaro* and *La Caricature*. What often happened in political cases of this kind was that sympathisers of the accused banded together to help pay the fine: the most famous instance of this had occurred under Charles X, in 1828, when a national subscription had paid the 10,000 francs which the republican song-writer, Béranger, had been fined for being rude about royalty. Stendhal himself attached great importance to the freedom of the press, the political influence of which had grown immensely since the Restoration (see commentary VIII), and that is why he singles out this incident (which he does not further explain) as indicative of an autocratic desire to suppress free speech.

It is noteworthy that the prefect is obsessed with the idea of spying. He goes to ridiculous extremes to obtain clandestine information about the doings of the opposition parties, through his cook, his barber and the Crown attorney, and he is continually on his guard against the suspected spies of the other side; he even worries about whether Lucien and Coffe have secret sources of intelligence about his own activities. No doubt this obsession springs in part from his timorous character and the need he feels to ingratiate himself with the minister on whom his livelihood depends, but Stendhal makes it clear that he too takes seriously the existence of such miniature espionage systems: Lucien and Coffe are careful to ensure that the reports they send back to Paris are in code, addressed to a go-between, and posted elsewhere than in the town they are visiting. One of the things which make the prefect so wary of the Bishop is that the latter's letters are not sent through the public post, hence making it impossible for him to intercept and scrutinise them. Considering that the legitimists and the republicans were both striving to topple the *régime* and that the Government itself was resorting to large-scale chicanery in elections, the atmosphere of mutual suspicion and petty conspiracy which Stendhal evokes may be supposed to be less caricatural than it appears.

Indeed, Stendhal's picture of an election in 1834 is strikingly corroborated by Balzac's very similar account of an election in 1839 in *Le Député d'Arcis*, a novel which was still unfinished when he died. There is the same emphasis on local gossip, on elaborate and unscrupulous manœuvring, on disgruntled legitimists in the background, on interference by an emissary of the Minister of the Interior. Of the two, Stendhal's picture is the more acidly etched, even though Balzac, as a legitimist, was in principle more strongly opposed to Louis-Philippe's *régime*; but this comes about because Balzac wanted to see his novel in print without official censure, while Stendhal, as a consular official, knew that he would never be able to publish his anyway. A third novel, Louis Reybaud's *Jérôme Paturot à la recherche d'une situation sociale* (1843), further confirms this impression of electoral campaigns during the July Monarchy. Its hero becomes a Governmental candidate because he is noted for his denunciations of the freedom of the press, he scares the local prefect just as much as Lucien and Coffe do, and he owes his election to intimidation, wholesale bribery and underhand trickery. It was indeed accusations of corruption in elections which eventually sparked off the 1848 Revolution and caused the fall of the *régime*.

The local personalities mentioned by the prefect provide an interesting sidelight on class and politics under Louis-Philippe. The active politicians in Champagnier appear to be the Crown attorney, the lawyer, the Bishop and the rich young men—in other words, the moneyed classes rather than the aristocracy, who prefer to brood in solitude (except for those of their sons who rebelliously support the republicans). The workers are mentioned only incidentally but are obviously a source of anxiety, though they too, like the nobles, if for very different reasons, stand outside the main arena of political activity. This is because, under Louis-Philippe, the middle classes were powerful as never before in political matters. With 1830, the nobility had lost their grip on political life; the proletariat, still deprived of the vote, had not yet found any legal means of making their opinion count. The governing class, severely restricted by the *cens* (the tax qualification for the vote), thus consisted largely of farmers and professional men. Louis-Philippe himself, *le roi bourgeois* with his umbrella, his unpretentiousness and his easy-going manner, was their symbol as well as their leader. Nor is it without significance that the prefect should take money matters as a gauge of political feelings: money-making was the prime concern of the middle classes, money was the key to the vote, and, as Balzac so often insisted, money was rapidly becoming the standard by which all values were judged. It was in Louis-Philippe's reign that a minister launched the slogan: 'Enrichissez-vous!'

Lucien Leuwen is perhaps the most revealing satire of political life during the July Monarchy, and this passage ironically displays many of the forces which were moulding government at the time and which, to different degrees, were permanent features of the political scene in nineteenth-century France: the monopoly of power by the *bourgeoisie*, the reactionary pressure from discontented nobles, the menacing rise of the working classes, the dissensions which continually split the moderates, the tension between Catholics and anti-clericals, the fear of the press, the constant worry that extremists of the Left or the Right would seek redress of their grievances through revolution. As Stendhal well knew, it was becoming almost impossible to depict the life of the times without taking sides in politics. As he says in his preface to *Lucien Leuwen*:

> Pour peu qu'un roman s'avise de peindre les habitudes de la société actuelle, avant d'avoir de la sympathie pour les personnages, le lecteur se dit : « De quel parti est cet homme-là ? ».[1]

Present-day readers of nineteenth-century novels may not want to ask exactly that question, but they will risk understanding very imperfectly the works of the period unless they know something of the political background.

FURTHER READING

R. SOLTAU, *French Political Thought in the Nineteenth Century* (New Haven, Yale University Press; 1931).

[1] *Lucien Leuwen*, vol. I, p. 2.

VII

Félicité de Lamennais

(1782–1854)

FROM *Paroles d'un croyant*

Comprenez bien comment on se rend libre.

Pour être libre, il faut avant tout aimer Dieu, car si vous aimez Dieu, vous ferez sa volonté, et la volonté de Dieu est la justice et la charité, sans lesquelles point de liberté.

Lorsque, par violence ou par ruse, on prend ce qui est à autrui; lorsqu'on l'attaque dans sa personne; lorsqu'en chose licite on l'empêche d'agir comme il veut, ou qu'on le force d'agir comme il ne veut pas; lorsqu'on viole son droit d'une manière quelconque, qu'est-ce que cela? Une injustice. C'est donc l'injustice qui détruit la liberté.

Si chacun n'aimait que soi et ne songeait qu'à soi, sans venir au secours des autres, le pauvre serait obligé souvent de dérober ce qui est à autrui, pour vivre et faire vivre les siens, le faible serait opprimé par un plus fort, et celui-ci par un autre encore plus fort; l'injustice règnerait partout. C'est donc la charité qui conserve la liberté.

Aimez Dieu plus que toutes choses, et le prochain comme vous-mêmes, et la servitude disparaîtra de la terre.

Cependant ceux qui profitent de la servitude de leurs frères mettront tout en œuvre pour la prolonger. Ils emploieront pour cela le mensonge et la force.

Ils diront que la domination arbitraire de quelques-uns et l'esclavage de tous les autres est l'ordre établi de Dieu; et, pour conserver leur tyrannie, ils ne craindront point de blasphémer la Providence.

Répondez-leur que leur Dieu à eux est Satan, l'ennemi de la race humaine, et que le vôtre est celui qui a vaincu Satan.

Après cela, ils déchaîneront contre vous leurs satellites; ils feront bâtir des prisons sans nombre pour vous y enfermer; ils vous poursuivront avec le fer et le feu, ils vous tourmenteront et répandront votre sang comme l'eau des fontaines.

Si donc vous n'êtes pas résolus à combattre sans relâche, à tout supporter sans fléchir, à ne jamais vous lasser, à ne céder jamais, gardez vos fers et renoncez à une liberté dont vous n'êtes pas dignes.

La liberté est comme le royaume de Dieu : elle souffre violence, et les violents la ravissent.

Et la violence qui vous mettra en possession de la liberté n'est pas la violence féroce des voleurs et des brigands, l'injustice et la vengeance, la cruauté; mais une volonté forte, inflexible, un courage calme et généreux.

La cause la plus sainte se change en une cause impie, exécrable, quand on emploie le crime pour la soutenir. D'esclave l'homme de crime peut devenir tyran, mais jamais il ne devient libre.

FÉLICITÉ DE LAMENNAIS, Paroles d'un croyant, XXII,
in Œuvres complètes (Paris, Pagnerre; 1844), vol. x, pp. 69–72

The Industrial Revolution reached France somewhat later than England, and it was during the July Monarchy that its effects first made themselves felt on a massive scale. The proportion of the population living in large towns grew from 15 per cent in 1830 to 25 per cent in 1846, and as workers poured in from the countryside, so wages decreased and unemployment rose. In 1832 one person in seven in Paris was dependent on charity, only a third of the population of France was able to afford meat, children were working as cheap labour in factories and mines, and the working day could be as much as sixteen hours. The formation of this vast depressed class, herded together in great cities, neglected by the Government, periodically breaking out in riots like those in Lyons in 1831 and 1834, drew the attention of social reformers to the fact that it was monstrously unjust that such abysmal poverty should exist alongside the riches coined by the factory-owners and capitalists, with the result that innumerable schemes for the reorganisation of the country's economy on a socialist basis were propounded in the 1830s and 1840s. Perhaps the most resounding of these calls for reform was the <i>Paroles d'un croyant</i>, by the abbé Félicité de Lamennais, which stirred the conscience of the whole of Europe on its publication in 1834.

When Lamennais talks about liberty, as he does here, he is thinking less of freedom of political action (as eighteenth-century reformers and revolutionaries had done) than of freedom to earn a living—phrases like 'lorsque, par violence ou par ruse, on prend ce qui est à autrui' or 'ceux qui profitent de la servitude de leurs frères' are clearly aimed at an economic system which in effect reduced the majority to slavery. It is true that for Lamennais economic evils are perpetuated by political means, and when he says: 'lorsqu'en chose licite on l'empêche d'agir comme il veut', he plainly has in mind the legislation of the early 1830s directed against workmen's associations. But for him as for most of his like-minded contemporaries, the root of the trouble lies not in the political institutions of the State but in an economic system based on the exploitation of the many by the few.

But while Lamennais passionately denounces social injustice and extols the spirit of Christian charity in this passage, there is no sign of any very positive doctrine of economic reorganisation, and this is where he tends to differ from other social reformers of his time. Most of them had a more or less practical system to expound; Lamennais's indignation remains primarily moral. The followers of the comte de Saint-Simon (1760–1825), for instance, saw the solution in increasing industrial production with the State ensuring that the proceeds were fairly distributed among the various classes. On the other hand, Charles Fourier (1772–1837) wanted society to be regrouped in a series of co-operative *phalanges*, with agriculture as their basis. Another group of thinkers, including Pierre Leroux, Blanqui and Louis Blanc, held that capital ought to be common property. After Marx and Engels had produced their *Communist Manifesto* in 1848, writers like Proudhon denounced the whole idea of property as immoral. It is difficult to find any such theories in Lamennais's works. What he counts on is the religious impulse towards justice: 'Pour être libre, il faut avant tout aimer Dieu', 'aimez Dieu plus que toutes choses, et le prochain comme vous-mêmes, et la servitude disparaîtra de la terre'.

It was natural that Lamennais, who in 1834 was still in Holy Orders and who had attained considerable eminence as a Catholic apologist, should maintain that the disorders of society could be extirpated by a practical application of the teachings of Christ. But he was far from alone in linking social reform and religious ardour. In their different ways, almost all the socialist systems of the 1830s and 1840s sought to give a semi-mystical colouring to their ideas. Prosper Enfantin, who in 1829 had become one of the joint heads of the Saint-Simonian sect, set up a religious hierarchy, proclaiming Saint-Simon as the new Messiah, giving himself the title 'Père', founding a kind of pseudo-religious community at Ménilmontant and eventually setting out for the East in search of a 'Femme-Messie' (the emancipation of women was an important article of faith in many of these creeds). Fourier's social theories rested on a set of mystical notions of 'universal analogy' and 'passionate attraction'. Others like George Sand's friend Pierre Leroux made democracy itself the object of a veritable cult. The connections between socialism and religion are illuminated by a fragment of dialogue from *Le Meunier d'Angibault*, written by George Sand in 1845. The speakers are, respectively, an honest miller and a rich and grasping farmer:

> — Et nous autres paysans, nous sommes comme les femmes, nous avons besoin de religion.
> — Eh bien! vous en avez une sous la main; allez à la messe, je ne vous en empêche pas, pourvu que vous ne me forciez pas d'y aller.
> — Cela peut arriver cependant, si la religion que nous avons redevient fanatique et persécutante comme elle l'a été si fort et si souvent.
> — Elle ne vaut donc rien? laissez-la tomber. Je m'en passe bien, moi!
> — Mais puisqu'il nous en faut une, absolument, à nous autres, c'est donc une autre qu'il faudrait avoir?
> — Une autre! une autre! diable! comme tu y vas! Fais-en donc une, toi!
> — J'en voudrais avoir une qui empêchât les hommes de se haïr, de se craindre et de se nuire.
> — Ça serait neuf, en effet! J'en voudrais bien une comme ça qui empêcherait des métayers de me voler mon blé la nuit, et mes journaliers de mettre trois heures par jour à manger leur soupe.
> — Cela serait, si vous aviez une religion qui vous commandât de les rendre aussi heureux que vous-même.[1]

This dialogue, while stressing the widely felt need of a religious basis for social reform, by its denunciation of Catholicism as having failed, shows up the whole anomaly of Lamennais's position. On the one hand, he was a liberal democrat preaching reform, and on the other he was a priest of a Church which at that time was associated throughout Europe with conservative monarchical *régimes*. Lamennais himself longed above all to re-inspire the Church with the spirit of primitive Christianity and to make it a regenerative force in society. Instead, he found his *Paroles d'un croyant* condemned by the Pope in words which left no doubt about the side on which the Church intended to align itself:

> Nous réprouvons, condamnons et voulons qu'à perpétuité on tienne pour condamné et réprouvé le livre dont nous venons de parler, qui a pour titre

[1] *Le Meunier d'Angibault* (Paris, Nelson; 1962), p. 142.

Paroles d'un croyant, où, par un abus impie de la parole de Dieu, les peuples sont criminellement poussés à rompre les liens de tout ordre public, à renverser l'une et l'autre autorité, à exciter, à nourrir, étendre et fortifier les séditions dans les empires, les troubles et les rébellions.[1]

One could hardly imagine a more direct conflict than that which opposes this condemnation to Lamennais's prediction: 'Ils diront que la domination arbitraire de quelques-uns et l'esclavage de tous les autres est l'ordre établi de Dieu'. The break was inevitable, and though Lamennais at first tried to submit to the Pope's judgment, it was not long before he found himself divorced from the Church, lonely and disappointed.

In this as in so many other things, Lamennais's fate typifies that of many men of letters of his generation, who found themselves unable to reconcile their reforming zeal with the reactionary policies of the Church: Lamartine and Hugo, for instance, both former Catholic Royalists, abandoned orthodoxy for reasons which were largely social and political. After the alliance between Napoleon III and the Church, the hostility between republican and Catholic opinion grew ever sharper, and the Third Republic was the theatre of numerous quarrels between the two groups—over the nomination of bishops, over the authorisation of religious Orders, over the laicisation of education and the like. When in commentary xx we analyse Anatole France's comments on the Dreyfus case, we shall see how envenomed the dispute had become. Flaubert's caricatural opposition of the free-thinking Left-winger Homais and the complacently conservative abbé Bournisien represents one of the fundamental divisions that split France in the nineteenth century. At the same time, one can trace back to Lamennais a current of liberal Catholicism which managed to combine religious orthodoxy and concern with social reform. Men like Lacordaire, Montalembert and Ozanam lent it their support, and after Leo XIII in his encyclical *Rerum novarum* in 1891 had enjoined Catholics to re-examine the situation of the working classes in modern industrial society, it became a real force in French politics.

Though Lamennais failed to convert the Church into an organ of social renovation, he did exercise a profound influence on the literature of his time. The pressure which socialist thinkers exerted on literature

[1] From the encyclical letter *Singulari vos*.

during the July Monarchy was very heavy, so heavy that one could say
it changed the whole direction of the Romantic movement. The necessity for drastic changes in the structure of society, the intolerable condition of the poor and the suppression of individual liberty through
economic tyranny shocked almost all the leading Romantics after
1830, in many cases through personal contacts with Lamennais or
one or other of the socialist groups of the day. The result is that
much post-1830 Romantic literature is, directly or indirectly, propaganda pleading for a complete reform of society. The outstanding
example is of course supplied by Victor Hugo. As he said in *Écrit
en 1846*:

> J'ai, dans le livre, avec le drame, en prose, en vers,
> Plaidé pour les petits et pour les misérables,
> Suppliant les heureux et les inexorables.[1]

The preliminary note to *Les Misérables* (1862) makes the reforming
intention even clearer:

> Tant qu'il existe, par le fait des lois et des mœurs, une damnation sociale
> créant artificiellement, en pleine civilisation, des enfers, et compliquant
> d'une fatalité humaine la destinée qui est divine; tant que les trois pro-
> blèmes du siècle, la dégradation de l'homme par le prolétariat, la déchéance
> de la femme par la faim, l'atrophie de l'enfant par la nuit, ne seront pas
> résolus; tant que, dans certaines régions, l'asphyxie sociale sera possible;
> en d'autres termes, et à un point de vue plus étendu encore, tant qu'il y
> aura sur la terre ignorance et misère, des livres de la nature de celui-ci
> pourront ne pas être inutiles.[2]

One even finds one of the favourite themes of Hugo's social literature
anticipated by Lamennais here when he declares that, if there were
neither charity nor justice, 'le pauvre serait obligé souvent de dérober
ce qui est à autrui, pour vivre et faire vivre les siens'. The noble brigand
had been a Romantic commonplace for long enough, largely because he
corresponded to an individualistic contempt for the rules and regulations of society. But after 1830 Hugo tends to transform the idea into
that of the man who, from the sheer necessity of keeping alive, is compelled to commit what society pitilessly regards as crimes—above all,

[1] *Les Contemplations*, p. 264.
[2] *Les Misérables* (Paris, Imprimerie Nationale; 1908), vol. I, p. 3.

the Jean Valjean of *Les Misérables*. Lamennais would certainly have agreed with Hugo that:

> La faim, c'est le regard de la prostituée,
> C'est le bâton ferré du bandit, c'est la main
> Du pâle enfant volant un pain sur le chemin.[1]

Like many of Hugo's later works, a large number of George Sand's novels are devoted to urging the need for action to improve the lot of the poor: *Spiridion*, *Consuelo* and *Le Meunier d'Angibault* all preach a socialist thesis. Vigny's *Chatterton* echoes socialist thought on the exploitation of the poor: the heartless John Bell boasts:

> La terre est à moi parce que je l'ai achetée; les maisons, parce que je les ai bâties; les habitants, parce que je les loge; et leur travail, parce que je le paye. Je suis juste selon la loi.[2]

Lamartine moves from solitary melancholy to active social republicanism, founds a *Parti social*, and eventually takes a leading part in the February Revolution of 1848, a development which typifies the evolution of Romanticism in general and which Lamartine himself summarises thus:

> Jeune, j'ai partagé le délire et la faute,
> J'ai crié ma misère, hélas, à voix trop haute :
> Mon âme s'est brisée avec son propre cri!
> De l'univers sensible atome insaisissable,
> Devant le grand soleil j'ai mis mon grain de sable,
> Croyant mettre un monde à l'abri.
>
> Puis, mon cœur, insensible à ses propres misères,
> S'est élargi plus tard aux douleurs de mes frères;
> Tous leurs maux ont coulé dans le lac de mes pleurs,
> Et, comme un grand linceul que la pitié déroule,
> L'âme d'un seul, ouverte aux plaintes de la foule,
> A gémi toutes les douleurs.[3]

Even some of the writers who are not normally thought of as having social preoccupations participated at one time or another in the move-

[1] *Chose vue un jour de printemps*, in *Les Contemplations*, p. 118.
[2] *Chatterton*, p. 830.
[3] *A M. Félix Guillemardet sur sa maladie* (1837), in *Recueillements poétiques* (Paris, Gosselin; 1847), pp. 56-7.

ment for reform. Sainte-Beuve sympathised successively with the Saint-Simonians and with Lamennais, Leconte de Lisle for a time was a regular contributor to the Fourierist periodical *La Phalange*, Baudelaire knew the works of Fourier and had socialist leanings before 1848, Balzac (whose politics were highly conservative) gives a favourable portrait of a Saint-Simonian in the person of Michel Chrestien in *Illusions perdues*.

One of the consequences of this desire to depict contemporary conditions in such a way as to make people want to change them is an increasing trend towards realism during this period. Lamennais's eloquent indignation has a timeless quality, but many of his contemporaries believed that the best way of correcting social abuses was to show concrete examples of them from their own time. The tendency is visible in George Sand, in Balzac (though the ills and remedies he discusses are not those the socialists diagnosed), in Eugène Sue and in later Hugo. The Left-wing press of the time was continually exhorting the Romantics to pay more attention to the problems of their own age, and even turned momentarily benevolent towards Dumas in gratitude for *Antony*. But at the same time, this movement towards utilitarian literature provoked a reaction in the opposite direction on the part of those who felt that art ought to remain independent of didactic or social intentions, and Gautier's preface to *Mademoiselle de Maupin*, written in the same year as the *Paroles d'un croyant*, shows violent hostility to the invasion of art by non-artistic preoccupations. In this manifesto of *l'art pour l'art* he is particularly severe on religious and socialist writers, among whom he mentions Lamennais—'quelques-uns font infuser dans leur religion un peu de républicanisme; ce ne sont pas les moins curieux'.[1] Gautier himself, the Parnassians and Baudelaire all support the idea of the autonomy of art which was eventually to find its apotheosis in the cult of art practised by the Symbolists (see commentary XVII).

But if the social theories formulated under the July Monarchy had a multiple effect on literature, literature in turn helped to give those theories an audience and an efficaciousness which they might otherwise have lacked. Lamennais and Hugo probably did more than anyone to jolt the society of Louis-Philippe's time into awareness of its own failings and injustices, and socialist ideas gained as much currency among

---

[1] *La Préface de « Mademoiselle de Maupin »*, (Paris, Droz; 1946), p. 6.

the general public through the novels of George Sand and the songs of Béranger, albeit in vague and simplified forms, as they did through the less accessible treatises of the sociologists and political philosophers. One can see in the powerful biblical simplicity of Lamennais's language a determined and successful effort to speak to the people in terms they would both understand and feel to be true; the printer in charge of *Paroles d'un croyant* in 1834 is reported to have said: 'Mes ouvriers eux-mêmes ne peuvent le composer sans en être comme soulevés et transportés; l'imprimerie est tout en l'air'.[1] It is this spirit that led to the 1848 Revolution (which in the last paragraphs of this passage Lamennais seems both to foresee and to fear, lest it should compromise the purity of the cause of the poor); without taking it into account, one can scarcely understand the events of that year.

FURTHER READING

D. O. EVANS, *Social Romanticism in France 1830–48* (Oxford, Clarendon Press; 1951).

H. J. HUNT, *Le Socialisme et le Romantisme en France* (Oxford, Clarendon Press; 1935).

D. G. CHARLTON, *Secular Religions in France 1815-70* (Oxford University Press; 1963).

A. J. GEORGE, *The Development of French Romanticism: the Impact of the Industrial Revolution on Literature* (Syracuse, Syracuse University Press; 1955).

[1] Quoted by Claude Carcopino, in *Les Doctrines sociales de Lamennais* (Paris, Presses Universitaires de France; 1942), p. 205.

VIII

Honoré de Balzac

(1799–1850)

FROM *Illusions perdues*

Toujours la même ardeur précipite chaque année, de la province ici, un nombre égal, pour ne pas dire croissant, d'ambitions imberbes qui s'élancent la tête haute, le cœur altier, à l'assaut de la Mode, cette espèce de princesse Tourandocte des *Mille et un Jours* pour qui chacun veut être le prince Calaf! Mais aucun ne devine l'énigme. Tous tombent dans la fosse du malheur, dans la boue du journal, dans les marais de la librairie. Ils glanent, ces mendiants, des articles biographiques, des tartines, des faits-Paris aux journaux, ou des livres commandés par de logiques marchands de papier noirci qui préfèrent une bêtise débitée en quinze jours à un chef-d'œuvre, qui veut du temps pour se vendre. Ces chenilles, écrasées avant d'être papillons, vivent de honte et d'infamie, prêtes à mordre ou à vanter un talent naissant, sur l'ordre d'un pacha du *Constitutionnel*, de la *Quotidienne* ou des *Débats*, au signal des libraires, à la prière d'un camarade jaloux, souvent pour un dîner. Ceux qui surmontent les obstacles oublient les misères de leur début. Moi qui vous parle, j'ai fait pendant six mois des articles où j'ai mis la fleur de mon esprit pour un misérable qui les disait de lui, qui sur ces échantillons a passé rédacteur d'un feuilleton : il ne m'a pas pris pour collaborateur, il ne m'a pas même donné cent sous, je suis forcé de lui tendre la main et de lui serrer la sienne.

— Et pourquoi? dit fièrement Lucien.

— Je puis avoir besoin de mettre dix lignes dans son feuilleton, répondit froidement Lousteau. Enfin, mon cher, travailler n'est pas le secret de la fortune en littérature, il s'agit d'exploiter le travail d'autrui. Les propriétaires de journaux sont des entrepreneurs, nous sommes des maçons. Aussi plus un homme est médiocre, plus promptement arrive-t-il ; il peut avaler des crapauds vivants, se résigner à tout, flatter les petites passions basses des sultans littéraires, comme un nouveau venu de Limoges, Hector Merlin, qui fait déjà de la politique dans un journal du centre droit, et qui travaille à notre petit journal : je l'ai vu ramasser le chapeau tombé d'un rédacteur en chef. En n'offusquant personne, ce garçon-là passera entre les ambitions rivales pendant qu'elles se battront.

HONORÉ DE BALZAC, Illusions perdues,
ed. A. Adam (Paris, Garnier; 1956), pp. 274–6

The second part of Balzac's *Illusions perdues*, entitled *Un Grand Homme de province à Paris* and first published in 1839, uses the dramatic story of Lucien de Rubempré's rise and fall as a journalist in order to produce a long and searching analysis of the world of the press and publishing in Paris.[1] The talented but immature Lucien is constantly torn between genuine devotion to literature (represented by his idealistic friends in the *Cénacle*) and desire for success at any price (represented by the cynical and unscrupulous newspapermen who persuade him that ruthlessness, a lively style and a liking for intrigue are all that he needs to win fame and riches through the press). The most clear-sighted of these disillusioned hacks is Étienne Lousteau, who in the course of the long conversation with Lucien from which this extract is taken expounds to him the immoral, venal, egoistic habits of the career on which he is about to embark.

Newspapers were not by any means a new invention at this time. They had originated in the privately circulated news letters of the seventeenth century, had developed in the eighteenth century as influential organs of opinion, usually as periodicals rather than as dailies, had multiplied under the Revolution, had further enhanced their importance under Napoleon and the Restoration, despite the repressive censorship to which they were subjected, and had by 1830 attained such power over the public that they were largely responsible for mobilising hostility to Charles X and bringing about the July Revolution. But they continued to be relatively expensive objects until the mid-1830s when Émile de Girardin altered the whole nature of journalism by selling his new paper *La Presse* at half the usual price. From then on, newspapers became more and more the staple reading matter of the literate classes, whose numbers were expanding rapidly with the spread of elementary education. The great organs of opinion which Balzac enumerates here reached what was for those days a large public: in 1824, about the time when Balzac situates the action of

---

[1] Journalists and the press figure in various other novels of the *Comédie humaine* too, notably *César Birotteau* (where Balzac investigates the effects of commercial publicity, through the press), and *Une Fille d'Ève*.

Illusions perdues, *Le Constitutionnel*, of liberal tendencies, had over 16,000 subscribers, *La Quotidienne*, ultra-Royalist, had nearly 6,000, and *Le Journal des débats*, Royalist, had 13,000 (and they were all read by far more people than those who could afford to take them regularly). By 1839, when Balzac was writing *Illusions perdues*, the total sale of Parisian dailies was nearing 100,000 and provincial papers probably sold half as many again. When one considers that the total electorate did not greatly exceed that number, it becomes clear that what by present-day standards would be a very modest circulation represented then a position of considerable political power.

The rush to Paris by young men with literary ambitions was not a new phenomenon either. It had existed at least since the time when the centralising forces of the seventeenth century had conferred on the capital its undisputed pre-eminence as the centre of cultural as well as political life. But in Balzac's view, the process had been greatly accelerated since the beginning of the nineteenth century by two factors: one was the enormous growth in the prestige of the national press, and the other was the relative democratisation of public and artistic activity which had taken place since the Revolution. The result is that there are, in the *Comédie humaine* (as in novels like *Le Rouge et le Noir* or *L'Éducation sentimentale*), swarms of youths like Lucien de Rubempré who fondly imagine that because their works have been applauded in some provincial *salon* they have only to move to Paris in order to achieve a national success.

But Balzac, always alive to the economic laws of artistic production, realised that such young men were, at the outset of a literary career, faced with the problem of subsistence, since large-scale works were liable to demand months or even years of labour without any cash returns in the meantime. The obvious expedient, for someone intending to make a living as a writer, was to work for newspapers and reviews; but this often proved so time-consuming, so exhausting and so soul-destroying that a man's talent could be completely eroded by it. Balzac consequently denounces journalism as the graveyard of true literature; as Fulgence Ridal, one of the members of the *Cénacle*, warns Lucien:

> Le journalisme est un enfer, un abîme d'iniquités, de mensonges, de trahisons, que l'on ne peut traverser et d'où l'on ne peut sortir pur, que protégé comme Dante par le divin laurier de Virgile.[1]

[1] *Illusions perdues*, p. 250.

Exactly the same bitter reproaches are levelled at journalism by the hero of the Goncourt brothers' novel *Charles Demailly*, in which they anatomised the press of 1860 as Balzac had done that of the Restoration. Charles Demailly exclaims to his colleagues on *Le Scandale* who have been mocking his pretensions as a writer:

> Eh bien! oui, je fais du petit journal... Je fais des articles, je fais de l'esprit... je joue de l'orgue et de la clarinette... Il y a des choses que je signe : en les signant, je sais qu'elles n'auront pas plus d'immortalité qu'un gâteau monté... Le plus bas métier du monde, mes amis! Vous avez bien raison; ma conscience me le chante depuis assez longtemps; vous la doublez, je vous dois quelque chose! Parbleu! si vous croyez que je suis arrivé là du premier coup!... J'ai eu l'âge où l'on présente une tragédie à l'Odéon... Je cherchais la petite bête... Je voulais souffler dans mes doigts, creuser dans mon coin, faire un beau livre... J'avais des illusions, des idées... Dites donc, est-ce que vous me prenez pour un homme de lettres? Un homme de lettres, moi? Allons donc! je suis un cheval de fiacre : touchez là, mes amis![1]

Like Lucien, Charles is torn between journalism and serious literature, and though he tries to escape from the world of the gutter press, like Lucien he is destroyed by his former friends.

There is no doubt that in the nineteenth century there were many able and original writers who wasted their creative talents on ephemeral journalism, Balzac himself among them, but also Gautier, Nerval, Barbey d'Aurevilly, Zola and Maupassant. In some cases, what they wrote for newspapers retains the qualities of their other work, but for the most part it is of minor and transitory interest. Most often it was financial necessity which compelled them to write for newspapers. Sometimes, especially with those numerous writers—among them Chateaubriand, George Sand, Victor Hugo and dozens of Symbolist poets—who founded or edited periodicals, they wanted to produce propaganda for some political or literary ideology. Sometimes, with writers like Sainte-Beuve, Anatole France or Brunetière, they practised journalism because their ability as critics rendered them invaluable in the day-to-day assessment of the literary life of the country. Sometimes, as in the case of Balzac's own abortive attempts to found and run reviews on his own, the lure was doubtless the power over men's minds which the press represented. But in all these instances, it seems likely

---

[1] *Charles Demailly* (Paris, Flammarion and Fasquelle; 1926), p. 40.

that the pressure of journalistic production interfered with the possible elaboration of works of more permanent value, and that the persistence of journalistic habits of presentation vitiated the quality of some of their major projects.

The result of catering for an enormous public which did not buy its newspapers for any pieces of literature they might contain, and which had no intention of reading them very carefully anyway, was to lower the artistic standards of the people who wrote for them. The 'logiques marchands de papier noirci' set out simply to satisfy existing tastes, however low they might be, and produced during the July Monarchy and afterwards a commercialisation of art on a scale never before experienced. The Goncourts are scathing about this development:

> Plus de public; une certaine quantité de gens seulement qui aiment lire pour leur digestion, comme on boit un verre d'eau après une tasse de chocolat, gens demandant une prose coulante et claire, de l'eau de Seine clarifiée; gens aimant à se faire raconter en voyage, en voiture, en chemin de fer, des histoires par un livre qui en contient beaucoup; gens qui lisent, non pas un livre, mais pour vingt sous.[1]

An editor in Villiers de l'Isle-Adam's satirical tale *Deux Augures* (1883) likewise tells a budding author:

> Tout journaliste vraiment digne de ce grand titre doit n'écrire qu'au trait de la plume, n'importe ce qui lui passe par la tête, — et, surtout, sans se relire! Va comme je te pousse! Et avec des convictions dues seulement à l'humeur du moment et à la couleur du journal. Et marche!... Le Public ne lit pas un journal pour penser ou réfléchir, que diable! — On lit comme on mange.[2]

This general preference for what Lousteau calls 'une bêtise débitée en quinze jours' certainly had an effect on literary forms in the nineteenth century. In the 1830s, when Girardin was launching the first cheap mass-circulation newspapers, it became customary for papers to serialise new novels, often commissioning them specially from authors who knew how to maintain suspense from episode to episode. The great master of the *roman-feuilleton*, as it was called,[3] was Eugène Sue, whose

[1] *Charles Demailly*, p. 78.
[2] *Œuvres complètes*, vol. II, pp. 50, 53.
[3] The *feuilleton* was originally the literary and critical part of the paper, as distinct from the news pages.

Juif errant is reputed to have attracted 15,000 new subscribers to *Le Constitutionnel* and to have brought him in 100,000 francs, but Dumas *père* ran him a close second, while Balzac himself and George Sand were also much in demand. The limited space which a daily paper could allot to fiction likewise helped to promote the fortunes of the short story: the eagerness of newspapers to buy his wares explains the often hasty and uninspired nature of much of Maupassant's massive output.

Balzac points out that the growth of the press has led to a concentration of literary power in the hands of newspaper editors and critics. The influence of the press became vital in securing the success of new books which had to reach a wider public than ever before if they were to prove economically viable. Lousteau is right to point out that newspaper proprietors, who exploit other people's work, hold the key to fame and fortune in modern conditions; he is also right to emphasise how much (and sometimes for what irrelevant reasons) critics can affect the reception accorded to an unknown author. The critics of the big newspapers—men like Sainte-Beuve, Jules Janin or Francisque Sarcey—could make and break reputations easily if they set their mind to it. For instance, if Sainte-Beuve had ever condescended to write the article on Baudelaire which he was constantly promising, he might have changed the whole attitude of the public towards the poet. On the other hand, Maeterlinck's emergence from obscurity was due largely to a sensational article in *Le Figaro*, in which Octave Mirbeau compared him to Shakespeare. As Lousteau tells Lucien, measuring their chances of success as journalists against those of d'Arthez, the writer of genius who is the moving spirit of the *Cénacle*:

> Quand d'Arthez sera devenu aussi instruit que Bayle et aussi grand écrivain que Rousseau, nous aurons fait notre fortune, nous serons maîtres de la sienne et de sa gloire.[1]

As for the intrigues, the flattery, the backbiting, the jealousy which, according to Balzac, dominate life on newspapers, it is difficult to know how far the picture has been deliberately darkened for dramatic effect. At all events, Lousteau's views are no more cynical than those one finds in other nineteenth-century novels dealing with the press. Charles Demailly's associates are quite as vile as the men of whom Lousteau is speaking; the hero of Maupassant's *Bel-Ami* (1885) establishes himself

---

[1] *Illusions perdues*, p. 328.

as a prominent journalist by a judicious use of his skill as a seducer; two of the young men in Maurice Barrès's *Les Déracinés* (1897) even commit murder to gain funds for the paper *La Vraie République*. The only novel to portray a journalistic *milieu* with some degree of sympathy is Remy de Gourmont's *Sixtine* (1890), and there, since he is describing one of the literary reviews of the Symbolist period, his characters are men of letters rather than professional journalists. Generally speaking, novelists were agreed that the ruthless competition on newspapers led to corruption, dishonesty and selfishness.

If novelists were so derogatory about the influence, the customs and the values of the press, it is at least in part because they knew what immense power for good or evil it could wield and felt that it was failing to live up to its responsibilities. According to one of the newspapermen in *Illusions perdues*:

> Le Journal au lieu d'être un sacerdoce est devenu un moyen pour les partis; de moyen, il s'est fait commerce; et comme tous les commerces, il est sans foi ni loi.[1]

Few men of letters were able to resist the temptation of journalism; few seem to have had much respect for it as a calling. But none denied the vital role which the press had come to play in the life of the nation. If Balzac scornfully referred to it as 'les coulisses de la vie littéraire',[2] he also said of it:

> La presse a organisé la pensée et la pensée va bientôt exploiter le monde. Une feuille de papier, frêle instrument d'une immortelle idée, peut niveler le globe.[3]

It is this ambivalence which characterises the relationship between literature and journalism throughout the century.

FURTHER READING

Charles LEDRÉ, *Histoire de la presse* (Paris, Arthème Fayard; 1958).

[1] *Illusions perdues*, p. 356.
[2] ibid., p. 270.
[3] Quoted by Maurice Nadeau, 'Balzac et la presse', in *L'Œuvre de Balzac* (Paris, Club français du livre; 1962), vol. III, p. v.

IX

Victor Hugo

(1802–85)

FROM *Océan*

L'amour, c'est le fond de l'homme.
L'amour, c'est l'antique pomme
    Qu'Ève cueillit.
L'ombre passe, l'amour reste,
Il est astre au dais céleste,
    Perle en ton lit.

Nos inventions nouvelles
Prendront à tes vents des ailes;
    Dieu nous sourit;
Nous monterons sur ta rage,
Nous attellerons l'orage
    A notre esprit.

Oui, malgré tes chocs sauvages,
Nous lierons tes deux rivages
    D'un trait de feu;
L'avenir aura deux Romes,
Et, près de celle des hommes
    Celle de Dieu.

L'avenir aura deux temples,
Deux lumières, deux exemples,
    Un double hymen,
La liberté, force et verbe,
L'unité, portant la gerbe
    Du genre humain.

Tais-toi, mer! Les cœurs s'appellent,
Les fils de Caïn se mêlent
    Aux fils d'Abel;
L'homme, que Dieu mène et juge,
Bâtira sur toi, déluge,
    Une Babel.

A cette Babel morale
Aboutira la spirale
  Des deux Sions,
Où sans cesse recommence
Le fourmillement immense
  Des nations;

Et tu verras sans colère,
Du tropique au flot polaire,
  Dieu te calmant,
Au-dessus de l'eau sonore,
Se construire dans l'aurore
  Superbement

Les progrès et les idées,
Pont de cent mille coudées
  Que rien ne rompt,
Et sur tes sombres marées
Ces arches démesurées
  Resplendiront!

VICTOR HUGO, *Océan*, in *La Légende des siècles*
(Paris, Imprimerie Nationale; 1906), vol. II, pp. 170–3

The early nineteenth century saw great strides in almost all the sciences. New discoveries and inventions were constantly being made which not only helped to transform everyday life (gas lighting was first introduced towards the end of the previous century, the first railway in France was opened in 1837, the electric telegraph came into use in the 1840s) but also raised hopes that man would eventually understand the whole universe and harness it to his needs. Many of France's most famous scientists—men like Cuvier, Lamarck, Ampère and Arago— were alive then, and the prestige of science had risen to heights it had never known before.[1] As there were in the same period innumerable schemes for the rational reorganisation of society to the greater benefit of all its members, and as various philosophical systems, notably those of Hegel and Auguste Comte, postulated the progress of the world to some realisable goal, it seemed to many people that there was now nothing to stop humanity advancing to general unity and happiness; there was widespread confidence in the inevitability of movement towards a utopian future. Victor Hugo was one of those who were most

[1] In commentaries XII and XV, we shall see some of the consequences of the continuance of this movement in the second half of the century.

fired by such optimism, and his works are full of lyrical outbursts of
hope like the hymn to progress we have here. It is part of a poem
written in 1854 in which the ocean defies man to subject it to the
slavery into which he is throwing the rest of nature; man then replies
with this triumphant proclamation of faith in his ability to extend his
peaceful conquests over all the world.

One may distinguish in it two main themes: the glorification of
science and its 'inventions nouvelles' which will enable man to sub-
jugate nature, and the belief that 'les progrès et les idées' will lead to a
new era of happiness and harmony. These are recurrent themes in
Hugo's work. The novel *Les Travailleurs de la mer* is inspired by the
idea of the dramatic victory of man over the hostile forces of nature.
In *Tout le passé et tout l'avenir*, from *La Légende des siècles*, there are
ecstatic expressions of joy at the imminent liberation and fraternisation
of all peoples:

> Nous allons à l'amour, au bien, à l'harmonie...
> Les peuples trouveront de nouveaux équilibres;
> Oui, l'aube naît, demain les âmes seront libres.[1]

Plein Ciel, also in *La Légende des siècles*, is another paean of praise to
science, in which the flight of an imaginary airship serves to symbolise
the moral regeneration of humanity through scientific progress:

> Où va-t-il, ce navire? Il va, de jour vêtu,
> A l'avenir divin et pur, à la vertu,
>   A la science qu'on voit luire,
> A la mort des fléaux, à l'oubli généreux,
> A l'abondance, au calme, au rire, à l'homme heureux;
>   Il va, ce glorieux navire,
>
> Au droit, à la raison, à la fraternité,
> A la religieuse et sainte vérité
>   Sans imposture et sans voiles,
> A l'amour, sur les cœurs serrant son doux lien,
> Au juste, au grand, au bon, au beau... — Vous voyez bien
>   Qu'en effet il monte aux étoiles![2]

Hugo may surpass everyone else in the fervour of his enthusiasm, but
he is far from being alone in supposing that a golden future is opening

---

[1] *La Légende des siècles*, vol. II, p. 200.
[2] ibid., p. 397.

out for humanity. Renan's *L'Avenir de la science*, published only in 1890 but written in 1848 (the fateful year which is the high-water mark of this kind of humanitarian optimism), is a long and glowing account of what he hopes science may accomplish. His programme is extraordinarily ambitious:

> ORGANISER SCIENTIFIQUEMENT L'HUMANITÉ, tel est donc le dernier mot de la science moderne, telle est son audacieuse, mais légitime prétention.[1]

Vast privileges and responsibilities are conferred on it:

> La science, et la science seule, peut rendre à l'humanité ce sans quoi elle ne peut vivre, un symbole et une loi.[2]

It is raised to the status of a religion and becomes the supreme hope of mankind:

> La science est donc une religion; la science seule fera désormais les symboles; la science seule peut résoudre à l'homme les éternels problèmes dont sa nature exige impérieusement la solution.[3]

And like Hugo, Renan is confident that one day humanity will enter upon an era of joyful unity:

> O jour où il n'y aura plus de grands hommes, car tous seront grands, et où l'humanité revenue à l'unité marchera comme un seul être à la conquête de l'idéal et du secret des choses![4]

Even towards the end of the century, when the tide of faith in science and progress was ebbing, writers like Zola, who had a naïve admiration for anything scientific, still excitably prophesied the advent of a millennium brought about by science and echoed Hugo's predictions of complete human mastery over nature:

> Admettons que la science ait marché, que la conquête de l'inconnu soit complète : l'âge scientifique que Claude Bernard[5] a vu en rêve sera réalisé. Dès lors, le médecin sera maître des maladies; il guérira à coup sûr, il agira sur les corps vivants pour le bonheur et pour la vigueur de l'espèce. On

---

[1] *L'Avenir de la science* (Paris, Calmann-Lévy; 1890), p. 37.
[2] ibid., p. 31.
[3] ibid., p. 108.
[4] ibid., p. 409.
[5] Claude Bernard (1813–78) was a celebrated physiologist on whose scientific thought Zola tried to base his literary theories. See commentary XV.

entrera dans un siècle où l'homme tout puissant aura asservi la nature et utilisera ses lois pour faire régner sur cette terre la plus grande somme de justice et de liberté possible.[1]

The internationalism which dominated Hugo's grandiose visions of the amity of nations (and which led him to propose the foundation of the United States of Europe) occurs also in the works of Lamartine, notably in *La Marseillaise de la paix*, written in 1841 on the occasion of a Franco-German dispute over the Rhine. There he emphasises the fundamental unity of mankind:

> Ce ne sont plus des mers, des degrés, des rivières
> Qui bornent l'héritage entre l'humanité :
> Les bornes des esprits sont leurs seules frontières;
> Le monde en s'éclairant s'élève à l'unité.[2]

The same sentiments recur in his *Toast porté a un banquet national des Gallois et des Bretons à Abergavenny dans le pays de Galles* [3] :

> L'esprit des temps rejoint ce que la mer sépare;
> Le titre de famille est écrit en tout lieu.
> L'homme n'est plus Français, Anglais, Romain, Barbare;
> Il est concitoyen de l'empire de Dieu!
> Les murs des nations s'écroulent en poussières,
> Les langues de Babel retrouvent l'unité,
> L'Évangile refait avec toutes ses pierres
>   Le temple de l'humanité.

Lamartine indeed came near to realising at least part of this fraternal ideal when the February Revolution of 1848 made him briefly head of the provisional Government and enabled him to see a large part of Europe apparently on the point of founding a new society based on justice, co-operation and freedom. The spirit of 1848 is to a large extent the spirit of Hugo's *Océan*.

But while 1848 highlights these hopes of a better world, it also very soon marked the limits of such a belief, when the Revolution crumbled and the old order reasserted itself under a new name, with the accession to power of Napoleon III. The contrast is dramatically pointed by

[1] Émile Zola, *Le Roman expérimental* (Paris, Charpentier; 1894), p. 23.
[2] Alphonse de Lamartine, *Mélanges* (Paris, Gosselin; 1847) p. 435.
[3] *Recueillements poétiques*, p. 78.

Flaubert in his *Bouvard et Pécuchet*, where the two retired clerks, infatuated with science and social progress, are abruptly brought face to face with the disagreeable reality of the *coup d'état* of 2nd December 1851:

> Bientôt ils arrivèrent à la question du Progrès.
> Bouvard n'en doutait pas dans le domaine scientifique. Mais, en littérature, il est moins clair; et si le bien-être augmente, la splendeur de la vie a disparu.
> Pécuchet, pour le convaincre, prit un morceau de papier.
> — Je trace obliquement une ligne ondulée. Ceux qui pourraient la parcourir, toutes les fois qu'elle s'abaisse, ne verraient pas l'horizon. Elle se relève pourtant, et malgré ses détours, ils atteindront le sommet. Telle est l'image du progrès.
> Mme Bordin entra.
> C'était le 3 décembre 1851. Elle apportait le journal.[1]

And a few days later we find Bouvard exclaiming in disgust: 'Hein, le Progrès, quelle blague!' [2] For Flaubert, though he admired science, was too deeply mistrustful of human nature ever to have much faith in the indefinite continuance of progress. Even Renan himself subsequently said of *L'Avenir de la science*: 'L'erreur dont ces vieilles pages sont imprégnées, c'est un optimisme exagéré',[3] and sought to set his youthful enthusiasm in its historical context by adding the sub-title *Pensées de 1848*.

Just as some people like Hugo and Zola never gave up their belief in progress, however much history might seem to give the lie to it, others had always strenuously objected to its implications. Sometimes it was because they were sceptical about the supposition on which the idea rested, namely that, as Hugo puts it, 'l'amour, c'est le fond de l'homme': this was the case with Flaubert. Notable among the detractors of the concept of progress who held that human nature was fundamentally corrupt was Baudelaire, whose passionate belief in the reality of sin made him bitterly scornful of a theory which simply ignored it (Renan, when asked what he did with original sin in his philosophy, is said to have replied: 'Ma foi, je crois que je le supprime'). Baudelaire writes with angry verve:

[1] *Bouvard et Pécuchet* (Paris, Conard; 1923), p. 224.
[2] ibid., p. 226.
[3] *L'Avenir de la science*, p. ix.

Il est encore une erreur fort à la mode, de laquelle je veux me garder comme de l'enfer. — Je veux parler de l'idée du progrès. Ce fanal obscur, invention du philosophisme actuel, breveté sans garantie de la nature ou de la Divinité, cette lanterne moderne jette des ténèbres partout sur tous les objets de la connaissance; la liberté s'évanouit, le châtiment disparaît. Qui veut y voir clair dans l'histoire doit avant tout éteindre ce fanal perfide. Cette idée grotesque, qui a fleuri sur le terrain pourri de la fatuité moderne, a déchargé chacun de son devoir, délivré toute âme de sa responsabilité, dégagé la volonté de tous les liens que lui imposait l'amour du beau; et les races amoindries, si cette navrante folie dure longtemps, s'endormiront sur l'oreiller de la fatalité dans le sommeil radoteur de la décrépitude. Cette infatuation est le diagnostic d'une décadence déjà trop visible.[1]

Just as Rousseau had done with Voltaire, so Baudelaire retorts that modern times show evidence of decadence rather than of progress; the idea rapidly gains favour in the second half of the century.

Others, like Balzac or Barbey d'Aurevilly, took sides against the idea because of its social and political overtones. Since socialist thinkers tended to look forward to some kind of utopia, Balzac's monarchical conservatism made him suspect that progress would mean the ruin of his own ideals. So he produces an absurd list of the moral and material improvements which, according to him, were confusedly implied by adherence to the ideal of progress:

Se dire un homme de progrès, c'était se proclamer philosophe en toute chose et puritain en politique. On se déclarait ainsi pour les chemins de fer, les mackintosh, les pénitenciers, le pavage en bois, l'indépendance des nègres, les caisses d'épargne, les souliers sans couture, l'éclairage au gaz, les trottoirs en asphalte, le vote universel, la réduction de la Liste Civile. Enfin, c'était se prononcer contre les traités de 1815, contre la branche aînée, contre le colosse du Nord, la perfide Albion, contre toutes les entreprises bonnes ou mauvaises du gouvernement. Comme on le voit, le mot *progrès* peut aussi bien signifier : Non! que Oui!... C'était le réchampissage du mot *libéralisme*, un nouveau mot d'ordre pour des ambitions nouvelles.[2]

Though the passage obviously exaggerates for comic effect, there is more than a grain of truth in it. Upholders of the concept of progress, from Hugo to Zola, did tend to be men of the Left, who wanted to see the old order change, and they did tend (as *Océan* and *Plein Ciel* show)

[1] *L'Exposition universelle de 1855*, in *Œuvres complètes*, p. 685.
[2] *Le Député d'Arcis*, in *La Comédie humaine*, vol. VII, pp. 659-60.

to think in strangely mixed terms of spiritual uplift and semi-scientific gadgetry.

In other cases, the tendency for the scientific associations of progress to give it a materialistic significance called forth vigorous opposition. Hugo managed to combine his vague adulation of science with religious mysticism, but writers like Renan and Zola saw the advance of science as eradicating revealed religion for ever (an idea to be examined in more detail in commentaries XII and XIII). That is why Catholics like Villiers de l'Isle-Adam were inclined to denounce progress as destructive of man's higher instincts. Villiers maintained that progress is meaningless in that it denies mankind any transcendental goal outside this life:

Ah! comment vous suffit-il de ne vous développer, vous Homme, qu'à travers une série d'expressions relatives dont la somme constitue votre Science! Dans ce cas, au lieu d'être de parfaits animaux, nous sommes, seulement, des animaux qui s'améliorent et qu'un Progrès indéfini enferme à jamais dans une loi proportionnelle! Si même la chose était absolument vraie, ce ne serait point là de quoi nous enorgueillir, car, dans mille ans, avec ce système, nous creuserions encore, comme les taupes : qu'importe la grandeur, la splendeur et la profondeur du trou, si nous savons que ce trou doit ensevelir toute notre destinée ? si nous sommes voués à la Mort, enfin, vers laquelle nous marcherons d'un pas toujours plus rapide, — les cieux, d'après les affirmations même de la Science la plus positive, devant se faire, tôt ou tard, brûlants ou mortels.[1]

Océ ... thus typifies one attitude on one of the great subjects of dispute in the middle of the nineteenth century. On the one hand are aligned inordinate ambitions for the future of science, confidence in the goodness of human nature and the limitless potentialities of human intelligence, joyful expectations of a regeneration of mankind, and a general hope that it will not be long before the scientific reorganisation of the world's resources solves humanity's troubles. On the other side are fixed loyalties to the traditional values of religion and society which seem in danger of being swept away by progress, a deep-rooted conviction that men are too wicked and too selfish ever to live together in concord, mistrust of the pretensions and methods of science, and a feeling that the world is already less worth living in than it used to be. By the end of the century, the scepticism induced by the repeated failure of social revolution, the humiliating loss of a major war, the inability of

[1] *Claire Lenoir*, in *Œuvres complètes*, vol. III, pp. 142–3.

science to provide the promised final solutions had shaken the exaggerated optimism of the earlier period. Pre-1848 confidence in the future is replaced by post-1870 gloom. In the meantime, the great debate on progress had profoundly marked the literature and the thought of the time; it was an issue on which few people failed to take up a position, on one side or the other.

FURTHER READING

C. A. FUSIL, *La Poésie scientifique de 1750 à nos jours* (Paris, 1918).

X

Gustave Flaubert

(1821–80)

FROM *L'Éducation sentimentale*

Le Citoyen employait ses jours à vagabonder dans les rues, tirant sa moustache, roulant des yeux, acceptant et propageant des nouvelles lugubres; et il n'avait que deux phrases : « Prenez garde, nous allons être débordés! » ou bien : « Mais, sacrebleu! on escamote la République! » Il était mécontent de tout, et particulièrement de ce que nous n'avions pas repris nos frontières naturelles. Le nom seul de Lamartine lui faisait hausser les épaules. Il ne trouvait pas Ledru-Rollin « suffisant pour le problème », traita Dupont (de l'Eure) de vieille ganache; Albert, d'idiot; Louis Blanc, d'utopiste; Blanqui, d'homme extrêmement dangereux; et, quand Frédéric lui demanda ce qu'il aurait fallu faire, il répondit en lui serrant le bras à le broyer :

— Prendre le Rhin, je vous dis, prendre le Rhin! fichtre!

Puis il accusa la réaction.

Elle se démasquait. Le sac des châteaux de Neuilly et de Suresne, l'incendie des Batignolles, les troubles de Lyon, tous les excès, tous les griefs, on les exagérait à présent, en y ajoutant la circulaire de Ledru-Rollin, le cours forcé des billets de Banque, la rente tombée à soixante francs, enfin, comme iniquité suprême, comme dernier coup, comme surcroît d'horreur, l'impôt des quarante-cinq centimes! — Et, par-dessus tout cela, il y avait encore le Socialisme. Bien que ces théories, aussi neuves que le jeu de l'oie, eussent été depuis quarante ans suffisamment débattues pour emplir des bibliothèques, elles épouvantèrent les bourgeois, comme une grêle d'aérolithes; et on fut indigné, en vertu de cette haine que provoque l'avènement de toute idée parce que c'est une idée, exécration dont elle tire plus tard sa gloire, et qui fait que ses ennemis sont toujours au-dessous d'elle, si médiocre qu'elle puisse être.

Alors, la Propriété monta dans les respects au niveau de la Religion et se confondit avec Dieu. Les attaques qu'on lui portait parurent du sacrilège, presque de l'anthropophagie. Malgré la législation la plus humaine qui fut jamais, le spectre de 93 reparut, et le couperet de la guillotine vibra dans toutes les syllabes du mot République; — ce qui n'empêchait pas qu'on la méprisait pour sa faiblesse. La France, ne sentant plus de maître, se mit à crier d'effarement, comme un aveugle sans bâton, comme un marmot qui a perdu sa bonne.

GUSTAVE FLAUBERT, *L'Éducation sentimentale*
(Paris, Conard; 1923), pp. 424-5

L'Éducation sentimentale, which appeared in 1869, is a novel with two purposes. One is to show the high hopes and ideals of its young hero, Frédéric Moreau, and their gradual erosion until his life degenerates into empty disillusionment. The other is to describe the events that led up to the February Revolution of 1848 which deposed Louis-Philippe, the vast expectations of social and political improvement which it awakened, and their frustration in the rise of a wave of reaction which eventually resulted in the establishment of the dictatorial Second Empire. The two themes echo each other constantly throughout the work.

This passage, which is exclusively concerned with the historical situation, is placed somewhere about the middle of March 1848. The Revolution had broken out, spontaneously and unexpectedly, on 22nd February, as the result of a ban imposed by the unpopular Guizot Government on a meeting which was to have been held that day in Paris to call for reforms in the institutions of the State. Demonstrations turned into riots, and on the 23rd, Louis-Philippe tried to abdicate in favour of his grandson, but it was already too late. The mob invaded the Chamber of Deputies and compelled the Assembly to proclaim a provisional Government. This was formed on the 24th, with a coalition of moderate republicans including Dupont de l'Eure, Lamartine and Ledru-Rollin, and more Left-wing elements such as Louis Blanc and Albert. Louis-Philippe fled, France was declared a republic, and an immediate programme of social reform was instituted, embracing freedom of thought and expression, a democratic constitution, universal suffrage, changes in the structure of taxation, emancipation of the working classes, and ambitious schemes of work for all in national workshops. For the time being, the middle classes and the workers, united in their detestation of the July Monarchy, were animated by a common desire for social justice and political reform, and it seemed as though the Second Republic was to accomplish the foundation of true equality which neither 1789 nor 1830 had brought about.

But it was not long before dissensions split the ranks of the republicans and fear caused a change in public opinion, and it is at the moment when this is happening that Flaubert describes a meeting between his hero Frédéric and an old friend named Regimbart, whose republican opinions under the July Monarchy had earned him the nickname of 'le Citoyen'. Regimbart, eternally dissatisfied with the course of events and too much addicted to talk ever to take any effective part in them, is gloomily preoccupied with the signs of mounting reaction and with good reason fears that the Republic of his dreams will be 'escamoté' and that the genuine patriots will be 'débordés'.

Regimbart is one of the republicans who clamoured in vain for the Government to seek an immediate revision of the treaties of 1815 which had fixed the new frontiers of France, and his indiscriminate denigration of all the members of the provisional Government enables Flaubert to list the eminent politicians of the day. Lamartine comes first in Regimbart's catalogue of *bêtes noires*, partly because he was at that time still the popular hero of Revolution and partly because he was, as Minister for Foreign Affairs, responsible for the pacific foreign policy which so disgusts Regimbart. Ledru-Rollin, already a Left-wing deputy before 1848, was one of the key figures in the Government, since he not only occupied the vital post of Minister for the Interior but was also the only man capable of keeping the peace between the inimical factions of moderates and socialists in the Cabinet. It is because of this heavy burden that Regimbart regards him as not being 'suffisant pour le problème'. As for Dupont de l'Eure (the qualifying phrase was not part of his name but was usually added—sometimes in brackets—to distinguish him from other Duponts), he was President of the Council of Ministers; although he enjoyed immense respect after a long and honourable political career, his great age (he was eighty-one) goes some way to explaining Regimbart's disdainful epithet 'vieille ganache'. The moderates having thus been dismissed as incompetent, Regimbart goes on to display equal contempt for the socialists. Louis Blanc, journalist and political theorist, was the author of a treatise on *L'Organisation du travail* and was placed by the provisional Government at the head of a Commission of Workers designed to ensure full and equitable employment for all: the national workshops were a modified version of his plan for State regulation of labour. It is this desire to provide work for everyone which makes Regimbart call him a 'utopiste'. Albert was his ally, the only working-man member of the provisional Government, whose presence there appears to have been largely symbolic and who was in any case removed and imprisoned after a socialist demonstration had invaded the Assembly on 15th May. Finally comes Auguste Blanqui, 'homme extrêmement dangereux', who in 1848 was released from the prison sentence which he had been serving for revolutionary activities against Louis-Philippe and who then set about agitating to exert extremist pressure on the provisional Government through the secret societies and political clubs in which he was very powerful.

But if Regimbart has scant regard for the leading personalities striving to guide the new-born Second Republic, he is even more scornful of 'la réaction', the middle-class section of the population which was soon to thwart the social reforms that had been set in motion, and to repress once again the demands of the proletariat. This property-owning class, which had originally made common cause with the workers in the Revolution, had rapidly become alarmed at the way the situation was developing, and Regimbart lists their main grievances and worries. They fall into two categories: fright at the violence of some of the disorders which had occurred during the Revolution itself, and extreme distaste for some of the steps taken by the provisional Government. First there was the pillaging of some rich private houses, notably Louis-Philippe's summer residence at Neuilly and the Rothschild castle at Suresne. Then there were cases of incendiarism during the riots, notably in the Batignolles, a northern district of Paris. In the provinces, at Lyons and elsewhere, there had been attacks on factories and outbursts of machine-breaking. Lawlessness of this kind, though infrequent in February 1848, was nevertheless a source of disquiet to the peace-loving *bourgeoisie* who feared for their own dwellings and belongings.

Moreover, certain measures taken by the provisional Government hit their pockets and aroused anxiety for the whole future of private property. For instance, on 12th March, in a circular letter sent to the regional commissioners who had been appointed to replace Louis-Philippe's prefects, Ledru-Rollin gave warning that the Government intended to pursue a firmly Left-wing policy and insisted that candidates for the coming elections should all be democrats of long standing —'des républicains de la veille'—and not lukewarm opportunists. At the same time, a serious financial crisis was threatening the infant Republic with bankruptcy, and Government 5 per cent stock, quoted at 116 francs when the Stock Exchange closed on 23rd February, stood at only 97 francs 50 centimes when the market reopened on 7th March, and in the following days it fell swiftly, lower even than the 60 francs Flaubert mentions. The result was that many people living modestly on their investments were ruined. Various unpopular decrees were passed to palliate this state of affairs. There was a new issue of banknotes, which were not convertible into gold as they normally would have been, and on 18th March, Garnier-Pagès, newly appointed to the Ministry of Finance to succeed Goudchaux who had resigned in despair, announced that direct taxation was to be increased in the ratio of 45 centimes per franc—in other words, by 45 per cent—a step which brought forth howls of protest from the taxpayers, especially the provincial *bourgeoisie* and peasantry, who had not in any case had much to do with the setting up of the Republic, very largely a Parisian affair.

So, with commerce almost at a standstill, income from stocks and shares drastically reduced, taxation rising steeply, continual disturbances and demonstrations by workers, increasing pressure on the Government from its socialist and communist supporters, it is not surprising that the middle classes began to dread the advent of a social upheaval so momentous that they themselves would be swept away by it. That is why the principle of private property suddenly becomes sacred (Proudhon, one of the theorists of socialism, declared: 'La propriété, c'est le vol') and why the word 'Republic', at first the symbol of progress and justice, acquired sinister overtones of the Terror of 1793. This was the situation in mid-March 1848 which was soon to lead to demonstrations by the *bourgeois* National Guard, counter-demonstrations by the workers, the election of a largely conservative assembly in April, abortive Left-wing insurrections in May and June, after which General Cavaignac took over power until the presidential elections of December. Louis-Napoleon was then elected on a vaguely traditionalist programme and carried out an increasingly authoritarian and Right-wing policy until, taking advantage of a quarrel with the Assembly, he set up a dictatorship by the *coup d'état* of 2nd December 1851, proclaiming himself Emperor the following year. Thus the Revolution which had seemed destined to reform not only the political system but also the whole structure of society ended in the establishment of a *régime* even more reactionary and tyrannical than the one it had overthrown.

If one examines the way in which Flaubert presents his information and his analysis of the state of France in March 1848, it becomes clear that he is simultaneously pursuing two aims in this passage. The first and most obvious is that of using his novel to convey a full and accurate account of the history of his times. From this point of view, Regimbart is no more than a pretext for mentioning the names of the outstanding politicians, the most important events, the dominant currents of ideas— and Flaubert has done his work well. He used in *L'Éducation sentimentale* not only his own memories of the period and the published memoirs of his friend Du Camp, but also a whole library of historical works on 1848; in April 1867 he wrote to Louis Bouilhet: 'Je bûche la Révolution de 48 avec fureur. Sais-tu combien j'ai lu et annoté de volumes depuis six semaines? Vingt-sept, mon bon'.[1] The outcome of this meticulous documentation is a complete and faithful picture of the period: historians of the 1848 Revolution often quote *L'Éducation sentimentale* as evidence. As a historian, Flaubert lays claim to impartiality and objectivity:

> Je ne me reconnais pas le droit d'accuser personne. Je ne crois même pas que le romancier doive exprimer son opinion sur les choses de ce monde... Je me borne donc à exposer les choses telles qu'elles me paraissent, à exprimer ce qui me semble le vrai. Tant pis pour les conséquences.[2]

It is indeed true that any manual of history would give an impression of March 1848 substantially similar to that given by Flaubert.

But the second aim, more subtly insinuated, is that of making a sombre and satirical comment on the men and events of 1848, and through them, on humanity in general. Regimbart himself is a mildly ridiculous figure, talkative, mournful, hypercritical and ineffectual. Even so, the repetition of his derogatory views on the politicians of the day tends to cast discredit on them as well as on him. When he moves on to consider the dangers of reaction, the irony becomes much more marked. The fact that genuine grievances are now being exaggerated, that a new tax can be termed the height of iniquity, the last straw, the ultimate horror, that the *bourgeois* are frightened of socialism (although it is no more a novelty than the most ancient of children's games) as they would be of a shower of meteorites, that property is confused with

---

[1] Gustave Flaubert, *Correspondance* (Paris, Conard; 1929), vol. v, p. 293.
[2] ibid., p. 396 (to George Sand, 10th August 1868).

God, that offences against it are equated with cannibalism—all that indicates on Flaubert's part a withering contempt for the *bourgeois* reactionaries which far exceeds any scepticism about the republicans. This attitude is confirmed both by what he appears to have thought in 1848 and by what he said while writing the novel. He was sufficiently hostile to the July Monarchy to attend a reformist banquet at Rouen in December 1847, but came away angry and disillusioned:

> Quelque triste opinion que l'on ait des hommes, l'amertume vous vient au cœur quand s'étalent devant vous des bêtises aussi délirantes, des stupidités aussi échevelées.[1]

By May 1849, he was equally disgusted with all the parties:

> Républicains, réactionnaires, rouges, bleus, tricolores, tout cela concourt d'ineptie.[2]

And twenty years later, he forecast that 'les patriotes ne me pardonneront pas ce livre, ni les réactionnaires non plus'.[3] Even so, he detested the reactionaries more than the democrats because they were more *bourgeois*, and that, in Flaubert's eyes, was the one unforgivable sin: 'Les réactionnaires seront encore moins ménagés que les autres, car ils me semblent plus criminels'.[4]

That is why Flaubert seems momentarily to be defending socialism (with which he had in reality no great sympathy) when he talks about 'cette haine que provoque l'avènement de toute idée parce que c'est une idée, exécration dont elle tire plus tard sa gloire, et qui fait que ses ennemis sont toujours au-dessous d'elle, si médiocre qu'elle puisse être'. It is his habitual hatred of the *esprit bourgeois* in all its manifestations which leads him to this outburst, and which induces him to ridicule their fear of the guillotine by referring to 'la législation la plus humaine qui fut jamais'; there is no evidence that Flaubert felt any real enthusiasm for the reforms of the Second Republic. Flaubert uses comically incongruous similes to reinforce the climax of the ridicule which he heaps on middle-class France: 'La France... se mit à crier

---

[1] To Louise Colet, December 1847, *Correspondance*, vol. II, p. 79.
[2] To Ernest Chevalier, 6th May 1849, ibid., p. 87.
[3] To George Sand, 5th July 1868, vol. V, p. 385.
[4] To George Sand, 10th August 1868, ibid., p. 397.

d'effarement, comme un aveugle sans bâton, comme un marmot qui a perdu sa bonne'. In his pessimistic view of human nature, men lack the necessary intelligence to govern themselves, their affairs are consequently ruled by chance and by the least noble of their feelings, and ideas are the last things to affect their conduct.

The question remains how Flaubert manages to preserve a pretence of objectivity and yet work up to a paroxysm of ironic indignation at the end of the last paragraph. The key lies in his cunning use of indirect speech. Nominally, he is merely reporting Regimbart's opinions, for which as an author he bears no personal responsibility, and the 'Citoyen' is briefly and rather ludicrously evoked at the outset, 'tirant sa moustache, roulant des yeux'. Moreover, some of his remarks are given in direct speech, so that one is at first keenly aware of his presence. Then he goes on to charges against the reactionaries, and these are summarised, as one would expect, in the imperfect. But half-way through the paragraph, the tense changes without warning: 'Elles épouvantèrent les bourgeois'; a present tense intervenes as Flaubert generalises, and the remainder of the narration continues in the past definite. Once Flaubert drops the imperfect in favour of the past definite, he is speaking in his own name and not in Regimbart's, since the past definite cannot be used for reported speech. The end of the paragraph thus represents what Flaubert thinks and not what Regimbart says. In other words, he has just used Regimbart as a cover and has discarded him once he had served his purpose of disguising the introduction of Flaubert's own views. So the canon of historical objectivity and of literary impersonality which Flaubert preaches is really a way of masking the author's presence and not a way of eliminating it. He is vibrantly and vitally concerned here, full of vituperative scorn and blistering sarcasm.

The passage shows not only how the reproduction of thoroughly documented historical reality has become an integral part of novel-writing; it also reveals some of the secrets of a master-stylist who feels strongly and deeply but who believes that in his novels facts should speak for themselves (or at least should appear to do so) and who succeeds admirably in effacing himself behind his characters. Flaubert as a man, and 1848 as historical fact, are inseparable in this passage as they are throughout *L'Éducation sentimentale*, and one cannot understand the one without the other.

PLATE I *La Distribution des aigles* (from the painting by Louis David)

PETIT LEVER D'UN GRAND FEUILLETONISTE.

C'est un si beau sceptre que celui de la critique dramatique !

PLATE II *Petit Lever d'un grand feuilletoniste* (from the caricature by Grandville)

FURTHER READING

Jean POMMIER, *Les Écrivains devant la révolution de 1848* (Paris, Presses Universitaires de France; 1948).
Félix PONTEIL, *1848* (Paris, Armand Colin; 1937).

XI

Charles Baudelaire

(1821–67)

Correspondances

La Nature est un temple où de vivants piliers
Laissent parfois sortir de confuses paroles;
L'homme y passe à travers des forêts de symboles
Qui l'observent avec des regards familiers.

Comme de longs échos qui de loin se confondent
Dans une ténébreuse et profonde unité,
Vaste comme la nuit et comme la clarté,
Les parfums, les couleurs et les sons se répondent.

Il est des parfums frais comme des chairs d'enfants,
Doux comme les hautbois, verts comme les prairies,
— Et d'autres, corrompus, riches et triomphants,

Ayant l'expansion des choses infinies,
Comme l'ambre, le musc, le benjoin et l'encens,
Qui chantent les transports de l'esprit et des sens.

CHARLES BAUDELAIRE, *Correspondances*,
in *Les Fleurs du mal, Œuvres complètes*,
ed. Y.-G. Le Dantec (Paris, Pléiade; 1951), p. 85

Since the late eighteenth century, there had been in France an increasing curiosity about the various doctrines involving knowledge or use of mysterious forces and generically known as occultism. The reasons for this vogue are various. Orthodox religion appeared to be compromised by the criticisms of the rationalists, whereas, to those who still felt the need for religious consolation or experience, occultism could rebut all argument by the production of repeated revelations. The discovery of strange psychical phenomena, such as Mesmer's animal magnetism in the 1770s, mediumnistic communication with the spirits under the Restoration and table-turning in 1853, seemed to reinforce the claims of the mystics. The upsurge of emotionalism, irrationalism and fascination with the inexplicable which characterised Romanticism further reacted in its favour. To individualists who were repelled by the dogma and discipline of Catholicism (or by the Church's opposition to progressive social policies), it offered an entirely free field for independent speculation and experimentation. By 1830, there was a real if subterranean enthusiasm for occultism in all its different forms: the Jewish Kabbala, the mysticism of the eighteenth-century Swedish visionary Swedenborg, spiritualism and the innumerable and eccentric minor sects which multiplied around these major tendencies. Popularisers and charlatans of all sorts abounded: the baron Du Potet who was one of the leading figures among the *magnétiseurs*, Allan Kardec, the founder of spiritualism, the indefatigable Éliphas Lévi, whose numerous books on magic and occultism were avidly devoured by a vast public, Hugo's friend Alexandre Weill and dozens of others, all enjoying at least local celebrity, mixing with all classes of society and spreading their various gospels as hard as they could. Socialist doctrines too became involved with occultism—Pierre Leroux and Charles Fourier are cases in point (see commentary VII). Nor did the decline of Romanticism see any comparable decline in occultism. Orthodox religion having again been weakened by the prestige of positivism, occultism retained its fascination, and even Napoleon III called on the famous medium Daniel Dunglas Home to demonstrate his powers at the Tuileries. In the 1880s and 1890s, occultism basked in a positive blaze of publicity when idealism once again became fashionable, and on the fringes of literature there flourished scores of amateur or professional *magi*, preaching Rosicrucianism (there was for a time a Rosicrucian art exhibition, supported by the flamboyant Sâr Péladan, Barrès and others), Swedenborgianism, Kabbalism and even black magic. This persistence of esotericism helped to keep alive a certain religious spirit, a preoccupation with the other world and a confused belief in enigmatic powers at work behind the visible universe at a time when orthodox Christianity had lost much of its intellectual authority.

The influence of occultism on literature grew in proportion with its general popularity. Sometimes it was simply exploited for purposes of excitement and picturesqueness, as in novels like Gautier's *Avatar*,

Spirite and *Jettatura*. Sometimes its myths and symbols were incorporated into some personal religious vision, as happened in Nerval's poetry or his *Voyage en Orient* and Hugo's later works, notably *Les Contemplations*, *Dieu* and *La Fin de Satan*. Sometimes the intention was partly doctrinal and partly dramatic; this seems to be the case in works like Balzac's *Séraphîta* and *Ursule Mirouët*, George Sand's *La Comtesse de Rudolstadt* and Villiers de l'Isle-Adam's *Axël*. Occasionally, there was a documentary basis such as that which underlies *Là-bas*, J.-K. Huysmans's study of contemporary satanism. Frequently, authors of such books were only half convinced of the reality of the phenomena and the ideas which they were recounting; there is evidence of scepticism or hesitation in the attitudes of Gautier, Balzac and Villiers at least, and even as affirmative a believer as Hugo eventually deemed it expedient to leave well enough alone and abandon table-turning. But from beginning to end of the nineteenth century, occultism attracted men of letters and infiltrated, in one form or another, into their writings.

Baudelaire's sonnet *Correspondances*, the fourth poem in *Les Fleurs du mal*, marks what is perhaps the most significant occultist contribution in the period: its effect on aesthetic theory. In the title and in the first quatrain, Baudelaire is referring to the Swedenborgian belief that everything in the world is a symbol, or correspondence, for something in the spiritual world; he says elsewhere that 'c'est cet admirable, cet immortel instinct du beau qui nous fait considérer la terre et ses spectacles comme un aperçu, comme une correspondance du ciel'.[1] Similar assertions that a mysterious life inhabits every manifestation of nature and obscurely bodies forth the existence of another world are to be found in the writings of other poets at about the same time (it is a tenet common to several occultist systems). In *Ce que dit la bouche d'ombre*, the poem of *Les Contemplations* in which Hugo expounds his individual version of the occultist cosmogony, the idea of life in inanimate objects is given the anthropomorphic formulation which is typical of him:

> Non, l'abîme est un prêtre et l'ombre est un poète.
> Non, tout est une voix et tout est un parfum;
> Tout dit dans l'infini quelque chose à quelqu'un;
> Une pensée emplit le tumulte superbe.

---

[1] Charles Baudelaire, 'Notes nouvelles sur Edgar Poe' (introducing the second volume of Baudelaire's translation of Poe's tales, *Nouvelles Histoires extraordinaires*).

Dieu n'a pas fait un bruit sans y mêler le verbe.
Tout, comme toi, gémit, ou chante comme moi ;
Tout parle. Et maintenant, homme, sais-tu pourquoi
Tout parle ? Écoute bien. C'est que vents, ondes, flammes,
Arbres, roseaux, rochers, tout vit ! Tout est plein d'âmes.[1]

Nerval, whose knowledge of occultist thought was encyclopaedic, propounds a similar theory in his *Vers dorés*:

Homme, libre penseur ! te crois-tu seul pensant
Dans ce monde où la vie éclate en toute chose ?
Des forces que tu tiens ta liberté dispose,
Mais de tous tes conseils l'univers est absent.

Respecte dans la bête un esprit agissant :
Chaque fleur est une âme à la Nature éclose ;
Un mystère d'amour dans le métal repose ;
Tout est sensible ! Et tout sur ton être est puissant.

Crains, dans le mur aveugle, un regard qui t'épie :
A la matière même un verbe est attaché...
Ne le fais pas servir à quelque usage impie !

Souvent dans l'être obscur habite un Dieu caché ;
Et comme un œil naissant couvert par ses paupières,
Un pur esprit s'accroît sous l'écorce des pierres ![2]

Even closer to Baudelaire is the explanation of Swedenborg's teachings which one finds in Balzac's *Séraphîta*:

Savoir les correspondances de la Parole avec les cieux, savoir les correspondances qui existent entre les choses visibles et pondérables du monde terrestre et les choses invisibles et impondérables du monde spirituel, c'est avoir *les cieux dans son entendement*... Les esprits angéliques connaissent donc essentiellement les correspondances qui relient au ciel chaque chose de la terre, et savent les sens intimes des paroles prophétiques qui en dénoncent les révolutions. Ainsi, pour ces esprits, tout ici-bas porte sa signifiance. La moindre fleur est une pensée, une vie qui correspond à quelques linéaments du grand tout, duquel ils ont une constante intuition.[3]

[1] *Les Contemplations*, p. 416.
[2] *Œuvres* (Paris, Pléiade; 1952), vol. I, pp. 38–9
[3] *Séraphîta*, in *La Comédie humaine* (Paris, Pléiade; 1955), vol. x, pp. 507–8.

But Baudelaire does not rest content with what we have seen to be a relatively commonplace occultist view of the nature of the world—indeed, it is very hard to decide how seriously he takes it as a metaphysical statement. In the remainder of the sonnet, he moves on to another theme, which is related to the first one but not identical with it: that of the correspondences which exist between the impressions received by the different senses. The line: 'Les parfums, les couleurs et les sons se répondent' is a clear statement of what is known as synaesthesia, and the tercets serve to give examples of it, chosen, characteristically for Baudelaire, from perfumes, which evoke sensations of sound, touch and colour. The idea that the impressions made on one sense could correspond to those made on another sense was not a new one: it was dear to the German novelist E. T. A. Hoffmann, one of Baudelaire's favourite authors, and it is mentioned by Mme de Staël[1] and by Théophile Gautier.[2] What is new about Baudelaire's use of it, apart from the firmness with which it is proclaimed, is its insertion into a quasi-mystical context. He sets up an implied connection between the 'confuses paroles' of the second line and the instances of sense correspondences which he adduces, and then hints at a resumption of the theme in the concluding reference to 'les transports de l'esprit et des sens', which appears to refer to states in which one is vouchsafed some experience of another world. The logical link between the two kinds of correspondence—the 'vertical' ones between the two planes of reality and the 'horizontal' ones between different sense impressions—is left vague, and one must assume it to lie in the idea that the world is a 'ténébreuse et profonde unité'. Elsewhere he says it is not the least strange that sounds can suggest colours or colours melodies,

> les choses s'étant toujours exprimées par une analogie réciproque, depuis le jour où Dieu a proféré le monde comme une complexe et indivisible totalité.[3]

In Baudelaire's own poetry, contrary to what one might expect, these ideas did not lead to an extensive use of synaesthesia, examples of which are comparatively rare in *Les Fleurs du mal*. What they did do was to justify a new attitude towards metaphor, which in Baudelaire's hands

---

[1] In *De l'Allemagne.*
[2] In *Le Club des hachichins.*
[3] *Richard Wagner et Tannhäuser,* in *Œuvres complètes,* p. 1043.

ceases to be an arbitrary decoration and becomes instead an identification of two terms necessitated by the fact that they both evoke the same impression, a correspondence which in its turn creates the suggestion that some kind of higher meaning is being perceived behind the physical reality. But late in the century, images of synaesthesia became extremely popular with the poets of the Symbolist movement, particularly after Rimbaud had written his famous sonnet *Voyelles*:

> A noir, E blanc, I rouge, U vert, O bleu, voyelles,
> Je dirai quelque jour vos naissances latentes.[1]

One group of Symbolists, René Ghil and his *École instrumentiste*, even founded the whole of their poetic theory on an elaborate series of concordances between vowel sounds, colours, the timbre of musical instruments, and emotions. Many others, without subscribing to extravagances of that sort, frequently employed images of synaesthesia: in Mallarmé one finds 'le blanc souci',[2] 'les plis jaunes de la pensée',[3] in Rimbaud 'ces parfums pourpres',[4] 'le sommeil bleu',[5] in Verlaine 'la chanson grise',[6] in Maeterlinck 'les mauvaises tendresses noires',[7] 'un sanglot glauque',[8] and so on. By then, largely prompted by the example of Baudelaire's sonnet, the imagery of synaesthesia had become a recognised part of the language of poetry, even for a time one of its *clichés*.

It is however equally characteristic of Symbolism that such imagery is often held to have a symbolic function. In Symbolist theory, the world was not to be described for its own sake, since it was only an illusory veil cast over reality; instead, its objects were to be utilised in poetry for what, in essence, they were: symbols. The connection with Swedenborgian and other occultist doctrines is obvious, and the contribution of occultism to Symbolist thought, acknowledged and unacknowledged, is considerable. Among the masters of the movement, Villiers de l'Isle-Adam had thought deeply about occultism, Rimbaud was familiar with various works on it, and Mallarmé showed a sympathetic if remote interest in it, while among lesser figures Gourmont, Dujardin,

[1] *Œuvres complètes* (Paris, Mercure de France; 1952), p. 69.
[2] *Salut.*   [3] *Hérodiade.*
[4] *Métropolitain.*   [5] *Les Premières Communions.*
[6] *Art poétique.*   [7] *Oraison nocturne.*
[8] *Serre d'ennui.*

Morice and Mauclair were all at one time or another in contact with it.
One might take the following statement by the critic Camille Mauclair
as a fair definition of the standard Symbolist view of the world, and its
indebtedness to Swedenborg is plain:

> Tout objet est le symbole passager de son idée-même. Le monde n'est
> qu'un système de symboles subordonné à un système d'idées pures qui sont
> régies par des lois cosmiques, et dont la réunion constitue la divinité.
> L'univers est pour ainsi dire une écriture immense dont chaque objet est
> une lettre et dont le total raconte le divin.[1]

The connection between this type of idea and synaesthesia is no more
explicit than in Baudelaire's sonnet, but it seems nevertheless to have
been vaguely present in the minds of many of the poets of the 1880s.

A further ramification of these lines of thought is the collaboration—
or confusion—of the arts so much in evidence in the Symbolist period.
If Baudelaire is right in postulating that sense data are merely different
ways of perceiving aspects of the same 'ténébreuse et profonde unité',
then the diverse arts too must be expressing the same things in different
ways. Equivalences can consequently be established between them and
they can be made to assist and reinforce each other, even to take over
each other's functions. We shall see, in commentary XIX, some of the
ways in which poetry tried to assume the character of music. But on a
more ambitious scale, ideas of this kind, especially with the impetus
given by the music-dramas of Wagner, led to a desire to produce a total
work of art (Wagner's *Gesamtkunstwerk*) which would unite all the arts
to express the whole of reality. Intentions of that sort lie behind
Mallarmé's concept of 'l'Œuvre', in which all the arts would be resumed
by that of poetry and would contribute to the final synthesis of the meaning of the universe, Villiers de l'Isle-Adam's vast tragedy *Axël*, and the
theatre of Paul Claudel, which in its chaotic complexity is meant to be
an image of creation itself.

It is not too much to say that Baudelaire's *Correspondances* is the
poem of its century which is most pregnant with meaning. The occultist
tradition and the perception of new modes of feeling and new pos-
sibilities of language make it a programmatic summary for the evolution
of French poetry in the second half of the century.

[1] *L'Art en silence* (Paris, Ollendorf; 1900), p. 190.

FURTHER READING

Jean POMMIER, *La Mystique de Baudelaire* (Paris, Les Belles Lettres; 1932).

Auguste VIATTE, *Les Sources occultes du Romantisme* (Paris, Champion; 1928).

A. MERCIER, *Les Sources ésotériques et occultes de la poésie symboliste (1870–1914)* (Paris, Nizet; 1969).

A. G. LEHMANN, *The Symbolist Aesthetic in France 1885–1895* (Oxford, Blackwell; 1950).

XII

Ernest Renan

(1823–92)

FROM *Vie de Jésus*

Encore moins connut-il l'idée nouvelle, créée par la science grecque, base de toute philosophie et que la science moderne a hautement confirmée, l'exclusion des dieux capricieux auxquels la naïve croyance des vieux âges attribuait le gouvernement de l'univers. Près d'un siècle avant lui, Lucrèce avait exprimé d'une façon admirable l'inflexibilité du régime général de la nature. La négation du miracle, cette idée que tout se produit dans le monde par des lois où l'intervention personnelle d'êtres supérieurs n'a aucune part, était de droit commun dans les grandes écoles de tous les pays qui avaient reçu la science grecque. Peut-être même Babylone et la Perse n'y étaient-elles pas étrangères. Jésus ne sut rien de ce progrès. Quoique né à une époque où le principe de la science positive était déjà proclamé, il vécut en plein surnaturel. Jamais peut-être les Juifs n'avaient été plus possédés de la soif du merveilleux. Philon, qui vivait dans un grand centre intellectuel, et qui avait reçu une éducation très-complète, ne possède qu'une science chimérique et de mauvais aloi.

Jésus ne différait en rien sur ce point de ses compatriotes. Il croyait au diable, qu'il envisageait comme une sorte de génie du mal, et il s'imaginait, avec tout le monde, que les maladies nerveuses étaient l'effet de démons, qui s'emparaient du patient et l'agitaient. Le merveilleux n'était pas pour lui l'exceptionnel; c'était l'état normal. La notion du surnaturel, avec ses impossibilités, n'apparaît que le jour où naît la science expérimentale de la nature. L'homme étranger à toute idée de physique, qui croit qu'en priant il change la marche des nuages, arrête la maladie et la mort même, ne trouve dans le miracle rien d'extraordinaire, puisque le cours entier des choses est pour lui le résultat de volontés libres de la divinité. Cet état intellectuel fut toujours celui de Jésus. Mais dans sa grande âme, une telle croyance produisait des effets tout opposés à ceux où arrivait le vulgaire. Chez le vulgaire, la foi à l'action particulière de Dieu amenait une crédulité niaise et des duperies de charlatans. Chez lui, elle tenait à une notion profonde des rapports familiers de l'homme avec Dieu et à une croyance exagérée dans le pouvoir de l'homme; belles erreurs qui furent le principe de sa force; car si elles devaient un jour le mettre en défaut aux yeux du physicien et du chimiste, elles lui donnaient sur son temps une force dont aucun individu n'a disposé avant lui ni depuis.

ERNEST RENAN, *Vie de Jésus*
(Paris, Calmann-Lévy; 1960), pp. 108–9

When Ernest Renan's *Vie de Jésus* appeared in 1863, it had an immense *succès de scandale*, became one of the best-selling books of the century and caused its author to be deprived of his Chair at the Collège de France. It was read even by idle young men-about-town like the Anatole Durand of Taine's *Thomas Graindorge*, of whom his uncle said disparagingly:

Je crois qu'il a parcouru *la Vie de Jésus*, encore était-ce pour en pouvoir parler, être à la mode.[1]

It owed its popularity largely to the fact that it was the first book in France accessible to laymen which applied to Biblical studies the principles of positivism and the methods of historical scholarship used for profane subjects. Both these attitudes are exemplified in the present passage, which occurs when Renan is discussing the education of Jesus and the type of mentality which could most probably be attributed to him.

The positivism which governs Renan's analysis of the life of Jesus is, in its original form, the belief that science provides the model of the only kind of knowledge we can attain. This doctrine had first been formulated by the philosopher Auguste Comte in the 1830s, and the immense strides made by the natural sciences since then had invested it with such authority that, under the Second Empire, it had become by far the most vigorous force in the intellectual life of France. As Renan himself says in *L'Avenir de la science*:

La religion, la philosophie, la morale, la politique trouvent de nombreux sceptiques; les sciences physiques n'en trouvent pas (au moins quant à leur partie définitivement acquise et quant à leur méthode). La méthode de ces sciences est ainsi devenue le *criterium* de certitude pratique des modernes; cela leur paraît certain et scientifique, qui est acquis d'une manière analogue aux résultats des sciences physiques.[2]

[1] Hippolyte Taine, *Vie et opinions de M. Frédéric Thomas Graindorge* (Paris, Hachette; 1959), p. 120.
[2] *L'Avenir de la science*, p. 442.

But, like many of his contemporaries, Renan was so dazzled by the prestige of scientific method that he tended to go beyond this relatively cautious position and to affirm that anything not susceptible of scientific proof did not exist at all. So it is that the *Vie de Jésus* and the succeeding volumes of his *Histoire des origines du christianisme* are dominated by the categorical assertion that there is no supernatural. This we find postulated in the preface to the work:

> La question du surnaturel est pour nous tranchée avec une entière certitude, par cette seule raison qu'il n'y a pas lieu de croire à une chose dont le monde n'offre aucune trace expérimentale.[1]

That was the certainty which had been gradually hardening in Renan's mind ever since he had defected from the seminary where he was training for the priesthood, and which he had noted fifteen years earlier in *L'Avenir de la science*:

> Ce n'est pas d'un raisonnement, mais de tout l'ensemble des sciences modernes que sort cet immense résultat : Il n'y a pas de surnaturel.[2]

The consequences of this attitude are clearly visible in the extract under consideration. The idea that nature is not governed by the whim of the gods is extolled as the 'base de toute philosophie'; 'la négation du miracle' is claimed to be the 'principe de la science positive'; 'l'inflexibilité du régime général de la nature' is taken as an axiom of modern thought. Renan's criterion of judgment is scientific opinion: 'la science grecque' appears as the originator of philosophic certainty and 'la science moderne' as its ultimate arbiter. 'La science positive', 'la science expérimentale de la nature' form the key to any reasonable understanding of the world, and it is the physicist and the chemist alone who are qualified to pronounce on its workings. Patently, Renan's admiration for scientific method knows no bounds.

Under these conditions Renan and his contemporaries are convinced that only those disciplines, like history, which can somehow be made to conform to scientific method, constitute modes of philosophic investigation which can yield positive results. Recent advances in subjects like Egyptology and comparative philology gave added plausibility to the supposition that a real analogy could be drawn between science and

---

[1] *Vie de Jésus*, pp. 16–17.
[2] *L'Avenir de la science*, p. 47.

history. In the dedication of *L'Avenir de la science*, Renan writes to Eugène Burnouf, the famous orientalist, that his lectures had demonstrated the realisation of what had hitherto seemed only a dream: 'la science devenant la philosophie, et les plus hauts résultats sortant de la plus scrupuleuse analyse des détails'.[1] This desire to reform every branch of intellectual activity as a kind of science extended also to literature, and Zola in particular, in *Le Roman expérimental*, tried to found a doctrine of novel-writing on the *Introduction à l'étude de la médecine expérimentale* by the great physiologist Claude Bernard. There one finds this hope expressed:

> Puisque la médecine, qui était un art, devient une science, pourquoi la littérature elle-même ne deviendrait-elle pas une science, grâce à la méthode expérimentale?[2]

The concluding words of Zola's treatise sum up his view of the dominance of scientific method over the whole realm of human endeavour:

> En somme, tout se résume dans ce grand fait : la méthode expérimentale, aussi bien dans les lettres que dans les sciences, est en train de déterminer les phénomènes naturels, individuels et sociaux, dont la métaphysique n'avait donné jusqu'ici que des explications irrationnelles et surnaturelles.[3]

It proved much harder than Zola had imagined to impose a programme of that kind on literature, but the ambition to give art a scientific basis was responsible for the crystallisation of the more diffuse trends of realism into the strict dogma of Naturalism (the very name of the school betrays its scientific pretensions). Even writers who did not subscribe to this extreme position found themselves so impressed by science that they felt it necessary somehow to introduce it into the creation of their works. Flaubert, for instance, declares that 'le grand Art est scientifique et impersonnel',[4] the Goncourt brothers describe themselves, among other things, as 'des physiologistes', and Leconte de Lisle affirmed:

> L'art et la science, longtemps séparés par suite des effets divergents de l'intelligence, doivent donc tendre à s'unir étroitement, si ce n'est à se confondre.[5]

[1] *L'Avenir de la science*, p. 4.
[2] *Le Roman expérimental*, p. 30.
[3] ibid., p. 53.
[4] To George Sand, 15th–16th December 1866, *Correspondance*, vol. v, p. 257.
[5] Preface to *Poèmes antiques*, in *Derniers Poèmes*, p. 211.

Equally apparent in the passage are the consequences of the new historical approach to Biblical scholarship. Renan has no wish to use his scientific certainty that miracles never happen to mock Christianity, like some latter-day Voltaire. What he wants to do is to reconstruct the mentality of an intelligent but uneducated Jew from a Palestinian village living at the time of the Emperor Tiberius, in order to discover what, in the light of the circumstances of his upbringing, he might have been expected to think, feel and believe, and thereby arrive at a better understanding of the historical origins of Christianity. In this way he comes to the conclusion that, although the rudiments of scientific method were known elsewhere, it would be unreasonable to suppose that Jesus could have been aware of them, and that, in view of the unquestioning acceptance of the marvellous among the Jewish people at that time, it was inevitable that Jesus too should have believed in the possibility of constant divine intervention in the natural order of things.

One can see in this sort of argument an attitude which the vast improvement in the method of historical studies had made characteristic of the mid-nineteenth century. Whereas the historians of the preceding ages had been content to regard history either as the piecing together of a coherent linear narrative of events, or as an excuse for moral philosophising on a grand scale, it had been increasingly realised since 1830 that a country's history and its great men could be properly understood only with an encyclopaedic knowledge of its ethnology, sociology, climate, physical circumstances, religion and customs. The study of history was henceforth to be carried out by the accumulation of provable details. The standards by which one assessed what happened in one age and country would be quite inappropriate to another age and country. Heavy stress was laid on the differences in human psychology which could be engendered by local circumstance; it was Renan's friend Taine who formulated the celebrated theory of *la race*, *le milieu* and *le moment*, the three essential factors conditioning the shape of any human mind. Two of these elements are present in this passage: the fervently religious cast of the Jewish mind and the kind of intellectual society in which Jesus lived; and the third, the particular conjuncture of events which had led, in Jesus's time, to a multiplication of revolutionary messianic movements, is added elsewhere. In adopting this kind of explanation, based on minute examination of the historical and archaeological evidence, as well as on first-hand experience of the country and people, Renan is conforming to the principles not only of Taine but also of the other great historians of the time—Fustel de Coulanges and Tocqueville, for example.

But while this attitude betokens a revolution in the writing and understanding of history, it also means far more than that. For men like Renan, the past can now be comprehended only in its own terms; each age has its centre of gravity within itself, and cannot be judged by eternal and unchanging standards as would have happened in the seventeenth century and to a large extent in the eighteenth too. Taine has this comment to make:

> Cette divination précise et prouvée des sentiments évanouis a, de nos jours, renouvelé l'histoire; on l'ignorait presque entièrement au siècle dernier; on se représentait les hommes de toute race et de tout siècle comme à peu près semblables, le Grec, le barbare, l'Hindou, l'homme de la Renaissance et l'homme du dix-huitième siècle comme coulés dans le même moule, et cela d'après une certaine conception abstraite, qui servait pour tout le genre humain. On connaissait l'homme, on ne connaissait pas les hommes; on n'avait pas pénétré dans l'âme; on ne savait pas que la structure morale d'un peuple et d'un âge est aussi particulière et aussi distincte que la structure physique d'une famille de plantes ou d'un ordre d'animaux.[1]

The development of the human race is now seen as a constantly changing part of a continuum of time, and the idea of unceasing change in the world and in the forces which govern it replaces the old concept of movement taking place only under the aegis of some permanent guiding power, be it God or reason. As Renan himself says in *L'Avenir de la science*:

> Le grand progrès de la réflexion moderne a été de substituer la catégorie du *devenir* à la catégorie de l'*être*, la conception du relatif à la conception de l'absolu, le mouvement à l'immobilité.[2]

That is why, later in the same work, he is able to claim that 'l'histoire est la vraie philosophie du XIXe siècle'.[3] It was no doubt something of the same idea that led Flaubert to write in 1859:

---

[1] *Histoire de la littérature anglaise* (Paris, Hachette; 1863), vol. I, pp. xi–xii of the Introduction.
[2] *L'Avenir de la science*, p. 182.
[3] ibid., p. 271.

Le *sens historique* est tout nouveau dans ce monde. On va se mettre à étudier les idées comme des faits et à disséquer les croyances comme des organismes. Il y a toute une école qui travaille dans l'ombre et qui fera quelque chose, j'en suis sûr.[1]

There is consequently in mid-nineteenth-century thought a strongly marked trend towards historical relativism and towards deterministic explanations of all the phenomena of human activity, of which religion becomes simply one manifestation among many, with forms as easily deducible from a given set of circumstances as those of political or social behaviour. Deformed echoes of this fundamental change in approach can be heard in Flaubert's *Bouvard et Pécuchet*, where one finds this analysis of a priest's reaction to modern scholarship:

M. Jeufroy tenait au surnaturel, ne voulait pas que le christianisme pût avoir humainement la moindre raison d'être, bien qu'il en vît chez tous les peuples des prodromes ou des déformations. L'impiété railleuse du XVIIIe siècle, il l'eût tolérée; mais la critique moderne, avec sa politesse, l'exaspérait. — J'aime mieux l'athée qui blasphème, que le sceptique qui ergote![2]

Christianity is just an historical phenomenon, and as such must be examined with the same dispassionate and critical realism that one would bring to a biological dissection or an account of some remote and long-forgotten battle.

As a result, to many Christians, Renan appeared as the arch-villain of modern disbelief. In Zola's words,

il devenait le géant de la négation, il symbolisait la science tuant la foi. En un mot, notre siècle d'enquête scientifique s'incarnait en lui.[3]

But Renan himself, despite his intellectual attachment to the scientific method in history and to positivism, did not find it easy to be consistent in accepting the conclusions which his principles forced on him. The end of this passage provides an illuminating example of the shifts in his thought, induced by a subjective desire to preserve something of the spirit of the religion to which he had once been so devoted, even after he had recognised the weight of the evidence assembled against it. After he has invoked so firmly the laws of science to disprove the

---

[1] *Correspondance*, vol. III, p. 207.
[2] *Bouvard et Pécuchet*, p. 333.
[3] *Lettre à la jeunesse*, in *Le Roman expérimental*, p. 70.

PLATE III *Le Génie de la science* (from the ceiling painting by Horace Vernet in the Salle des Pas perdus, Palais Bourbon)

—Vous verrez . . . . rien n'échappera à la baisse . . . . je parie qu'avant huit jours les pièces de cinq francs ne vaudront plus que trente sous . . . . rappelez vous ce que j'vous dis là, m'sieu Coquardeau !

PLATE IV *Rien n'échappera à la baisse* (from the caricature by Daumier)

supernatural, and after he has explained away a belief in it as the product of circumstance, he suddenly sheers away from the negative conclusions about Christianity which these preliminaries appear to portend, and launches instead into a panegyric of Jesus. With one of those consoling epithets which he manipulates so expertly, Renan transforms into 'belles erreurs qui furent le principe de sa force' what he might have presented as insuperable defects. The 'grande âme' of Jesus is somewhat patronisingly contrasted with 'le vulgaire'; a distinction is drawn between 'une crédulité niaise' and 'une notion profonde des rapports familiers de l'homme avec Dieu'. The ambivalence of Renan's position is even more clearly shown up by this passage from his essay on *La Méthode expérimentale en histoire religieuse* (a title which itself is indicative of the extent to which what purports to be scientific method has invaded domains originally quite foreign to it):

> Le développement des sciences critiques et des sciences naturelles, en changeant les idées de tous les peuples cultivés sur le surnaturel, c'est-à-dire sur la manière dont l'idéal fait son apparition dans les choses humaines, a modifié l'essence même de la religion... La religion, dès lors, s'est surtout réfugiée dans le cœur. Elle est devenue poésie et sentiment... Dieu nous garde de répudier ce beau nom de chrétien, qui nous met en rapport avec Jésus et l'idéal de l'Évangile, avec l'Église et tous les trésors de sainteté qu'elle a produits. Mais ne renions pas, non plus, notre passé naturaliste.[1]

In these unexpected twists, Renan is clearly abandoning any scientific standards of evidence in favour of a highly personal and speculative interpretation of things of which he can have no real knowledge. Such deviations from the canon of positivism are common in all Renan's writings and are responsible for the suspicion with which he was regarded by some of the more rigorous positivists of his time, among them Émile Littré, the scientist and lexicographer, Marcelin Berthelot, the chemist, and Taine himself, all of whom at one time or another expressed doubts about Renan's reliability as a supporter of the positivist cause. Zola eventually went so far as to denounce Renan for being a poet instead of a positivist:

> On a fini par comprendre que la *Vie de Jésus* était un aimable poème, dissimulant sous des fleurs romantiques quelques-unes des affirmations de l'exégèse moderne.[2]

---

[1] *Nouvelles Études d'histoire religieuse* (Paris, Calmann-Lévy; 1884), pp. 10–11.
[2] *Lettre à la jeunesse*, p. 73.

But as commentary XIII will show, Renan was only one of many who found the conclusions of positivism rationally irrefutable but emotionally unacceptable (though he was perhaps the only one who practised mental sleight-of-hand in order to elude the dilemma).

This passage demonstrates the power of the hold which science had taken on men's minds in the middle of the nineteenth century. Nor was it a naïve and uncritical admiration from the outside like Hugo's in *Océan*. The principles and methods of scientific investigators had inspired such respect in French thinkers from Auguste Comte onwards that they had invaded all sorts of other domains—philosophy, history and literature among them—and had come to assume the character of an infallible instrument of knowledge. But at the same time, Renan's reluctance to pursue his thought to its logical consequences betrays an uneasiness which many of his contemporaries were to feel at the apparently definitive disappearance of faith and which we shall see more clearly revealed in the next extract.

FURTHER READING

D. G. CHARLTON, *Positivist Thought in France during the Second Empire* (Oxford, Clarendon Press; 1959).

Louis HALPHEN, *L'Histoire en France depuis cent ans* (Paris, Armand Colin; 1914).

P. MOREAU, *L'histoire en France au XIXᵉ siècle* (Paris, Les Belles Lettres; 1935).

XIII

Leconte de Lisle

(1818–94)

FROM *La Paix des dieux*

Et l'Homme cria : — Dieux déchus de vos empires,
O Spectres, ô Splendeurs éteintes, ô Bourreaux
Et Rédempteurs, vous tous, les meilleurs et les pires,
Ne revivrez-vous plus pour des siècles nouveaux?

Vers qui s'exhaleront les vœux et les cantiques
Dans les temples déserts ou sur l'aile des vents?
A qui demander compte, ô Rois des jours antiques,
De l'angoisse infligée aux morts comme aux vivants?

Vous en qui j'avais mis l'espérance féconde,
Contre qui je luttais, fier de ma liberté,
Si vous êtes tous morts, qu'ai-je à faire en ce monde,
Moi, le premier croyant et le vieux révolté? —

Et l'Homme crut entendre alors dans tout son être
Une Voix qui disait, triste comme un sanglot :
— Rien de tel, jamais plus, ne doit revivre ou naître;
Les Temps balayeront tout cela flot sur flot.

Rien ne te rendra plus la foi ni le blasphème,
La haine, ni l'amour, et tu sais désormais,
Éveillé brusquement en face de toi-même,
Que ces spectres d'un jour c'est toi qui les créais.

Mais, va! Console-toi de ton œuvre insensée.
Bientôt ce vieux mirage aura fui de tes yeux,
Et tout disparaîtra, le monde et ta pensée,
Dans l'immuable paix où sont rentrés les Dieux.

LECONTE DE LISLE, *La Paix des dieux*,
in *Derniers Poèmes* (Paris, Lemerre; 1928), pp. 7–8

As we have seen in commentary II, the religious revival of the early years of the century was largely made possible by Chateaubriand's device of eluding the criticisms of eighteenth-century rationalism by proposing a purely emotional and aesthetic approach to the question. Voltairean objections were not so much refuted as ignored; a subjective need to believe was taken as being in itself a sufficient justification for belief. This attitude inevitably gave rise to a particularly emotional form of Catholicism, in which the individual's feeling for God was of primary importance, and during the Romantic period that kind of religion remained predominant. But even at that time there were a number of writers who found it difficult to suppress the claims of their intellect, however much they might want to preserve their faith. Lamartine's peremptory silencing of intelligence was not acceptable to everyone:

> Que ma raison se taise et que mon cœur adore![1]

Musset, for instance, makes exactly the same distinction between 'le cœur' and 'la raison', but is unable to decide between their contradictory conclusions:

> Ma raison révoltée
> Essaye en vain de croire et mon cœur de douter.[2]

For him the anti-religious arguments of Voltaire and the *philosophes* are—regrettably—unanswerable; God has been killed by them:

> Et que nous reste-t-il, à nous, les déicides?
> Pour qui travailliez-vous, démolisseurs stupides,
> Lorsque vous disséquiez le Christ sur son autel?...
> Vous vouliez pétrir l'homme à votre fantaisie;
> Vous vouliez faire un monde. — Eh bien, vous l'avez fait.
> Votre monde est superbe, et votre homme est parfait!
> Les monts sont nivelés, la plaine est éclaircie;
> Vous avez sagement taillé l'arbre de vie;
> Tout est bien balayé sur vos chemins de fer,
> Tout est grand, tout est beau, mais on meurt dans votre air.[3]

Nerval too complains that the legacy of eighteenth-century scepticism makes belief impossible;[4] Vigny anxiously scrutinises the heavens for a sign, but, in *Le Mont des Oliviers*, is forced to admit that none will come.

[1] *La Semaine sainte*, in *Méditations poétiques*, p. 197.
[2] *L'Espoir en Dieu*, in *Poésies*, p. 350.
[3] *Rolla*, in *Poésies*, p. 294.   [4] See p. xv.

This conflict between heart and reason was still unresolved when a new element was introduced into the situation by the positivist reassessment of the religious phenomenon, typified by Renan's *Vie de Jésus*. This time there seemed to be no doubt at all. Not only was it impossible to accuse men like Renan and Taine of systematic hostility to Christianity, as one could accuse Voltaire and his associates; it was also apparently impossible even to think of rebutting their arguments, since these rested on incontrovertible scientific certainty. Religion had been definitively assigned to its proper place as a transient phenomenon in the progress of human evolution; it could be inspected like a pre-historic relic in a museum, but there was no point in harbouring any very strong feelings about it, since it had simply ceased to exist.

This attitude to the history of religion, whether Christian or pagan, is typical of many of Renan's generation, not least of Leconte de Lisle. *La Paix des dieux*, though it was first published in 1888, towards the end of its author's life, sums up the moods and the ideas which were already characteristic of him at a much earlier stage. In it Man, insatiably curious about the secrets of eternity, begs the Spectre to show him the charnel-house of the dead gods. The Spectre tells him to look in his own heart, and there he sees a vast procession of the gods of past ages, ending with Christ. The poem concludes with the stanzas quoted here. The various gods which humanity has worshipped are thus presented as the emanations of an irrational desire to believe in something outside life; now, historical and anthropological research has revealed them all to be equally vain, and they have passed away for ever. From the idols of savage tribes to Christ himself, they are treated with the same pains-taking attention to racial and linguistic detail, because it is philological and archaeological investigation of comparative religion which has demonstrated their common origin in human needs and delusions.

The connection with Renan's views is obvious. Indeed, the *Souvenirs d'enfance et de jeunesse* (first published in 1883, five years before *La Paix des dieux*) contains, in *La Prière sur l'Acropole*, a paragraph which reads almost as a summary of Leconte de Lisle's poem (except for its much more conciliatory tone):

Un immense fleuve d'oubli nous entraîne dans un gouffre sans nom. Ô abîme, tu es le Dieu unique. Les larmes de tous les peuples sont de vraies larmes; les rêves de tous les sages renferment une part de vérité. Tout n'est ici que symbole et que songe. Les dieux passent comme les hommes, et il

ne serait pas bon qu'ils fussent éternels. La foi qu'on a eue ne doit jamais
être une chaîne. On est quitte envers elle quand on l'a soigneusement
roulée dans le linceul de pourpre où dorment les dieux morts.[1]

The whole course of Leconte de Lisle's poetry seems to be anticipated
in another sentence from *L'Avenir de la science*:

> Les mythologies ne sont plus pour nous des séries de fables absurdes et
> parfois ridicules, mais de grands poèmes divins, où les nations primitives
> ont déposé leurs rêves sur le monde suprasensible.[2]

Leconte de Lisle's utilisation of Greek, Scandinavian, Celtic, Germanic
and Oriental mythology in the *Poèmes antiques* and the *Poèmes barbares*
is a development of the same idea, and Flaubert's *La Tentation de Saint
Antoine* is based on a similar intention.

But however final this clinical review of deceased religions may
appear, and however anti-Christian Leconte de Lisle may be elsewhere,
he is obviously suffering from a sense of frustration at his own discoveries. Like Renan himself, he is aghast at the thought that the solace
of religion, illusory as it was, will henceforward be denied to the world.
Man is alone, and the prospect is a chilling one. The dilemma of reason
and feeling thus reasserts itself in an even more acute form—more
acute because there is now no chance at all of suppressing the evidence
of reason. Only Renan still contrives to turn the question by continuing to talk about God while making mental reservations that he
really means 'la catégorie de l'idéal'; for Leconte de Lisle and many
others of his generation, all that remains is a nostalgic despair at a loss
which seems to be irreparable. The theme is a recurrent one in Leconte
de Lisle's poetry:

> Plus de transports sans frein vers un ciel inconnu,
> Plus de regrets sacrés, plus d'immortelle envie!
> Hélas! des coupes d'or où nous buvions la vie
> Nos lèvres et nos cœurs n'auront rien retenu!
>
> O mortelles langueurs, ô jeunesse en ruine,
> Vous ne contenez plus que cendre et vanité!
> L'amour, l'amour est mort avec la volupté;
> Nous avons renié la passion divine![3]

[1] *Souvenirs d'enfance et de jeunesse*, p. 72.
[2] *L'Avenir de la science*, p. 266.
[3] *L'Anathème*, in *Poèmes barbares* (Paris, Lemerre; 1927), p. 350.

These feelings of dismay at the emotional consequences of being intellectually certain that God does not exist are shared by many of his contemporaries. In 1858, the young Villiers de l'Isle-Adam looks back longingly at former ages of unquestioning faith:

> Car, en ces temps évanouis,
> Croire n'était pas difficile...
> Mais le monde a changé depuis.[1]

Des Esseintes, the hero of Huysmans's *A Rebours* (1884), finds himself imprisoned in the same dilemma:

A mesure même que sa faim religieuse s'augmentait, à mesure qu'il appelait, de toutes ses forces, comme une rançon pour l'avenir, comme un subside pour sa vie nouvelle, cette foi qui se laissait voir, mais dont la distance à franchir l'épouvantait, des idées se pressaient dans son esprit toujours en ignition, repoussant sa volonté mal assise, rejetant par des motifs de bon sens, par des preuves de mathématique, les mystères et les dogmes!

Il faudrait pouvoir s'empêcher de discuter avec soi-même, se dit-il douloureusement; il faudrait pouvoir fermer les yeux, se laisser emporter par ce courant, oublier ces maudites découvertes qui ont détruit l'édifice religieux, du haut en bas, depuis deux siècles.[2]

The most characteristic reactions are perhaps those of two poets deeply interested in positivist thought, Louise Ackermann and Sully Prudhomme. It would be difficult to find a more succinct and revealing statement of the hesitations and anxieties of the post-positivist generations than Mme Ackermann's *Le Positivisme*, written in the 1870s:

> Il s'ouvre par delà toute science humaine
> Un vide dont la Foi fut prompte à s'emparer.
> De cet abîme obscur elle a fait son domaine;
> En s'y précipitant, elle a cru l'éclairer.
> Eh bien! nous t'expulsons de tes divins royaumes,
> Dominatrice ardente, et l'instant est venu :
> Tu ne vas plus savoir où loger tes fantômes;
>   Nous fermons l'Inconnu.
>
> Mais ton triomphateur expiera ta défaite.
> L'homme déjà se trouble, et, vainqueur éperdu,
> Il se sent ruiné par sa propre conquête :

[1] *Découragement*, in *Premières Poésies, Œuvres complètes*, vol. x, p. 137.
[2] *A Rebours* (Paris, Charpentier; 1947), p. 288.

En te dépossédant nous avons tout perdu.
Nous restons sans espoir, sans recours, sans asile,
Tandis qu'obstinément le Désir qu'on exile
Revient errer autour du gouffre défendu.[1]

Sully Prudhomme expresses the same regret in many of his poems, for
example *Intus*, which dates from the mid-1860s:

L'intelligence dit au cœur :
« Le monde n'a pas un bon père.
Vois, le mal est partout vainqueur ».
Le cœur dit : « Je crois et j'espère.

Espère, ô ma sœur, crois un peu :
C'est à force d'aimer qu'on trouve;
Je suis immortel, je sens Dieu ».
— L'intelligence lui dit : « Prouve! »[2]

Neither Mme Ackermann nor Sully Prudhomme has anything like the
poetic force of feeling and expression which Leconte de Lisle can
muster, but they are excellent witnesses to the state of mind of their
times, and Sully Prudhomme's summing-up of the mid-century
religious problem is pertinent and penetrating:

La science froide et sûre en face d'un spectre religieux qui ne veut pas lui
céder la place, voilà le drame *moderne* de la pensée humaine.[3]

Leconte de Lisle's position is further complicated by the violent
antipathy which he feels for Christianity and for its God. This means
that he not only laments the passing of 'la foi' and 'l'amour' but also
regrets 'le blasphème' and 'la haine'. If God is dead, so is the Devil,
and there is no longer even any sense in rebelling against the supposed
injustices of God under the banner of Satan or Cain. Such movements
of revolt had frequently flared up in Leconte de Lisle's earlier poetry,
for instance in *Le Runoïa* or *Qaïn*, the hero of which had defiantly
cried:

---

[1] *Poésies philosophiques* (Paris, Lemerre; n.d.), pp. 91–2.
[2] *Poésies 1865–7* (Paris, Lemerre; 1883), pp. 37–8.
[3] *Journal intime, Lettres—Pensées* (Paris, Lemerre; 1922), pp. 186–7; quoted by D. G.
Charlton in *Positivist Thought in France*, p. 193.

Dieu triste, Dieu jaloux qui dérobes ta face,
Dieu qui mentais, disant que ton œuvre était bon,
Mon souffle, ô Pétrisseur de l'antique limon,
Un jour redressera ta victime vivace.
Tu lui diras : Adore! Elle répondra : Non![1]

This kind of outburst against God often occurs in the works of writers
of the second half of the century. It usually constitutes a last desperate
attempt to jolt God into some sort of action by insulting Him, and it
tends chiefly to affect those who would secretly like to accept God and
render Him responsible for their inability to do so. It colours much of
Baudelaire's work, especially of course the section *Révolte* in *Les Fleurs
du mal*; it is an important element in Rimbaud's *Une Saison en enfer*;
and it dominates the venomous diatribes against the deity which form
Lautréamont's *Chants de Maldoror*. Traces of the same attitude are
present in some of Nerval's works (for example the sonnet *Antéros* and
the *Histoire de la reine du matin*), in one or two of Mallarmé's early
poems, and in Villiers de l'Isle-Adam's novel *L'Ève future*. The
obsession with evil in Barbey d'Aurevilly's *Les Diaboliques* is a related
phenomenon, and J.-K. Huysmans's *Là-bas*, a detailed account of
Satanism in Parisian society, shows how a belief in the Devil can even
lead to a return to belief in God. Such manifestations reveal the persistence of a religious spirit in circumstances when its normal forms
have been rendered untenable. In these cases worship of the Devil
constitutes a perverted form of belief.

Other writers tried other ways of keeping the notion of religion alive.
Flaubert is particularly perceptive in a comment he makes on the
situation of thinking men now that science has formally confirmed the
demise of religion:

> La base théologique manquant, où sera maintenant le point d'appui de cet
> enthousiasme qui s'ignore? Les uns chercheront dans la chair, d'autres
> dans les vieilles religions, d'autres dans l'art.[2]

For 1852 that was a remarkably accurate forecast of some of the dominant trends of intellectual life during the Second Empire: an almost
hysterical quest for pleasure and entertainment, an archaeological
resurrection of past religions, and a fanatical devotion to art. For

[1] *Poèmes barbares*, p. 18.
[2] To Louise Colet, *Correspondance*, vol. III, pp. 16–17.

Renan, Leconte de Lisle and to some extent Flaubert himself, the study of the forms religion had assumed through the ages was an aid to oblivion of its present non-existence. For Leconte de Lisle again, Baudelaire, Flaubert, Mallarmé and many Symbolists, art was elevated to the rank of a religion (we shall examine this in more detail in commentary XVII). Other trends not mentioned by Flaubert also have the character of substitutes for religion: the attempts of thinkers like Fourier and Auguste Comte to transform social doctrines into lay religions (see commentary VII), the quasi-mystical cult of science by Zola, Renan in his earlier period, and on occasion Hugo (see commentary IX), and the constant temptation to dabble in occultism (see commentary XI). It would seem that the gap left by the disappearance of religion had to be filled somehow and that those who saw it passing could not bear to accept the idea that it would not return in some form or other. The note of desperation in *La Paix des dieux*, unexpected from a man who had been as bitterly opposed to Christianity as Leconte de Lisle was, is an echo of this anguish.

The only thing which appears to afford him any consolation now is the contemplation of 'l'immuable paix' into which the gods, the world and Man himself will eventually vanish. This idea, which recurs constantly in his poetry, is itself derived from the study of hitherto ill-known religions, especially Buddhism. The influence of Eastern thought is an important development in the intellectual world of the mid-century. Hand in hand with detailed inquiries into the nature and origins of the world's religions had come a vastly increased knowledge of Oriental and especially Indian beliefs. Eugène Burnouf had expounded Buddhism to the French public, and the great Indian poems had been translated. The consequences of this discovery of a new civilisation were so far-reaching that it has even been termed the Oriental Renaissance. Writers as diverse as Vigny, Quinet, Michelet, Hugo and Jules Laforgue, as well as Leconte de Lisle, felt the attraction of Eastern doctrines, and by the end of the century pessimism often took the form of a fascination with *nirvana*, of the type which marks the end of *La Paix des dieux*. The popularity which Schopenhauer's works enjoyed in France after 1870 reinforced this influence, since Schopenhauer himself had been an ardent admirer of Buddhism and had incorporated Buddhistic elements into his own philosophy. A further indirect support came from Wagner's music-dramas, since Wagner was a disciple of Schopenhauer, had once planned a Buddhist opera, and had as the climax of *Götterdämmerung* a vision of the end of all things.

Absolute but gloomy acceptance of the conclusions of positivism, nostalgia for the passing of religion, muted echoes of Cainist revolt and semi-Buddhist pessimism combine to make *La Paix des dieux* a conspectus of mid-century religious attitudes. The shadow of Renan's *Vie de Jésus* hangs over it, as it does over the minds of many Frenchmen in the 1860s and 1870s.

FURTHER READING

Raymond SCHWAB, *La Renaissance orientale* (Paris, Payot; 1950).

XIV

Hippolyte Taine

(1823–93)

FROM *Vie et opinions de M. Frédéric Thomas Graindorge*

4 janvier. — *Alceste* à l'Opéra.

Le public était très froid et ne s'est trouvé émoustillé que par le ballet. Ce public se compose pour les trois quarts de gens qui veulent s'amuser, et qui viennent écouter un grand poème dramatique, comme on va au café ou au Vaudeville. Scribe, Alexandre Dumas père, Adolphe Adam donnent la mesure du Français. Pourtant, à cause du terreau parisien, il y a une petite élite de vrais juges, et, à la rigueur, les autres peuvent être soulevés jusqu'à eux. Mais la sympathie native, l'intelligence innée du beau, la capacité d'illusion sont en Italie et en Allemagne. A Berlin, on écoute la musique en silence, aussi attentivement qu'à l'église. Ici on raille.

Par suite, les bévues abondent. Les ronds des arrosoirs sur le plancher sont vus des meilleures loges et salissent l'imagination. L'expression ennuyée, effrontée des figurants fait contraste avec la musique; ils se poussent du coude, se gouaillent dans les coulisses. Le ballet est ignoble. C'est une exposition de filles à vendre. Elles ont les gestes et les basses petites minauderies de l'emploi, la fadeur voluptueuse et voulue. Il n'y a pas dix pour cent dans un ballet de beauté vraie. Tout est provocation comme sur un trottoir; les jambes en maillot rose se montrent jusqu'aux hanches : l'attitude est celle des danseuses de corde; avec leurs vilaines pattes de grenouille moderne, avec leurs bras filamenteux d'araignée, avec leurs ronds de jambe qui sentent l'école du saltimbanque, elles s'imaginent représenter les nobles processions de la Grèce antique.

Des gens du monde qui vivent pour le plaisir et l'attrapent une fois sur dix, des bourgeois qui courent après sans l'atteindre, des filles et une populace interlope qui le vendent ou le filoutent : voilà Paris.

Un seul but : jouir et paraître.

HIPPOLYTE TAINE, *Vie et opinions de M. Frédéric Thomas Graindorge* (Paris, Hachette; 1959), pp. 10–11

Hippolyte Taine is best known as a philosopher, an historian and a literary critic. But in 1863 an old friend of his named Marcelin who had become editor of *La Vie parisienne*, a light, satirical review, persuaded him to write a long series of notes and sketches on the Paris of the Second Empire. These took the form of the diary and reflections of an imaginary American oil magnate of French origins, M. Frédéric Thomas Graindorge, and were published in book form in 1867. It is from this work that the present bitterly critical impression of an evening at the opera is taken.

The dominant impression of Parisian society which Taine, in the person of Graindorge, seeks to convey in this revealing miniature, is one of a frantic, undignified scramble for pleasure—and pleasure on a superficial, frivolous, sensual plane. 'Jouir' is the keynote; the audience at one of Gluck's most grave and moving operas wants only to 's'amuser', to be 'émoustillé' as it would be by a few glasses of champagne; Paris is occupied above all with the industry of 'le plaisir'. Taine was far from alone in picking out this lust for pleasure as the most striking feature of life in France under the Second Empire. Victor Hugo, for instance, said much the same in 1870 when he cast a sombre backward glance over the fallen Empire:

> Naguère, aux jours d'orgie où l'homme joyeux brille,
>   Et croit peu,
> Pareils aux durs sarments desséchés où pétille
>   Un grand feu,
>
> Quand, ivre de splendeur et de songes,
>   Tu dansais
> Et tu chantais, en proie aux éclatants mensonges
>   Du succès,
>
> Alors qu'on entendait ta fanfare de fête
>   Retentir,
> O Paris, je t'ai fui comme le noir prophète
>   Fuyait Tyr.[1]

About the same time Renan was writing:

Paris était envahi par l'étranger viveur, par les provinciaux, qui n'y encourageaient qu'une petite presse ridicule et la sotte littérature, aussi peu

[1] *Au moment de rentrer en France*, in *Les Châtiments* (Paris, Imprimerie Nationale; 1910), p. 7.

parisienne que possible, du nouveau genre bouffon. Le pays, en attendant, s'enfonçait dans un matérialisme hideux.[1]

Most contemporaries and historians agree that the Second Empire was a time of luxury, of high living, of open-handed spending and of strenuous entertainment. The reasons for this search for heedless pleasure are various. No doubt the main one was the vastly increased prosperity of France after 1852; the process of growth begun under Louis-Philippe proceeded apace. France's colonial empire, started by the conquest of Algeria during the July Monarchy, was extended by leaps and bounds, in Senegal, in the Middle East and in Indo-China; her railway network was trebled between 1851 and 1859 alone; her industries grew enormously (the great iron-works at Le Creusot produced five times as much in 1867 as they had in 1855); new banks were founded at regular intervals to finance the continual expansion of production; foreign trade increased threefold. The suddenness with which wealth had been thrust on a class not hitherto accustomed to it and with no real tradition of culture meant that money was often squandered fatuously: in that respect, the story of the meteoric rise and fall of Jansoulet, the good-natured but empty-headed millionaire from Tunis, which Daudet relates in his novel *Le Nabab*, is symptomatic of the 1860s. Then there was a general turning away from the serious pursuit of politics, partly encouraged by Napoleon III as a guarantee of the stability of his own *régime* and partly an instinctive reaction to the disappointments of 1848. When Graindorge says of his young nephew:

Quant aux théories politiques, elles sont tombées dans l'eau en 1848; à ses yeux, les phrases qu'on fait sur les affaires publiques ne sont qu'un moyen d'accrocher une place,[2]

he is defining the state of mind of a disillusioned generation. To these factors must be added the decay of religion and the rise of positivism, which was often misconstrued as justifying exclusive concentration on material and temporal values; the personal example of Napoleon III and his court, fascinated with external glitter and pomp, easy-going and amoral, second-rate in their artistic taste; and the enormously enhanced importance of Paris as a centre of international tourist attractions, with

[1] *La Réforme intellectuelle et morale de la France* (Cambridge, Cambridge University Press; 1950), p. 28.   [2] op. cit., p. 123.

its increased ease of access by rail, its broad new thoroughfares laid out in the immense transformations undertaken by Baron Haussmann in the 1860s, and its two great exhibitions in 1855 and 1867.

It is no coincidence that Taine should situate this denunciation of French superficiality in the theatre. Paris in the 1850s and 1860s catered for the amusement of inhabitants and visitors by large numbers of theatres, opera houses, public balls, *cafés-concerts* and concert-halls, and the atmosphere of gaiety, of licence, of vapid enjoyment which reigned in most of them aptly symbolises the feckless, frivolous spirit of the times. The authors whom Taine disdainfully lists as manifestations of the French mentality all show the same characteristic of catering, competently and unambitiously, for a wide public which asked only for facile thrills and surface attractiveness: Dumas *père* with his interminable adventure stories, Scribe with his ingenious and undemanding plays, Adam with his tuneful but conventional light operas. The name which Taine surprisingly omits, no doubt because his greatest triumphs did not come until 1866 and 1867, is that of Offenbach, whose phenomenally successful partnership with the dramatists Meilhac and Halévy produced works like *La Belle Hélène*, *La Duchesse de Gérolstein* and *La Vie parisienne* which epitomise the life of their age perhaps better than anything else written then. Even Offenbach's contemporaries were inclined to see in his operettas, with their unbridled joyfulness, their disrespectful wit, their furious rhythms, their helter-skelter plots and their carefree self-indulgence, the symbol of Second Empire society. The refrain of the Augur's song in the last act of *La Belle Hélène* could well serve as the motto of the times:

Je suis gai, soyez gais, il le faut, je le veux![1]

and Jules Claretie, later Director of the Comédie-Française, was almost prophetic when he said to a friend as they left the première of *La Vie parisienne* in November 1866:

Si jamais l'on s'avise de faire une peinture allégorique de notre époque emportée par la fièvre de l'or et la frénésie de la jouissance, qu'on n'oublie pas surtout de mettre, au-dessus de notre sabbat épileptique, le maigre Offenbach conduisant la ronde en riant.[2]

[1] *La Belle Hélène* (Paris, Calmann-Lévy; 1955), p. 74.
[2] Letter from an unidentified correspondent, quoted by Léon Chancerel in *Le Siècle d'Offenbach*, Cahiers de la Compagnie Renaud-Barrault (Paris, Julliard; November 1958), p. 36.

An allegorical picture of that kind was in fact attempted by Zola in his *Nana*, an exposure of the corruption, decadence and triviality of Second Empire society, as seen through the brilliant career of the ex-prostitute Nana, who rises from playing the lead in what one is plainly intended to recognise as an Offenbach operetta to be one of the queens of the Parisian *demi-monde*. Zola's description of the audience at the first night of the operetta strongly recalls Taine's analysis of those present at *Alceste*:

> Paris était là, le Paris des lettres, de la finance et du plaisir, beaucoup de journalistes, quelques écrivains, des hommes de Bourse, plus de filles que de femmes honnêtes; monde singulièrement mêlé, fait de tous les génies, gâté par tous les vices, où la même fatigue et la même fièvre passaient sur les visages.[1]

Like Taine, Zola presents the chorus girls as so many 'filles à vendre' —so much so that Bordenave, manager of the theatre at which Nana is appearing, invariably corrects anyone who refers to his theatre with the coarse rejoinder: 'Dites mon bordel!' It is her stage appearances which enable Nana, like a great many theatrical stars of the time, to attract lovers from high society who, one after another, ruin themselves for her. Nor does Zola exaggerate the follies which men like Muffat were liable to commit for girls like Nana in those days: La Païva, a notorious Second Empire *prima donna*, was given by one of her admirers a mansion in the Champs-Élysées which, with its contents, was worth nearly half a million pounds. Indeed, Nana's own career, with its extravagant peaks and its tragic end, is in part modelled on that of Blanche d'Antigny, one of the leading operetta singers of the day. The social history of the time is full of the names of such beauties, spend-thrift, famous, adulated, and sometimes even with a modicum of talent —Hortense Schneider, Cora Pearl, Céline Montaland, Léonide Leblanc and so many others: to list their names is to characterise the Second Empire almost as surely as to list Napoleon's victories characterises the first.

Taine sees the immense popularity of the most trivial kind of enter-tainment in the Second Empire as a serious threat to more elevated forms of art. He admits the existence of 'une petite élite de vrais juges', but regards the majority as being either indifferent to beauty (like the

[1] *Nana* (Paris, Charpentier; n.d.), vol. I, pp. 12–13.

PLATE V   *Offenbach dressed as a pierrot* (from a caricature)

PLATE VI *Expérience de physiologie de Claude Bernard à la Sorbonne*
(from the painting by Lhermitte)

spectators at *Alceste*) or even hostile to it: 'Ici on raille'. Again, Taine is far from being alone among artists and intellectuals in protesting against the debasement of taste in the 1850s and 1860s. Flaubert and Baudelaire were resolute in affirming their own standards, but both found themselves prosecuted for their pains. Leconte de Lisle (though he accepted in secret subsidies from the imperial Government) was full of scathing contempt for the ignorance and philistinism of his contemporaries. Renan likewise denounced the degeneration of culture:

> L'abaissement de toute aristocratie se produisait en d'effrayantes proportions; la moyenne intellectuelle du public descendait étrangement. Le nombre et la valeur des hommes distingués qui sortaient de la nation se maintenaient, augmentaient peut-être; dans plus d'un genre de mérite, les nouveaux venus ne le cédaient à aucun des noms illustres des générations écloses sous un meilleur soleil; mais l'atmosphère s'appauvrissait; on mourait de froid.[1]

And Villiers de l'Isle-Adam, one of that category of *poètes maudits*, authors unpopular with public and publishers alike because of their high seriousness, remarked sadly as the Second Empire was nearing its end in 1870: 'Nous sommes devenus les amuseurs des autres nations'.[2]

The low standard of art in France in the 1860s stands out all the more clearly for Taine because of the contrast with other countries: 'La sympathie native, l'intelligence innée du beau, la capacité d'illusion sont en Italie et en Allemagne. A Berlin, on écoute la musique en silence, aussi attentivement qu'à l'église'. To many people at that time Germany more than any other country appeared as the real home of art and philosophy, a land which not only produced men of genius but encouraged them in their efforts and treated their works with a respect bordering on reverence. Taine himself owed much of his philosophic background to German sources, notably Hegel, as did his friend Renan, whose philological and Biblical researches would have been impossible without the studies previously carried out by German scholars like David Strauss, Creuzer, Jacobi and Max Müller. In the middle of the century the intellectual debt of France to Germany was enormous. But here Taine is thinking more of the gulf in musical taste which separated the two countries, and it was probably in this domain that the shallowness of the reactions of the French public was most clearly

---

[1] *La Réforme intellectuelle et morale de la France*, p. 28.
[2] Preface to *La Révolte*, in *Œuvres complètes*, vol. VII, p. xx.

revealed. Wagner is the case which shows this most pointedly. By the 1860s Wagner's music-dramas, despite their revolutionary approach to operatic technique and their unconventional tonalities, were accepted and regularly performed in Germany, whereas in France the only attempt to stage one of them—*Tannhäuser* at the Opéra in 1861—had ended in disastrous failure, partly because the public was disconcerted by so lofty and uncompromising a conception of art, and partly because the members of the aristocratic and fashionable Jockey Club were furious that the second act contained no opportunity for their girl-friends in the *corps de ballet* to display their charms[1]—that same *corps de ballet* which Taine castigates as a collection of tarts. There is an ironic aptness in the fact that Offenbach's *Le Papillon* should have alternated with *Tannhäuser* during the latter's brief passage at the Opéra and that Offenbach himself should have composed more than one mocking and successful parody of Wagner. Those few Frenchmen who did feel themselves attracted by the idealism of Wagnerian art (most of them, like Baudelaire, poets and writers who were themselves objects of mistrust and derision in France) were for many years obliged to travel to Germany if they wished to see Wagner's works performed on the stage. The humiliation which this inflicted on Frenchmen anxious to restore dignity to the art of their own country was sharpened when, in 1876, Bayreuth became a veritable temple of Wagnerian music, thanks to the patronage of Ludwig II of Bavaria. As Villiers de l'Isle-Adam wrily asked after attending a Wagnerian festival in Germany in 1870:

> Où d'aussi surprenantes fantasmagories sont-elles réalisables, sinon dans ces contrées, tout artistiques, de l'Allemagne? [2]

The Second Empire is a period which can still evoke a certain nostalgia for irresponsible high spirits, lavish amusements and wild extravagances. As Renan foresaw,

> Il n'est pas douteux que le règne de Napoléon III restera pour certaines classes de la nation un véritable idéal,[3]

---

[1] It is true that Wagner had been prevailed upon to include a ballet in the first act, but that did not satisfy them, since they regarded it as beneath their dignity to arrive before the second act anyway—which in itself is a sufficient commentary on their attitude to art.

[2] *Le Tsar et les Grands-Ducs*, in *Œuvres complètes*, vol. v, p. 202.

[3] *La Réforme intellectuelle et morale de la France*, p. 27.

a judgment ironically echoed by Zola at the end of *Nana*, when one of the heroine's friends, a prostitute like her, exclaims:

Moi, j'ai vu Louis-Philippe, une époque de panés[1] et de grigous,[2] ma chère. Et puis est venue quarante-huit. Ah! une jolie chose, une dégoûtation, leur République! Après février, j'ai crevé la faim, moi qui vous parle!... Mais, si vous aviez connu tout ça, vous vous mettriez à genoux devant l'empereur, car il a été notre père, oui, notre père...[3]

Further confirmation is offered, strangely enough, by Ludovic Halévy himself, in his collection of short stories about back-stage life at the Opéra, entitled *La Famille Cardinal*. In *Monsieur Cardinal*, written while the Opéra was still closed after the war and the Commune of 1871, Mme Cardinal bewails her misfortune, since one of her two daughters in the *corps de ballet* has still not found a protector:

J'avais encore une fille à caser, et je me disais : « Avec tout ça l'Opéra est fermé depuis neuf mois... et quand rouvrira-t-il? Et Pauline n'est pas casée, et j'aurai probablement du mal à la caser sous la République, tandis que sous l'Empire, il faut être juste, ça allait tout seul ».[4]

But if the *demi-monde* mourned the passing of the Second Empire, it was also a time when, the divorce between public taste and serious art being almost complete, the greatest creative writers were either solitary and unhappy figures like Baudelaire, Flaubert and Leconte de Lisle, or young anti-conformist rebels such as Verlaine, Villiers de l'Isle-Adam and Mallarmé. Taine's intelligence, his acuteness of observation and his incisive powers of analysis have enabled him to make an apparently innocuous diary entry recording a visit to the opera into a concise and telling delineation of a whole epoch.

FURTHER READING

Léon GUICHARD, *La Musique et les lettres au temps du wagnérisme* (Paris, Presses Universitaires de France; 1963).
Le Siècle d'Offenbach, Cahiers de la Compagnie Renaud-Barrault (Paris, Julliard; November 1958).

[1] Slang: 'stony broke'. [2] Slang: 'skinflints'. [3] *Nana*, vol. II, pp. 266-7.
[4] *La Famille Cardinal* (Paris, Calmann-Lévy; n.d.), p. 45.

XV

Edmond and Jules de Goncourt

(1822-96)   (1830-70)

FROM *Sœur Philomène*

Elle redoutait beaucoup de voir un mort. Elle en vit un qui venait de mourir. Il avait les deux mains étendues et posées à plat sur le lit. Un tricot brun mal boutonné sur sa poitrine. Deux oreillers lui soulevaient le corps; sa tête, un peu sur le côté, se renversait en arrière. On voyait le dessous de son cou, une barbe forte et noire, un nez pincé, des yeux creux. Autour de sa tête ses cheveux plaquaient à l'oreille comme des cheveux en sueur. Sa bouche béante était restée toute grande ouverte dans une aspiration suprême : la vie semblait l'avoir forcée pour en sortir. Il était là tout chaud et déjà enveloppé et raidi dans le suaire invisible de la mort... La sœur regarda : elle resta pour s'éprouver, longtemps à le regarder : elle ne sentit pas plus d'émotion devant ce cadavre que devant une cire.

Elle se soutint pendant quelques jours dans cet état de fermeté naturelle et de courage sans effort. C'était une grande surprise et un grand contentement pour elle d'échapper si facilement à la lâcheté de ses sens, aux défaillances qu'elle avait redoutées. Elle commençait à se croire aguerrie déjà, lorsque, regardant un soir une malade qui dormait toute pâle, le cœur lui manqua : elle fut obligée de se retenir à la colonnette du lit pour ne pas tomber. Jusque-là, par la volonté, par l'application de toutes ses forces à son rôle, à sa tâche de dévouement, elle s'était dérobée à l'impression et au contre-coup de ce qu'elle voyait. L'heure était venue où toutes les émotions amassées en elle à son insu, éclataient sans motif. Elle cédait à un malaise indéfini, à l'ébranlement de toutes les secousses qu'elle n'avait pas perçues sur le moment. Ses nerfs, tenus par le spectacle de l'hôpital dans une irritation continue, avaient un jeu fébrile, une sensibilité agacée et maladive; et certains bruits, comme la chute d'un gobelet d'étain, lui donnaient un tressaillement douloureux.

Puis elle voyait tous les jours un peu plus de ce que l'hôpital cache si admirablement aux premiers regards. Les têtes des jeunes étudiants penchés à la visite sur un lit n'étaient pas quelquefois si rapprochées que son œil, malgré elle, ne passât au travers et ne touchât, sur un membre entrevu, une plaie nue et vive. La mort, elle la croisait à toute heure dans cette affreuse boîte brune, portée par deux infirmiers, qui voile le cadavre et donne la terreur du mystère à l'horreur de la mort. Toutes sortes d'objets, dont le sens lui échappait aux premiers temps, prenaient pour elle une signification qui s'emparait de sa pensée au passage. Elle ne pouvait les rencontrer de l'œil sans y trouver un souvenir qui lui faisait peur, une image qui lui faisait mal. Les choses évoquaient l'ombre des souffrances qu'elles avaient touchées. Elle revoyait sur le brancard de bois renversé en l'air dans l'antichambre, à l'entrée de la salle, ces femmes que presque chaque jour le brancard emportait pâles à la salle des opérations et rapportait plus pâles. Tout alors lui parlant et allant jusqu'au fond de ses entrailles, elle éprouvait un serrement sous les côtes, et elle se sentait les jambes à la fois molles et légères, avec un froid dans les os descendant de la rotule au bout de l'orteil.

EDMOND AND JULES DE GONCOURT, *Sœur Philomène*
(Paris, Lemerre; 1890), pp. 99–101

La science approche enfin, et approche de l'homme; elle a dépassé le monde visible ou palpable des astres, des pierres, des plantes, où, dédaigneusement, on la confinait; c'est à l'âme qu'elle se prend, munie des instruments exacts et perçants dont trois cents ans d'expérience ont prouvé la justesse et mesuré la portée. La pensée et son développement, son rang, sa structure et ses attaches, ses profondes racines corporelles, sa végétation infinie à travers l'histoire, sa haute floraison au sommet des choses, voilà maintenant son objet.[1]

So wrote Hippolyte Taine in his *Histoire de la littérature anglaise* in 1863, and his claim reads almost like an analysis of the novel in the 1860s and 1870s. The progress of medical science in the nineteenth century, through men like Claude Bernard, Pasteur, Raspail and a whole company of brilliant surgeons, had been so sensational that it was inevitable that both physiologists and philosophers should begin to wonder if increased knowledge of the functions of the body would not also soon cover the functions of the brain. Taine himself, in his treatise *De l'Intelligence* (1870) and in his critical essays, was one of the first to sketch a theory of mental processes in the context of a deterministic physiology, in which he implies that it will eventually prove possible to account for mental, moral and spiritual processes in the same way as modern medicine is accounting for physical processes:

[1] Hippolyte Taine, *Histoire de la littérature anglaise* (Paris, Hachette; 1863), vol. III, pp. 611–12.

Que les faits soient physiques ou moraux, il n'importe, ils ont toujours des causes; il y en a pour l'ambition, pour le courage, pour la véracité, comme pour la digestion, pour le mouvement musculaire, pour la chaleur animale. Le vice et la vertu sont des produits comme le vitriol et le sucre, et toute donnée complexe naît par la rencontre d'autres données plus simples dont elle dépend.[1]

Ideas of this kind, which were spreading rapidly round 1860, naturally caused novelists to re-examine the traditional concept of psychology in fiction, which had hitherto tended to play itself out in a privileged sphere, remote from interference from the grosser bodily sensations. Balzac had already firmly suggested that the mental and physical attributes of a person were inseparable, and that was one of the many reasons for his popularity with his Realist and Naturalist successors. Flaubert too, with the clinical detachment of *Madame Bovary* and the meticulous medical documentation of episodes like the arsenic poisoning, had given further impetus to the trend. Indeed, it was *Madame Bovary* which provoked Sainte-Beuve's famous exclamation: ' Anatomistes et physiologistes, je vous retrouve partout!' [2] But it was the Goncourt brothers who first systematically sought in their fiction to make psychology into a branch of physiology, and *Sœur Philomène*, the second of their mature novels, provides a good example of their technique.

It is the story of a poor orphan girl who becomes a nun and works in the hospital of La Charité in Paris. The passage we have here describes Philomène's first reactions when she begins her training as a nurse, and the method of the description makes it clear how intimately her feelings depend on physical sensations. The almost photographic evocation of the corpse is followed by a reference to 'la lâcheté de ses sens', designed to bring out the extent to which the nun's involuntary feelings are at odds with her will-power. When she does eventually succumb to the horrors of hospital life, it is because of a physical impression, 'une malade qui dormait toute pâle', and results in a physical weakness: 'le cœur lui manqua : elle fut obligée de se retenir à la colonnette du lit pour ne pas tomber'. The further analysis of her disturbed state is carried on in terms which are at least as much physical as they are emotional: 'un malaise indéfini', 'l'ébranlement de toutes les secousses',

---

[1] *Histoire de la littérature anglaise* p. xv of the Introduction.
[2] *Causeries du lundi* (Paris, Garnier; 1858), vol. XIII, p. 297.

'une irritation continue', 'ses nerfs... avaient un jeu fébrile, une sensibilité agacée et maladive', 'un tressaillement douloureux'. At the end,
a remarkably precise physical notation is used to convey the nun's
continued perturbation at the contact of death: 'Elle éprouvait un
serrement sous les côtes, et elle se sentait les jambes à la fois molles et
légères, avec un froid dans les os descendant de la rotule au bout de
l'orteil'.

If one compares this description to most previous evocations of the
fear aroused by the proximity of death—Mme de Lafayette's account
of the death of the prince de Clèves, for instance, Chateaubriand's
idealised description of the death and burial of Atala, or even Hugo's
numerous expressions of the horror of death in *Les Contemplations*—
one is immediately struck by the exactness and the fullness of the
physical detail, both in the realistic picture of the corpse and in the
minute notations which mark the stages of Philomène's reactions. The
Goncourts, it is true, come nowhere near the insistence on the revolting
facts of illness and decomposition which distinguishes some of Zola's
novels, notably *L'Assommoir* and *La Débâcle*; what they say about the
seamier side of hospital life is relatively restrained. But their main
interest nevertheless remains the rendering of Philomène's states of
mind in physiological terms, and in some of their later novels they go
so far as to make the whole conception of a character dependent on a
pathological condition—the hysteria of Germinie Lacerteux or the
tuberculosis of Mme Gervaisais, for example. They even call *Germinie
Lacerteux* 'la clinique de l'amour'.[1] The list of works they consulted for
some of these novels reads like the catalogue of a medical library, and
the same could be said of the sources of certain episodes in Flaubert's
works, such as the death of Félicité in *Un Cœur simple* or the illness of
Mme Arnoux's son in *L'Éducation sentimentale*. With Zola, the habit is
yet more marked. For *Germinal*, he read up the illnesses endemic in
mining communities, and then distributed them among his characters.
He even made Taine's already quoted aphorism about vice and virtue
the epigraph to *Thérèse Raquin* (1867) and boldly proclaimed his
pseudo-biological intentions by subtitling the Rougon-Macquart series
Histoire naturelle et sociale d'une famille sous le Second Empire. As far as
characterisation is concerned, the whole trend of the Realist novel of
the 1860s and 1870s is towards physiological determinism, and Zola is

[1] *Germinie Lacerteux* (Paris, Flammarion and Fasquelle; 1930), p. 5.

only slightly exaggerating a widely held belief when he writes in *Le Roman expérimental*:

> Un jour, la physiologie nous expliquera sans doute le mécanisme de la pensée et des passions; nous saurons comment fonctionne la machine individuelle de l'homme, comment il pense, comment il aime, comment il va de la raison à la passion et à la folie.[1]

This is one reason why, in the same period, the trivial objects of the outside world come to assume a new significance in the novel. Once more Balzac had led the way, with descriptive catalogues like the furnishings of Mme Vauquer's boarding-house in *Le Père Goriot*, and Flaubert had used the same sort of device in his novels—one thinks of Emma Bovary's irritation at Charles's squeaking boots, for instance. In the present passage the idea is the same. Philomène's worst moments are caused by insignificant but concrete happenings like 'la chute d'un gobelet d'étain', and recurrences of her weakness are brought on by apparently innocuous objects like the wooden stretcher: 'Toutes sortes d'objets... prenaient pour elle une signification qui s'emparait de sa pensée au passage... Les choses évoquaient l'ombre des souffrances qu'elles avaient touchées'. This belief in the influence of the objects with which we have to live is one of the determining factors in the Naturalist predilection for lengthy passages of description; it is another aspect of Taine's theory of *le milieu*.

But it is not only in their meticulous attentiveness to the slightest nervous impressions and their mental consequences that the Goncourts represent the tendencies of the Realist novel; it is also in the nature of their subject-matter. Just as they rehabilitate the workings of the body ignored by most previous schools, so they rehabilitate characters and classes hitherto neglected. Philomène (by her real name Marie Gaucher) is of the most humble origins, leads a humble and humdrum life and passes her life among people as humble and obscure as herself (the nameless patients of La Charité, like the corpse in this extract, are people, too poor to pay for private treatment, who are reduced to public charity). The urban poor play little part in the *Comédie humaine*, Balzac being too obsessed with great interests to accord them much attention; George Sand's peasants are depicted in lyrical, idyllic tones; *Les Misérables*, in any case subjected to the deforming exaggeration of

[1] *Le Roman expérimental*, pp. 18–19.

Hugo's chaotic imagination, came only after the Goncourts' first novels. The Goncourts deliberately make it their business to deal with drab, poverty-stricken existences, which they set out with as much fidelity to real life as they can achieve. In their preface to *Germinie Lacerteux* (1864) they explain thus what had made them write both that work and 'l'humble roman de *Sœur Philomène*':

> Vivant au dix-neuvième siècle, dans un temps de suffrage universel, de démocratie, de libéralisme, nous nous sommes demandé si ce qu'on appelle « les basses classes » n'avait pas droit au Roman; si ce monde sous un monde, le peuple, devait rester sous le coup de l'interdit littéraire et des dédains d'auteurs qui ont fait jusqu'ici le silence sur l'âme et le cœur qu'il peut avoir.[1]

From then on the way was open for novelists to justify Flaubert's axiom that 'en art, il n'y a ni beaux ni vilains sujets',[2] and they took advantage of it with such vigour that the commonest complaint against the Naturalists was that of their excessive fondness for the commonplace and the sordid.

As far as the Goncourts were concerned, their justification for a passage on a disagreeable subject such as the one we are discussing would have been that such things are the stuff of which the greater part of reality is made.

> Aujourd'hui que le roman s'élargit et grandit, qu'il commence à être la grande forme sérieuse, passionnée, vivante, de l'étude littéraire et de l'enquête sociale, qu'il devient, par l'analyse et par la recherche psychologique, l'Histoire morale contemporaine, aujourd'hui que le Roman s'est imposé les études et les devoirs de la science, il peut en revendiquer les libertés et les franchises.[3]

But if this claim is to have any meaning, their novels must be genuine documents about their own time and not merely imaginative fantasies. To this end they take great pains to ensure the accuracy of their observation and the directness of their knowledge of a subject. For example, before completing *Sœur Philomène*, they spent some days in La Charité, acquainting themselves with conditions there:

---

[1] *Germinie Lacerteux*, pp. 5–6.
[2] *Correspondance*, vol. II, p. 345.
[3] *Germinie Lacerteux*, p. 6.

Il nous faut faire pour notre roman de sœur philomène, des études à l'hôpital, sur le *vrai*, sur le *vif*, sur le *saignant*.[1]

The present passage shows how faithfully they utilised the notes they took there. The corpse which Philomène sees is the corpse which they themselves saw on 23rd December 1860 (which explains the minor inconsistency that it is the corpse of a man, though we are told that Philomène worked in the women's wards). Apart from one or two slight literary embellishments and the suppression of an irrelevant association of their own, the picture is almost word for word the same as that to be found in their diary:

> Nous arrivons au lit d'un phtisique qui vient de *passer* à l'instant même. Je regarde et je vois un homme de quarante ans, le haut du corps soulevé par des oreillers, un tricot brun mal boutonné sur la poitrine, les bras tendus hors du lit, la tête un peu de côté et renversé en arrière. On distingue les cordes du dessous du cou, une barbe forte et noire, le nez pincé, des yeux caves; autour de sa figure, sur l'oreiller, ses cheveux, étalés, sont plaqués ainsi qu'un paquet de filasse humide. La bouche est grande ouverte, ainsi que celle d'un homme dont la vie s'est exhalée en cherchant à respirer, sans trouver d'air. Il est encore chaud, sous la sculpture profonde de la mort sur un vieux cadavre. Ce mort a réveillé une image dans ma mémoire : le supplicié par le garot de Goya.[2]

Even the symptoms of Philomène's nervous exhaustion are those they had observed on themselves in the same circumstances. Like her, they had at first stood up well to the strain of being in the hospital, only to collapse suddenly, like her, for a seemingly insignificant reason, after which they reacted exactly as Philomène does to unexpected noises, like the dropping of a pewter cup:

> Le soir nous avons les nerfs si malades qu'un bruit, qu'une fourchette qui tombe, nous donne un tressaillement par tout le corps, et une impatience presque colère.[3]

The curious sensation noted at the end is the one they had experienced as they followed the surgeon Velpeau on his rounds:

> Nous nous sentons les jambes, comme si nous étions ivres, avec un senti-ment de la rotule dans les genoux, et comme du froid dans la moelle des tibias.[4]

---

[1] Edmond and Jules de Goncourt, *Journal*, vol. 1, p. 272.   [2] ibid., p. 273.
[3] ibid., p. 278.   [4] ibid., p. 272.

This cult of note-taking is one of the most striking features of the novel after 1860. Careful reading, on-the-spot investigations, questionings of experts became standard techniques of fiction-writing, and every Naturalist novelist from Zola to Daudet seems to have travelled with a notebook in his pocket, constantly questing for 'les petits faits significatifs' which, when accumulated in sufficient number, would confer on his novels the status of scientific inquiries. The Goncourt diaries are full of claims about the solid documentary value of their works.

> Un des caractères particuliers de nos romans, ce sera d'être les romans les plus historiques de ce temps-ci, les romans qui fourniront le plus de faits et de vérités vraies à l'histoire morale de ce siècle.[1]

> Le roman actuel se fait avec des *documents* racontés, ou relevés d'après nature, comme l'histoire se fait avec des documents écrits.[2]

> L'histoire est un roman qui a été; le roman est de l'histoire qui aurait pu être.[3]

Most of the other supporters of the Realist and Naturalist aesthetic would willingly have agreed with these and similar dicta, and there is no doubt that, in intention if not always in execution, the novel in France for three decades was moving away from imagination towards observation.

The advantages and shortcomings of this mode of literary creation have been well analysed by J.-K. Huysmans, who had at first been associated with Zola in the 'groupe de Médan' but who later became a dissident from the movement. At the beginning of his novel *Là-bas* (1891) two characters argue about Naturalism. One praises the unforgettable services which the Naturalists have rendered to art:

> Car, enfin, ce sont eux qui nous ont débarrassés des inhumains fantoches du romantisme et qui ont extrait la littérature d'un idéalisme de ganache et d'une inanition de vieille fille exaltée par le célibat! — En somme après Balzac, ils ont créé des êtres visibles et palpables et ils les ont mis en accord avec leurs alentours.[4]

But the other complains that this has led to a narrow, materialistic conception of human psychology:

[1] ibid., p. 279.
[2] ibid., vol. II, p. 183.
[3] ibid., vol. I, p. 305.
[4] *Là-bas* (Paris, Plon; 1949), p. 2.

Quand il s'est agi d'expliquer une passion quelconque, quand il a fallu sonder une plaie, déterger même le plus bénin des bobos de l'âme, il a tout mis sur le compte des appétits et des instincts. Rut et coup de folie, ce sont là ses seules diathèses.[1]

The present passage from *Sœur Philomène* enables one to appreciate the justice of both these comments.

FURTHER READING

J.-H. BORNECQUE and Pierre COGNY, *Réalisme et Naturalisme* (Paris, Hachette; 1959).

Pierre MARTINO, *Le Roman réaliste sous le Second Empire* (Paris, Hachette; 1913).

Pierre MARTINO, *Le Naturalisme français* (Paris, Armand Colin; 1923).

[1] J.-K. Huysmans, *Là-bas*, p. 2.

XVI

Émile Zola

(1840–1902)

FROM *La Débâcle*

En bas, sur le canapé, Maurice s'éveilla, au petit jour. Courbaturé, il ne bougea pas, les yeux sur les vitres, peu à peu blanchies d'une aube livide. Les abominables souvenirs lui revenaient, la bataille perdue, la fuite, le désastre, dans la lucidité aiguë du réveil. Il revit tout, jusqu'au moindre détail, il souffrit affreusement de la défaite, dont le retentissement descendait aux racines de son être, comme s'il en était le coupable. Et il raisonnait le mal, s'analysant, retrouvant aiguisée la faculté de se dévorer lui-même. N'était-il pas le premier venu, un des passants de l'époque, certes d'une instruction brillante, mais d'une ignorance crasse en tout ce qu'il aurait fallu savoir, vaniteux avec cela au point d'en être aveugle, perverti par l'impatience de jouir et par la prospérité menteuse du règne? Puis, c'était une autre évocation : son grand-père, né en 1780, un des héros de la Grande Armée, un des vainqueurs d'Austerlitz, de Wagram et de Friedland; son père, né en 1811, tombé à la bureaucratie, petit employé médiocre, percepteur au Chêne-Populeux, où il s'était usé; lui, né en 1841, élevé en monsieur, reçu avocat, capable des pires sottises et des plus grands enthousiasmes, vaincu à Sedan, dans une catastrophe qu'il devinait immense, finissant un monde; et cette dégénérescence de la race, qui expliquait comment la France victorieuse avec les grands-pères avait pu être battue dans les petits-fils, lui écrasait le cœur, telle qu'une maladie de famille, lentement aggravée, aboutissant à la destruction fatale, quand l'heure avait sonné. Dans la victoire, il se serait senti si brave et triomphant! Dans la défaite, d'une faiblesse nerveuse de femme, il cédait à un de ces désespoirs immenses, où le monde entier sombrait. Il n'y avait plus rien, la France était morte. Des sanglots l'étouffèrent, il pleura, il joignit les mains, retrouvant les bégaiements de prière de son enfance :

— Mon Dieu! prenez-moi donc... Mon Dieu! prenez donc tous ces misérables qui souffrent...

ÉMILE ZOLA, *La Débâcle*
(Paris, Charpentier; n.d.), vol. II, pp. 74–5

Zola's novel *La Débâcle* (1892) is based on the history of the Franco-Prussian War of 1870 and the Commune of the following year, when a Left-wing revolutionary Government briefly seized power in Paris, before being wiped out by the forces of the Third Republic which had retained control over most of the rest of France. These events are seen through the eyes of two soldiers, the honest, stolid peasant Jean Macquart, and his friend Maurice Levasseur, intelligent, dissipated, hypersensitive and middle-class. It is the latter whom we are shown here, waking up in the house of friends in Sedan, where he had taken refuge after the cataclysmic defeat which the French army had sustained the previous day (1st September 1870). The battle of Sedan did not bring the war to an end, since resistance to the Prussians was kept up, especially in the siege of Paris, until March 1871, but it was one of the most devastating military catastrophes France had ever endured. Over 80,000 men, with Napoleon III at their head, had to capitulate to the Prussians, the imperial *régime* disintegrated and all real hope of winning the war was lost.

The violence of Maurice's despair is partly explained by his character —the nervous, pleasure-seeking, unstable temperament which Zola thought typical of the Second Empire—and partly by the rapidity and unexpectedness of the disaster. Though Napoleon III had declared when he became Emperor in 1852: 'L'Empire, c'est la paix', he made much of the martial glories of his uncle, and soon found himself claiming that the Second Empire was a conquering force which would re-establish French predominance in Europe. Various military successes such as the extension of French colonial possessions in Senegal, the capture of Sebastopol in the Crimean War in 1855, a largely fortuitous victory over incompetently led Austrians in Italy in 1859, the Anglo-French punitive sortie against Peking in 1860 and an expedition to Syria in the same year had helped to maintain the myth of the invincibility of French arms, though the failure in 1867 of the attempt to set up a French puppet state in Mexico gave some warning of the hollowness of these supposed achievements. So when war eventually broke out with Prussia in August 1870, ostensibly over dynastic questions in Spain but in fact as a trial of strength between the two most powerful rivals for power in continental Europe, very few Frenchmen foresaw anything but an easy and speedy defeat of a nation which they mostly regarded as backward and impractical. In the event the

French were utterly crushed by the Prussian forces, and with such suddenness that there was no time for a gradual realisation of the truth. Maurice's anguish epitomises that of vast numbers of his countrymen, and is driven to its paroxysm by his visions of the past splendours of the Napoleonic era, when France held the whole of Europe at her mercy.

Zola goes further than simply characterising French feelings at the disaster; he wants also to diagnose its causes. That is why Maurice is made not only into a symbol of the average Frenchman ('le premier venu, un des passants de l'époque') but also into an introspective analyst of his share in the catastrophe ('... comme s'il en était le coupable. Et il raisonnait le mal, s'analysant, retrouvant aiguisée la faculté de se dévorer lui-même'). Zola says in his notes for the novel:

> La fatalité a pesé sur Sedan; un des écrasements de peuple les plus effrayants qu'on connaisse. Mais il y a eu des causes, et c'est justement l'étude de ces causes que je désire faire.[1]

The detailed external causes are listed elsewhere in the novel by a character named Weiss, whom Zola uses to put his own point of view: the weakness and demoralisation of the French Government, the outdated rigidity of army organisation, the incapacity of the generals and the vacillations of the Emperor himself. But most of all Zola incriminates the state of mind exemplified and identified by Maurice, which had been deliberately fostered by the imperial leaders—'l'impatience de jouir', bolstered up by 'la prospérité menteuse du règne'. We have seen in commentary XIV that many thinking men held that the outlook of the French people in the 1860s was materialistic, self-centred and frivolous; certainly the *régime* did all it could to encourage its subjects to immerse themselves in money-making and amusement, with the double aim of speeding up the commercial expansion of the country and damping down interest in politics. Maurice, in his representative capacity, now admits his share of guilt for the degradation of France; he and his fellow-citizens had allowed themselves to be deceived by these outward appearances. It is in symbolic expiation for these errors that at the end of the novel he dies as Paris goes up in flames during the dying throes of the Commune. The point is hammered home by the constant evocation, during the battle scenes of which the novel is

[1] *La Débâcle*, ed. M. Le Blond, (Paris, Bernouard; 1929), vol. II, p. 613.

largely composed, of the Emperor's enormous suite blundering around
from place to place, brilliant, noisy, cumbersome, extravagant and
completely useless. Faithful to his republican convictions, Zola arraigns
the Second Empire as the main cause for the sad waning of the fortunes
of his country.

With the usual desire of the Naturalists to lend an air of scientific
precision to their opinions, Zola talks about 'cette dégénérescence de la
race' of which Maurice is both a witness and an unconscious example,
and he draws a parallel with 'une maladie de famille' which immediately
reminds one of his use of the idea of heredity in the study of the
Rougon-Macquart family. The medical terminology is typical of the
cast of mind of Zola and his associates, and it is also typical of Zola that
he should have so arranged the family history of Maurice that it reflects
the general development of France since Napoleon's day. Maurice's
grandfather is a soldier and a hero, one of the supermen who conquered
Europe and to whom Musset's generation looked up with such admiration. His father, on the other hand, is reduced to the humdrum status
of a clerk in a government office—an image of the petty middle-class
existence led by the majority of Frenchmen in Louis-Philippe's time.
He himself has apparently risen in society and become a 'monsieur',
superficially well educated and prosperous. But, like the Second Empire
itself, his outward success hides inner corruption, and now the final
collapse has revealed all his shortcomings. In this as in so many things,
Maurice stands for the whole of France.

Implicit in the idea of a degenerate race is that of the vigour of its
youthful adversary, a vigour which shows above all in its readiness to
adopt modern scientific methods in all the branches of its corporate life.
This contrast between France and Prussia is openly discussed by Weiss,
who, as the war breaks out, sees with anxiety

> la Prusse grandie après Sadowa,[1] le mouvement national qui la plaçait à la
> tête des autres États allemands, tout ce vaste empire en formation, rajeuni,
> ayant l'enthousiasme et l'irrésistible élan de son unité à conquérir.[2]

In the great soul-searching which took place in France after the loss
of the Franco-Prussian War, one theme recurs time and again among
the commentators: that Prussia won because she was better organised,

---

[1] Sadowa was the battle at which the Prussians decisively defeated the Austrians in 1866,
thus establishing themselves as the leading power among the German-speaking countries.
[2] *La Débâcle*, vol. I, p. 23.

PLATE VII *Le Rêve* (from the painting by Detaille in Le Musée de l'Armée)

PLATE VIII   *Encore une maison où nous ne dînerons plus!* (from a caricature)

more scientifically equipped, more intelligently led. To many people, education seemed to be the key of Prussian superiority, and the figure of the Prussian schoolmaster was popularly credited with having done the groundwork for the Prussian victory. Maurice, like France itself, is said to be 'certes d'une instruction brillante, mais d'une ignorance crasse en tout ce qu'il aurait fallu savoir'. This is a theory which Zola develops more fully in *Lettre à la jeunesse*, written long before *La Débâcle*:

> Ce qu'il faut confesser très haut, c'est qu'en 1870 nous avons été battus par l'esprit scientifique. Sans doute l'imbécillité de l'empire nous lançait sans préparation suffisante dans une guerre qui répugnait au pays... Nous avons été écrasés par des masses manœuvrées avec logique, nous nous sommes débandés devant une application de la formule scientifique à l'art de la guerre.[1]

The unexpected consequence of this widely held belief is that the various projects for the reorganisation of French institutions proposed or carried out after 1870 nearly all rely heavily on German models. The prestige of Germany in artistic and intellectual matters already stood high in France in the 1860s, as we saw in commentary XIV; in philosophy, history, linguistics and archaeology French scholars tended to acknowledge that the Germans were in the lead. Victor Cousin, Michelet, Quinet, Taine and Renan all incurred heavy debts to German thought and learning. The defeat of 1870, instead of nullifying this tendency, gave it a new lease of life, after an initial period of hesitation and disenchantment. The reform of the educational system, the introduction of general conscription, the rearrangement of the structure of the army were all inspired by the Prussian example (though with the aim, avowed or unspoken, of securing revenge on Prussia).

As Maurice is intended to represent, at least in part, the French character, his reactions to the defeat do no more than magnify those of the majority of his compatriots and which Zola himself had observed in 1870. The shame he experiences when he thinks of the heroes of Napoleonic times is shared by Sully Prudhomme:

> Ces noms dont notre gloire a si longtemps vécu,
> Je ne peux les entendre aujourd'hui, je leur creuse
> Une tombe en mon cœur, muette et ténébreuse;
> Leur beau son me fait mal comme un sarcasme aigu.[2]

[1] In *Le Roman expérimental*, p. 97.
[2] *Poésies 1868–78* (Paris, Lemerre; 1884), p. 270.

The same idea is developed with a great rhetorical flourish by Victor Hugo (who, like Zola, mingles distress at the fall of France with satisfaction at the disappearance of the Emperor):

> Alors la Gaule, alors la France, alors la gloire,
> Alors Brennus, l'audace, et Clovis, la victoire,
> Alors le vieux titan celtique aux cheveux longs,
> Alors le groupe altier des batailles, Châlons,
> Tolbiac la farouche, Arezzo la cruelle,
> Bouvines, Marignan, Baugé, Mons-en-Puelle,
> Tours, Ravenne, Agnadel sur son haut palefroi,
> Fornoue, Ivry, Coutras, Cérisoles, Rocroy,
> Denain et Fontenoy, toutes ces immortelles
> Mêlant l'éclair du front au flamboiement des ailes,
> Jemmape, Hohenlinden, Lodi, Wagram, Eylau,
> Les hommes du dernier carré de Waterloo,
> Et tous ces chefs de guerre, Héristal, Charlemagne,
> Charles-Martel, Turenne, effroi de l'Allemagne,
> Condé, Villars, fameux par un si fier succès,
> Cet Achille, Kléber, ce Scipion, Desaix,
> Napoléon, plus grand que César et Pompée,
> Par la main d'un bandit rendirent leur épée.[1]

Jules Simon, later to become Prime Minister, declared as early as 1871 that the French had been responsible for their own defeat by their thoughtless hedonism during the Second Empire:

> Est-ce bien le spectacle que nous avons vu? Est-ce bien la société que nous avons été? Et, s'il en est ainsi, ne devons-nous pas confesser, malgré les héros et les martyrs de la dernière heure, que nous étions vaincus avant Sedan? Oui, nous portions en nous la cause de la défaite. Oui, nous avons été presque aussi coupables que malheureux. Oui, nous avons à guérir l'âme même de la France.[2]

The sense of stunned consternation at the loss of the war is exemplified in Alphonse Daudet's story *Le Siège de Berlin*, which is about an old officer who believes so firmly that the French must be approaching Berlin that he dies of shock when he sees the Prussian troops marching down the Champs Élysées. The feeling of heightened love for France in her misfortunes is noted by Taine, who wrote to his mother in

---

[1] *L'Année terrible* (Paris, Imprimerie Nationale; 1914), p. 28.
[2] In a speech to the Five Academies on 28th October 1871.

December 1870: 'Je ne savais pas qu'on tenait tant à sa patrie'.[1] That
is also the theme of Théodore de Banville's poem *A la Patrie*:

> Oui, je t'aimais alors, ô Reine,
> Menant dans tes champs magnifiques
> Brillants d'une clarté sereine
> Tous les triomphes pacifiques;
>
> Mais à présent, humiliée,
> Sainte buveuse d'ambroisie,
> Farouche, acculée, oubliée,
> Je t'adore! Avec frénésie
>
> Je baise tes mains valeureuses,
> A présent que l'éponge amère
> Brûle tes lèvres douloureuses
> Et que ton flanc saigne, — ma mère![2]

The idea that the defeat meant that a whole world was crumbling in
ruins is movingly confirmed by several writers, notably Flaubert, who
wrote not long after Sedan:

> J'ai le sentiment de la fin d'un monde. Quoi qu'il advienne, tout ce que
> j'aimais est perdu.[3]

Mallarmé likewise wrote to his friend Cazalis on 23rd April 1871 about
the death of the painter Henri Regnault, killed at Buzenval in an
attempt to break the siege of Paris:

> Je ne m'afflige pas vraiment, de penser qu'Henri s'est sacrifié pour la
> France, et que celle-ci ne soit plus. Sa mort a été plus pure.[4]

On hearing the news of the collapse, Prosper Mérimée, seriously ill at
Cannes, broke down in tears and said to his doctor: 'La France meurt,
je veux mourir avec elle'.[5] Clearly, Zola has given Maurice's behaviour
at the moment of crisis a representative value by making it an amalgam
of the feelings of people all round him.

Given that Maurice's desperate lament for France is only a heightened reproduction of what many of his fellow-countrymen felt, it is not

[1] *Hippolyte Taine, sa vie, sa correspondance* (Paris, Hachette; 1905), vol. III, p. 39.
[2] *Idylles prussiennes* (Paris, Lemerre; 1890), p. 68.
[3] *Correspondance*, vol. VI, p. 171.
[4] *Correspondance, 1862–71*, p. 351.
[5] Quoted by Robert Baschet, *Mérimée* (Paris, Nouvelles Éditions Latines; 1959), p. 258.

surprising that the years following 1870 were marked by a strong current of disillusionment and pessimism. If the values which had for so long seemed immutable could be so easily swept away, it was hard to believe that anything could be permanent and meaningful. Amid all the recriminations against Prussia, all the reassessments of French strengths and weaknesses, all the defiant calls for the liberation of the lost provinces of Alsace and Lorraine, all the schemes for the regeneration of France, there is a nagging awareness that things will never be the same again, that the memory of the immense humiliation suffered by France can never be wholly obliterated. Intellectually and emotionally, the twenty years between 1870 and 1890 are sombre and anxious ones. One cannot of course ascribe this solely to the results of 1870; other factors such as the fatalistic determinism of some scientific theory, the apparent decadence of religious life, the influence of Schopenhauer and Eastern thought all played their part in plunging thinking people into sceptical gloom. But it would nevertheless be hard to overestimate the extent of the ramifications of 1870 in French attitudes and ideas. It was indeed, as Maurice realised, the end of a world.

FURTHER READING

A. BAILLOT, *L'Influence de la philosophie de Schopenhauer en France* (Paris, Vrin; 1927).

Jean-Marie CARRÉ, *Les Écrivains français et le mirage allemand* (Paris, Boivin; 1947).

Claude DIGEON, *La Crise allemande de la pensée française 1870–1914* (Paris, Presses Universitaires de France; 1959).

XVII

Stéphane Mallarmé

(1842–98)

Les Fenêtres

Las du triste hôpital, et de l'encens fétide
Qui monte en la blancheur banale des rideaux
Vers le grand crucifix ennuyé du mur vide,
Le moribond sournois y redresse un vieux dos,

Se traîne et va, moins pour chauffer sa pourriture
Que pour voir du soleil sur les pierres, coller
Les poils blancs et les os de la maigre figure
Aux fenêtres qu'un beau rayon clair veut hâler,

Et la bouche, fiévreuse et d'azur bleu vorace,
Telle, jeune, elle alla respirer son trésor,
Une peau virginale et de jadis! encrasse
D'un long baiser amer les tièdes carreaux d'or.

Ivre, il vit, oubliant l'horreur des saintes huiles,
Les tisanes, l'horloge et le lit infligé,
La toux; et quand le soir saigne parmi les tuiles,
Son œil, à l'horizon de lumière gorgé,

Voit des galères d'or, belles comme des cygnes,
Sur un fleuve de pourpre et de parfums dormir
En berçant l'éclair fauve et riche de leurs lignes
Dans un grand nonchaloir chargé de souvenir!

Ainsi, pris du dégoût de l'homme à l'âme dure
Vautré dans le bonheur, où ses seuls appétits
Mangent, et qui s'entête à chercher cette ordure
Pour l'offrir à la femme allaitant ses petits,

Je fuis et je m'accroche à toutes les croisées
D'où l'on tourne l'épaule à la vie, et, béni,
Dans leur verre, lavé d'éternelles rosées,
Que dore le matin chaste de l'Infini

Je me mire et me vois ange! et je meurs, et j'aime
— Que la vitre soit l'art, soit la mysticité —
A renaître, portant mon rêve en diadème,
Au ciel antérieur où fleurit la Beauté!

Mais, hélas, Ici-bas est maître : sa hantise
Vient m'écœurer parfois jusqu'en cet abri sûr,
Et le vomissement impur de la Bêtise
Me force à me boucher le nez devant l'azur.

Est-il moyen, ô Moi qui connais l'amertume,
D'enfoncer le cristal par le monstre insulté
Et de m'enfuir, avec mes deux ailes sans plume
— Au risque de tomber pendant l'éternité?

STÉPHANE MALLARMÉ, *Les Fenêtres*, in
Œuvres complètes, ed. H. Mondor and G. Jean-Aubry
(Paris, Pléiade; 1945), pp. 32–3

In 1861, for their novel *Sœur Philomène*, the Goncourts took a hospital as the quintessential expression of that stark reality which it was the artist's business to record. Two years later, in 1863, in *Les Fenêtres*, Mallarmé chose a hospital as a symbol of the morbid, prison-like existence to which humanity is condemned and from which art must help it to escape. These two contrasting attitudes to the same image are symptomatic of a dichotomy which runs through much of nineteenth-century literature.

Already in Chateaubriand's time, longing for an unattainable ideal and distaste for the disappointing reality which everywhere obtruded itself form an important element in the Romantic mentality, as it is easy to see from *René*, the most sumptuous embodiment of *le mal du siècle*. Likewise, Hugo is speaking for many of his contemporaries when, in *Les Feuilles d'automne*, he avers that it is wiser not to try to realise one's dreams:

Gardons l'illusion; elle fuit assez tôt...
L'idéal tombe en poudre au toucher du réel.[1]

[1] *A mes amis L. B. et S.-B.*, in *Les Feuilles d'automne*, pp. 77–8.

But while the problem of the clash between the ideal and the real is implicit in much Romantic writing and is at the root of the world-weariness which characterises the period, it does not at that time become an obsessive literary theme, partly because most Romantics prefer singing about their melancholy to analysing the reasons for it, and partly because they are so eager to stimulate their emotions that they tend to ignore anything which would damp them down.

It is with the generation of Flaubert and Baudelaire that the conflict assumes such proportions that it is impossible to ignore it or to forget it. Both writers, brought up on the literature of the 1830s, still have an invincible desire for some experience which everyday reality cannot give them, but both are acutely aware that the sordid truth of life cannot honestly be ignored. *Madame Bovary* and *Les Fleurs du mal* are expressions of the irreconcilable and tragic contradiction between human desires and the human condition. That is what drives Emma Bovary to the realisation that

> Chaque sourire cachait un bâillement d'ennui, chaque joie une malédiction, tout plaisir son dégoût, et les meilleurs baisers ne vous laissaient sur la lèvre qu'une irréalisable envie d'une volupté plus haute.[1]

That too is what compels Baudelaire to fill his poetry with exemplary contrasts between the excitement of imagination and the triviality of experience, as in these lines, where the change in rhythm gives point to a deliberate effect of anti-climax:

> Mon cœur, comme un oiseau, voltigeait tout joyeux
> Et planait librement à l'entour des cordages;
> Le navire roulait sous un ciel sans nuages,
> Comme un ange enivré d'un soleil radieux.
>
> Quelle est cette île triste et noire? — C'est Cythère,
> Nous dit-on, un pays fameux dans les chansons,
> Eldorado banal de tous les vieux garçons.
> Regardez, après tout, c'est une pauvre terre.[2]

For both Flaubert and Baudelaire, trapped between an unrealisable ideal and an unacceptable reality, art was the only means of escape. Flaubert's letters are eloquent on the subject. He wrote to his mother

---

[1] *Madame Bovary* (Paris, Conard; 1930), pp. 392-3.
[2] *Un Voyage à Cythère*, in *Œuvres complètes*, p. 185.

that 'la banalité de la vie est à faire vomir de tristesse quand on la
considère de près,'[1] and affirmed that life was unbearable without an
aesthetic antidote to its poisons: 'Pour moi, je ne sais pas comment font
pour vivre les gens qui ne sont pas du matin au soir dans un état
esthétique'.[2] Art consequently became for him an alternative to life
(though at the same time his intellectual honesty would not allow him
in his works to embellish the truth as he saw it).

> La vie est une chose tellement hideuse que le seul moyen de la supporter,
> c'est de l'éviter. Et on l'évite en vivant dans l'Art, dans la recherche inces-
> sante du Vrai rendu par le Beau.[3]

The same attitude, in a form complicated by the intrusion of a religious
sensibility which was less strong in Flaubert, is visible behind much
that Baudelaire wrote. In *Le Mauvais Moine*, for example, the poet
deplores the difficulty of the task of artistic creation, which alone could
give meaning to his life:

> O moine fainéant! quand saurai-je donc faire
> Du spectacle vivant de ma triste misère
> Le travail de mes mains et l'amour de mes yeux?[4]

In other works, these themes are given a formulation which is much
closer to Mallarmé's *Les Fenêtres*. The title itself had already been used
by Baudelaire for one of his prose poems, which contains these lines,
Mallarméan in their refusal to accept the vileness of reality for what
it is:

> Qu'importe ce que peut être la réalité placée hors de moi, si elle m'a aidé
> à vivre, à sentir que je suis et ce que je suis?[5]

Another prose poem, *Anywhere out of the world—N'importe où hors
du monde*, introduces us to the image of the world as a hospital with
mankind as its patients:

> Cette vie est un hôpital où chaque malade est possédé du désir de changer
> de lit. Celui-ci voudrait souffrir en face du poêle, celui-là croit qu'il guéri-
> rait à côté de la fenêtre.[6]

[1] *Correspondance*, vol. II, p. 288.   [2] ibid., vol. I, p. 351.
[3] ibid., vol. IV, p. 182.   [4] *Œuvres complètes*, p. 89.
[5] ibid., p. 332.   [6] ibid., p. 347.

At the end of the poem, 'mon âme fait explosion, et sagement elle me crie : « N'importe où! pourvu que ce soit hors de ce monde! » '.[1]

Plainly, *Les Fenêtres* depends to a large extent on themes and images which had been suggested to Mallarmé by the works of Baudelaire, whom at the beginning of his career he revered beyond all other poets. The duality between the ideal and the real which characterises the writings of both men is expressed through the same images and sensations—the hospital, the window, the longing for escape, the heady feeling of danger, the commingling of art and religion. But *Les Fenêtres* was written when Mallarmé was still young, and he later came to concentrate more and more exclusively on the ideal. In the end, the refusal to take serious notice of the real world becomes so absolute that Mallarmé says to the poet about to compose a poem:

> Exclus-en si tu commences
> Le réel parce que vil.[2]

In his late poetry the world of ordinary reality exists by virtue of its absence. Art has become everything for him; it is near to being a complete substitute for life, from which it takes as little substance as possible.

Such extreme aversion for life in all its manifestations was given some kind of philosophic justification by the different forms of idealism which became popular in France in the second third of the century and which had as their common factor the proposition that the material world is illusory. Hegel was the first philosopher from whose works men of letters drew this lesson. He had been read in a quite different way by thinkers like Taine and Renan, who were interested above all in his historical determinism, and it was not until the 1860s that Villiers de l'Isle-Adam tendentiously interpreted his philosophy as a kind of solipsistic subjectivism, a view which was not without influence on Mallarmé. Villiers de l'Isle-Adam's character Élisabeth in *La Révolte* (1870) expresses what many laymen, especially among younger men of letters, were coming to regard as the fundamental tenet of German idealism, when she says:

> Comme le monde n'a de signification que selon la puissance des mots qui le traduisent et celle des yeux qui le regardent, j'estime que considérer

[1] *Œuvres complètes*, p. 348.
[2] *Toute l'âme résumée...*, in *Œuvres complètes*, p. 73.

toutes choses de plus haut que leur réalité, c'est la Science de la vie, de la seule grandeur humaine, du Bonheur et de la Paix.[1]

After 1870, Schopenhauer, more readable and more sympathetic because of his profound pessimism, supplanted Hegel in the favour of those who were looking for a philosophic sponsor for their idealistic tendencies, and his doctrines formed one of the mainstays of the metaphysical substructure of Symbolism.

By 1880 large numbers of young writers were coming to believe that the world as they saw it was, for philosophers, no more than a disagreeable illusion, and that consequently, the best way to bear it was to live in the creations of their own imagination—which would have at least as much reality as anything else. That is why Des Esseintes, the decadent hero of J.-K. Huysmans's *A Rebours* (1884), 'rêvait à une thébaïde raffinée, à un désert confortable, à une arche immobile et tiède où il se réfugierait loin de l'incessant déluge de la sottise humaine',[2] and constructs for himself an extraordinary fantasy life remote from common contingencies. Likewise, Villiers de l'Isle-Adam's Axël (in the play of the same name which first appeared in 1885) exclaims disdainfully: 'Vivre? les serviteurs feront cela pour nous',[3] and shuts himself away in a solitary castle, far from the sight of his fellow-men. Such a haughty refusal to contaminate oneself with ordinary human activities has as another of its poetic symbols the *femme froide*, the sterile woman resplendent in her own useless beauty. It is an image which recurs in Baudelaire's *Fleurs du mal*, in Villiers de l'Isle-Adam's *Isis* (1862), in Mallarmé's *Hérodiade* (1864) and in innumerable Symbolist plays and poems, down to Paul Valéry's *La Jeune Parque*. It is significant that it was while Zola was singing the praises of *Fécondité*, one of his *Quatre Évangiles*, that the Symbolists thus hymned sterility; while one group of writers enthusiastically accepted life in all its ugliness, another group turned away from it and sought only beauty.

In these circumstances art, as the supreme manifestation of what the mind can create outside all the transience and corruption of existence, assumes a special importance as a form of religion. We have already seen how religious feelings, deprived of their normal outlet by the

---

[1] *Œuvres complètes*, vol. VII, p. 25.
[2] *A Rebours* (Paris, Fasquelle; 1929), p. 9.
[3] *Œuvres complètes*, vol. IV, p. 265.

conclusions of positivism, tend to attach themselves to activities which can serve as a replacement for religion. The preoccupation with saints and asceticism in a man as little concerned with theology as Flaubert betrays a tendency to regard the artist as a similar kind of mediator, even a saviour. Baudelaire continually assigns quasi-religious tasks to the poet. Mallarmé himself, brought up as a Catholic and losing his faith, sees two possible windows through to whatever is on the other side of life: 'l'art' or 'la mysticité'—both apparently have exactly the same function. But the hesitation between them which is still evident here is later resolved entirely in favour of art; mysticity remains only in the religious ceremonial with which Mallarmé surrounded his poetry. For the Symbolists art is the central reality of the world, and their writings abound in often facile and exaggerated religious terminology. When they gathered round Mallarmé on Tuesday evenings in the Rue de Rome, the atmosphere was solemn and esoteric, and many of them saw in Mallarmé a high priest of art—a role in conformity with his own semi-messianic conception of the poet's function. Aestheticism in the 1880s and 1890s was a veritable cult, not only in its outward trappings, but also in its attempt to place art in the position once occupied in men's minds by religion.

The near-mystical adulation of beauty was accompanied by a preoccupation with occultism and magic (as in so many things, in this, too, Symbolism bears the mark of Baudelaire's influence). One of the many forms taken by 'la mysticité' was a fascination with heterodox modes of religious speculation and experimentation; indeed, suspicion of orthodox religion is implicit here in Mallarmé's reference to 'le grand crucifix ennuyé du mur vide'. We already know from commentary XI how profoundly theories of this kind affect the notion of the symbol and the poetic usage of synaesthesia in the closing years of the century, but while this interpenetration of the religious and aesthetic domains is typical of those two decades, it also indicates the extent to which the young writers of the time needed something new to excite their jaded curiosity. For many of them, the Church as an institution suffered from an excess of *bourgeois* respectability; the spice of unorthodoxy was a necessary adjunct to belief.

At the same time eccentric religious practices often led to more normal forms of experience, and there is an unmistakable Catholic revival among men of letters at the end of the century. Two typical cases of conversion by unusual routes are those of Huysmans and Claudel. The former found his way to Catholicism via an interest in Satanism and religious art; the latter was visited by a sudden mystical intuition of God after reading Rimbaud. Other writers who were converted in the same period include Verlaine, Bloy and Bourget, and in the last ten or twenty years of the century, religion figures more prominently in imaginative literature than it had done at any time since Chateaubriand. The increased prestige of Catholic thought and scholarship, the more positive social policies of the Church, the waning of confidence in science and materialism all helped to restore to Catholicism some of the prestige it had formerly enjoyed among men of letters.

Another way of escape from incarceration in the hospital of life was the violent one of smashing the window and bursting into another world through the influence of drink or drugs. The 'paradis artificiels' which Baudelaire studied so intently were an object of fascination for many nineteenth-century writers, who saw in them a means of release, if only briefly and illusorily, from the ordinary restrictions of the human condition. Gautier, Baudelaire, Rimbaud, Verlaine, Villiers all experimented with alcohol or hashish, less in the hope of discovering a new form of pleasure than as a way to flee the irremediable drabness of everyday existence. Gautier's *Le Club des hachichins*, Baudelaire's poems on *Le Vin* in *Les Fleurs du mal*, Rimbaud's *Illuminations* are the literary residue of these excursions into hallucination, but their most important consequence was the uncovering of regions of the personality hitherto repressed or hidden, which were now admitted to be a possible source of artistic inspiration. The imagery of Symbolism (and later of Surrealism) owes much to such experiments.

Les Fenêtres, in its amalgam of Baudelairean borrowings, specifically Mallarméan features (such as the reference to 'l'azur' and the involved and elliptical third stanza) and representative indications of contemporary preoccupations, is a rich and powerful evocation of some of the currents of emotion which eddied through literature in the second half of the century. In particular, its pitiless opposition between 'la Beauté' and 'la Bêtise' expresses a dilemma keenly felt by numerous artists in those years: is it the writer's duty to reproduce all the nastiness and flatness of life, as the Realists and Naturalists believed, or ought he not rather to provide a refuge from them by creating in his art a domain in which only the ideal exists, as most of the poets of the 1880s and

1890s maintained? The conflict is a fundamental one, and dominates most of the literary debates of the post-Romantic era, involving as it does questions of the artist's responsibility to society, of the philosophic interpretation of reality, of the nature of religion and of the individual's search for his own happiness. Mallarmé's own solution is unequivocal, despite the fact that, as in the last lines of *Les Fenêtres*, he often seems to despair of its success: it is to flee from everyday reality and to cling to

> toutes les croisées
> D'où l'on tourne l'épaule à la vie.

FURTHER READING

Guy MICHAUD, *Le Message poétique du Symbolisme* (Paris, Nizet; 1947).

R. GRIFFITHS, *The Reactionary Revolution. The Catholic Revival in French Literature 1870–1914* (London, Constable; 1966).

XVIII

Pierre Loti

(1850–1923)

FROM *Ramuntcho*

Pour regarder passer, très loin au-dessous de lui, un char à bœufs, il s'arrêta un instant, pensif. Le bouvier qui menait le lent attelage chantait aussi; par un sentier rocailleux et mauvais, cela descendait dans un ravin baigné d'une ombre déjà nocturne.

Et bientôt cela disparut à un tournant, masqué tout à coup par des arbres, et comme évanoui dans un gouffre. Alors Ramuntcho sentit l'étreinte d'une mélancolie subite, inexpliquée comme la plupart de ses impressions complexes, et, par un geste habituel, tout en reprenant sa marche moins alerte, il ramena en visière, sur ses yeux gris très vifs et très doux, le rebord de son béret de laine.

Pourquoi?... Qu'est-ce que cela pouvait lui faire, ce chariot, ce bouvier chanteur, qu'il ne connaissait même pas?... Évidemment rien... Cependant, de les avoir vus ainsi disparaître pour aller se gîter, comme sans doute chaque nuit, en quelque métairie isolée dans un bas-fond, la compréhension lui était venue, plus exacte, de ces humbles existences de paysans, attachées à la terre et au champ natal, de ces vies humaines aussi dépourvues de joies que celles des bêtes de labour, mais avec des déclins plus prolongés et plus lamentables. Et, en même temps, dans son esprit avait passé l'intuitive inquiétude des *ailleurs*, des mille choses *autres* que l'on peut voir ou faire en ce monde et dont on peut jouir; un chaos de demi-pensées troublantes, de ressouvenirs ataviques et de fantômes venait furtivement de s'indiquer, aux tréfonds de son âme d'enfant sauvage...

C'est qu'il était, lui, Ramuntcho, un mélange de deux races très différentes et de deux êtres que séparait l'un de l'autre, si l'on peut dire, un abîme de plusieurs générations. Créé par la fantaisie triste d'un des raffinés de nos temps de vertige, il avait été inscrit à sa naissance comme « fils de père inconnu » et ne portait d'autre nom que celui de sa mère. Aussi ne se sentait-il pas entièrement pareil à ses compagnons de jeux ou de saines fatigues.

Silencieux pour un moment, il marchait moins vite vers son logis, par les sentiers déserts serpentant sur les hauteurs. En lui, le chaos des choses *autres*, des *ailleurs* lumineux, des splendeurs ou des épouvantes étrangères à sa propre vie, s'agitait confusément, cherchant à se démêler... Mais non, tout cela, qui était l'insaisissable et l'incompréhensible, restait sans lien, sans suite et sans forme, dans des ténèbres...

A la fin, n'y pensant plus, il recommença de chanter sa chanson : elle disait, par couplets monotones, les plaintes d'une fileuse de lin dont l'amant, parti pour une guerre éloignée, tardait à revenir; elle était en cette mysté-rieuse langue euskarienne dont l'âge semble incalculable et dont l'origine demeure inconnue. Et peu à peu, sous l'influence de la mélodie ancienne, du vent et de la solitude, Ramuntcho se retrouva ce qu'il était au début de sa course, un simple montagnard basque de seize à dix-sept ans, formé comme un homme, mais gardant des ignorances et des candeurs de tout petit garçon.

PIERRE LOTI, *Ramuntcho*
(Paris, Calmann Lévy; London, Harrap; 1961), pp. 13–15

Pierre Loti was the pen-name of Julien Viaud, a French naval officer, and it is perhaps because his career took him many times round the world that his novels show such a strong feeling for local variations in speech, customs, character and scenery. Each of them is indissolubly linked with a particular place, in France or abroad, and *Ramuntcho* (1897) depends for its effect on its setting in the mountains of the Basque country, on the Spanish frontier near Hendaye. Ramuntcho, the hero of the novel, is a young Basque peasant, the illegitimate son of an uncultured Basque countrywoman and a *blasé*, intellectual Parisian artist, who had paid only a fleeting visit to that part of the country and then disappeared. It is this mixed ancestry which gives Ramuntcho the dual character to which we are introduced in this passage and which forms one of the novel's main centres of interest.

The psychological traits which Ramuntcho has inherited from his father—'l'intuitive inquiétude des *ailleurs*, des mille choses *autres* que l'on peut voir ou faire en ce monde et dont on peut jouir', 'le chaos des choses *autres*, des *ailleurs* lumineux, des splendeurs ou des épouvantes étrangères à sa propre vie'—are already familiar to us from *Les Fenêtres* (commentary XVII) as characteristics of the *fin de siècle* mentality. Dis-satisfaction with one's surroundings and ultimately with the human condition, vague longings for some rarefied ideal, and accompanying accesses of melancholy are commonplaces of the writing of the 1880s and 1890s, and it is more than likely that Loti was at least in part thinking of himself when he calls Ramuntcho's anonymous father 'un des raffinés de nos temps de vertige' (he had had more than one child by a Basque mistress of humble origins). What is special about the evocation of this state of mind here is its juxtaposition to the other side of Ramuntcho's nature, the side inherited from his mother, which means that at times he is just 'un simple montagnard basque de seize à dix-sept ans'.

The contrast between the over-refined, disillusioned products of urban civilisation and the unsophisticated, healthy children of nature is one which authors often point out in the closing years of the century, a reflection which came as a logical reaction to the attacks on nature so frequently made by post-Romantic writers. Baudelaire had been one of the first to declare his contempt for nature ('la femme est *naturelle*, c'est-à-dire abominable' [1]) and to turn for solace instead to the artificial creations of man; and the cult of art and the artificial had become one of the distinctive features of the poetic movement which originated with *Les Fleurs du mal*. Mallarmé, for instance, complains bitterly that

> Le printemps maladif a chassé tristement
> L'hiver, saison de l'art serein, l'hiver lucide,[2]

and Villiers de l'Isle-Adam is following a similar line of thought when he makes one of the characters in his *L'Ève future* exclaim:

> Adieu donc à la prétendue Réalité, l'antique dupeuse! Je vous offre, moi, de tenter l'ARTIFICIEL et ses incitations nouvelles! [3]

Together with a tendency for poetry to deal with urban subjects (as happens in the works of Baudelaire, Laforgue or Verhaeren, for example) and for emotions to become ever more extraordinary and unnatural (for instance, in the predilection for perversion and eccentricity in the writings of Huysmans, Mirbeau or Remy de Gourmont), this gave rise to a vague if general suspicion that civilisation had led Man to a decadent state in which he had lost touch with the primary realities of life. Sometimes, as with the group of poets who proudly dubbed themselves 'Décadents', this was an openly avowed doctrine; in other cases, it was more like a nostalgic recollection of lost innocence and an admission of irrevocable error. Both attitudes are exemplified

---

[1] *Œuvres complètes (Mon cœur mis à nu)*, p. 1199.
[2] *Œuvres complètes*, p. 34.   [3] *Œuvres complètes*, vol. I, p. 141.

in Huysmans's *A Rebours*, which is a veritable breviary of decadent habits and beliefs.

The shifts in Ramuntcho's moods in this passage correspond to an ambiguity in Loti's own opinions. Clearly, he himself was temperamentally closer to the city-bred artistic mentality, but at the same time he never rid himself of a deep attraction towards the natural, uncomplicated existence of those who earn their living with their hands. For all that he recognises the hardships such a life involves, there is a note of subdued envy in what he says about 'ces humbles existences de paysans, attachées à la terre et au champ natal', about Ramuntcho's 'compagnons de jeux ou de saines fatigues' and about the 'ignorances' and the 'candeurs' which people of that sort preserve. These feelings of course betoken a partial reversion to the cult of nature begun by Rousseau and practised with such enthusiasm by the Romantics. But now there are significant differences. Far from wanting to project his own emotions into nature (as we saw Chateaubriand doing), Loti is attracted by the country in so far as it enables him to forget his own neurotic preoccupations. Moreover, he is much more realistic in his awareness of how peasants really live; without placing the same emphasis on dirt, poverty and promiscuity as does Zola in *La Terre*, he avoids the idyllic misrepresentations which abound in Romantic literature, especially in the works of George Sand.

Perhaps the most notable feature of Loti's treatment of nature is the firmness with which he situates it in a particular corner of France. The mentions of the familiar woollen beret and 'cette mystérieuse langue euskarienne' fix the scene unmistakably in the Basque country, and later in the novel Loti makes great play with local peculiarities such as the game of pelota, the frequency of smuggling, Basque songs and dances and the like. Certain of the Romantics had already evoked with special affection parts of France which had personal associations for them: Chateaubriand and Brittany, Lamartine and Milly, Hugo and La Bièvre, Balzac and Touraine, and above all George Sand, who, despite her tendency to idealise all she saw, had sought in novels like *La Petite Fadette* and *François-le-Champi* to give an exact and detailed picture of her beloved Berry. The regionalism of the latter half of the century, however, though it proceeds from the fact that the Romantics inevitably linked their worship of nature with some particular spot, has as its main concern the preservation of local peculiarities in the teeth of the standardising forces of education, conscription and centralised government. The result is that, from about 1850 onwards, most provinces of France saw some sort of movement designed to give their heritage a lasting literary form. The most influential of such groups was the Félibrige, founded on 21st May 1854 by seven writers, including Mistral, Roumanille and Aubanel, for the defence and glorification of Provençal language and literature. Numerous novelists of the time made a name for themselves by specialising in works about a particular locality: Erckmann-Chatrian with Alsace, Daudet and Paul Arène with Provence, Barbey d'Aurevilly with the Cotentin peninsula, even to some extent Flaubert and Maupassant with Normandy. The growth of specifically national literatures in neighbouring countries meant that foreign novelists who wrote in French followed the same trend, so that there were now strictly localised novels about Switzerland by Toepffer or about Belgium by Camille Lemonnier, Georges Eekhoud and Georges Rodenbach (the most famous example is Rodenbach's *Bruges-la-Morte*).

At the same time there sprang up numerous learned societies which made it their business to collect linguistic or archaeological information about their own regions. The Provençal, Breton and Basque languages became an object of interest to philologists, who had no desire to see them sacrificed to the French of Paris. Local antiquaries grouped together to discover, catalogue and preserve the monuments, relics and manuscripts of the different provinces; it was during the nineteenth century that people settled down to serious researches among the riches of provincial libraries and archaeological sites. Prosper Mérimée, for many years Inspector-General of Historic Monuments, did much on his regular tours through the provinces to bring to light all the unsuspected treasures which were hidden there, and the M. de Peyrehorade whom he depicts in *La Vénus d'Ille* is typical of numerous local enthusiasts in his desire to show off the wealth of his homeland:

> Je ne vous lâche plus, sinon quand vous aurez vu tout ce que nous avons de curieux dans nos montagnes. Il faut que vous appreniez à connaître notre Roussillon, et que vous lui rendiez justice. Vous ne vous doutez pas de tout ce que nous allons vous montrer. Monuments phéniciens, celtiques, romains, arabes, byzantins, vous verrez tout, depuis le cèdre jusqu'à l'hysope. Je vous mènerai partout et ne vous ferai pas grâce d'une brique.[1]

[1] *Romans et nouvelles* (Paris, Pléiade; 1951), p. 443.

A great many of the provincial museums in France date from the same time, and were founded to accommodate the increasing number of discoveries which it was neither possible nor desirable to bring to Paris. The spread of the railway network also did much to make people conscious of the variety of the different provinces. It was in the second half of the nineteenth century that seaside resorts began to be popular for holidays—the number of hotels in Cannes, for example, rose from two in 1856 to twelve in 1863, and this was by no means an exceptional development. By the end of the century more people than ever before were conscious that France was composed of a number of distinct and characteristic regions, and that it was both socially and politically far from expedient to try to iron out the differences between them.

In some cases regionalism even acquired a philosophy of its own. This had been hinted as long ago as 1850 by Nerval, who throughout his life remained profoundly attached to his native Valois, when he wrote in *Angélique*:

> Quoi qu'on puisse dire philosophiquement, nous tenons au sol par bien des liens. On n'emporte pas les cendres de ses pères à la semelle de ses souliers, — et le plus pauvre garde quelque part un souvenir sacré qui lui rappelle ceux qui l'ont aimé. Religion ou philosophie, tout indique à l'homme ce culte éternel des souvenirs.[1]

The love for 'la terre et les morts' which Maurice Barrès inculcated into his admirers fifty years later, with its nationalist and racialist associations, is little more than an extension of Nerval's idea, intellectualised and given a strong political flavour. Barrès's jealous attachment to Lorraine makes him prize local and national virtues far higher than cosmopolitan or universal qualities, as witness *Les Déracinés*, in which he denounces the deleterious effects of centralisation in French education:

> Le Barrois, le pays de la Seille, la région de Longwy, les Vosges donnent à la Lorraine des caractères particuliers qu'il ne faut pas craindre d'exagérer, loin que cette province se doive effacer. Mais l'université méprise ou ignore les réalités les plus aisément tangibles. Ses élèves grandis dans une clôture monacale et dans une vision décharnée des faits officiels et de quelques grands hommes à l'usage du baccalauréat, ne comprennent guère que la race de leur pays existe, que la terre de leur pays est une réalité et que, plus existant, plus réel encore que la terre et la race, l'esprit de chaque petite patrie est pour ses fils instrument d'éducation et de vie.[2]

[1] *Œuvres*, vol. I, p. 213. [2] *Les Déracinés* (Paris, Plon; 1922), vol. I, pp. 36-7.

It is in this way that, about the turn of the century, regionalism even becomes a political force to be reckoned with.

Another aspect of regionalism in literature was likewise anticipated by Nerval: that is the influence on French poetry of the folk-song which enthusiasts began to collect in mid-century. In England, works like Percy's *Reliques*, or in Germany, Herder's *Stimmen der Völker* and Arnim and Brentano's *Des Knaben Wunderhorn*, had long since revealed all the inspiration which could be derived from anonymous folk-poetry, but in France interest for such things was so slow in awakening that as late as 1842 Nerval could end an essay on the *Chansons et légendes du Valois* with the words:

> Il serait à désirer que de bons poètes modernes missent à profit l'inspiration naïve de nos pères, et nous rendissent, comme l'ont fait les poètes d'autres pays, une foule de petits chefs-d'œuvre qui se perdent de jour en jour avec la mémoire et la vie des bonnes gens du temps passé.[1]

Such collections multiplied in the next decades (one of the most famous was made by a distant relative of Chateaubriand, Hersart de la Villemarqué), and post-Parnassian poetry shows, almost for the first time in France, apart from scattered exceptions, that cultivated poets can learn something from the casual, unpretentious simplicity of folk-song. Occasional experiments by Gautier and Banville (often under the title *Lied*, which shows the influence of Heine) were followed by a fuller exploitation of the vein by writers like Tristan Corbière, Verlaine, Rimbaud, Moréas, Laforgue, Kahn and Verhaeren. Symbolism thus becomes the first major poetic movement in France to assimilate the matter and manner of folk-song. It is in this context that one sees the real significance of Loti's sympathetic reference to 'la mélodie ancienne' sung by Ramuntcho.

Elements of this kind, reinforced by a recognition of the impossibility of living permanently in conformity with the tenets of an often exaggerated idealism, combine after 1890 to produce the break-up of the Symbolist movement. Nature, derided and despised by many of the hypersensitive poets of the 1880s, comes into its own again, and writers such as Francis Jammes and the Naturists preach a return to the simple, basic values of the countryside. Others, like Gide and Remy de Gourmont, react against the prejudices formerly current against nature

[1] *Œuvres*, vol. I, p. 308.

by declaring that whatever is in nature must by definition be good and wholesome. Loti does not go so far. Like one or two other authors of his generation, he is torn between what he suspects to be the degenerate pleasures of civilisation and nostalgia for a rougher, more instinctive way of life, without ever being able to opt finally for one or the other. Something of the same hesitation can be felt in Maupassant, who denounces the world as fit for only animals to live in, when in fact he himself found greater satisfaction than most people in purely animal pleasures:

> Contemple-la, cette terre, telle que Dieu l'a donnée à ceux qui l'habitent. N'est-elle pas visiblement et uniquement disposée, plantée et boisée pour des animaux? Qu'y a-t-il pour nous? Rien. Et pour eux, tout : les cavernes, les arbres, les feuillages, les sources, le gîte, la nourriture et la boisson. Aussi les gens difficiles comme moi n'arrivent-ils jamais à s'y trouver bien. Ceux-là seuls qui se rapprochent de la brute sont contents et satisfaits. Mais les autres, les délicats, les rêveurs, les chercheurs, les inquiets? Ah! les pauvres gens![1]

A reaction against sophistication, against a too exclusive devotion to art and abstract ideas, against the artificiality of city life and civilised occupations thus makes itself felt in literature as the century draws to a close. There were many writers who would not only have recognised in themselves the contradictory impulses which Loti attributes to Ramuntcho, but who would have approved—except perhaps for its political overtones—of the more extreme position adopted by Zola at the end of *La Débâcle*, where the death of the decadent Maurice at the hands of the peasant Jean is presented as the symbol of a future regeneration of France:

> C'était la partie saine de la France, la raisonnable, la pondérée, la paysanne, celle qui était restée le plus près de la terre, qui supprimait la partie folle, exaspérée, gâtée par l'Empire, détraquée de rêveries et de jouissances.[2]

---

[1] *L'Inutile Beauté*, in *Contes et Nouvelles* (Paris, Albin Michel; 1956), vol. I, p. 1159.
[2] *La Débâcle*, vol. II, p. 317.

FURTHER READING

A. E. CARTER, *The Idea of Decadence in French Literature* (Toronto, University of Toronto Press; 1958).

CHARLES-BRUN, *Le Régionalisme* (Paris, Bloud; 1911).

K. G. MILLWARD, *L'Œuvre de Pierre Loti et l'esprit fin de siècle* (Paris, Nizet; 1956).

K. W. SWART, *The Sense of Decadence in Nineteenth-Century France* (The Hague, Nijhoff; 1964).

M. DÉCAUDIN, *La Crise des valeurs symbolistes vingt ans de poésie française* (Toulouse, Privat; 1960).

XIX

Paul Verlaine

(1844–96)

Art poétique

De la musique avant toute chose,
Et pour cela préfère l'Impair
Plus vague et plus soluble dans l'air,
Sans rien en lui qui pèse ou qui pose.

Il faut aussi que tu n'ailles point
Choisir tes mots sans quelque méprise :
Rien de plus cher que la chanson grise
Où l'Indécis au Précis se joint.

C'est des beaux yeux derrière des voiles,
C'est le grand jour tremblant de midi,
C'est, par un ciel d'automne attiédi,
Le bleu fouillis des claires étoiles!

Car nous voulons la Nuance encor,
Pas la Couleur, rien que la nuance!
Oh! la nuance seule fiance
Le rêve au rêve et la flûte au cor!

Fuis du plus loin la Pointe assassine,
L'Esprit cruel et le Rire impur,
Qui font pleurer les yeux de l'Azur,
Et tout cet ail de basse cuisine!

Prends l'éloquence et tords-lui son cou!
Tu feras bien, en train d'énergie,
De rendre un peu la Rime assagie.
Si l'on n'y veille, elle ira jusqu'où ?

Ô qui dira les torts de la Rime?
Quel enfant sourd ou quel nègre fou
Nous a forgé ce bijou d'un sou
Qui sonne creux et faux sous la lime?

De la musique encore et toujours!
Que ton vers soit la chose envolée
Qu'on sent qui fuit d'une âme en allée
Vers d'autres cieux à d'autres amours.

Que ton vers soit la bonne aventure
Éparse au vent crispé du matin
Qui va fleurant la menthe et le thym...
Et tout le reste est littérature.

PAUL VERLAINE, *Art poétique*, in *Jadis et naguère*, *Œuvres poétiques complètes*, ed. Y.-G. Le Dantec (Paris, Pléiade; 1948), pp. 206–7

When Paul Verlaine wrote his *Art poétique* in 1874, he was protesting against two traditions firmly rooted in the poetry of the time: the tradition of pictorial description and the tradition of rhetoric. 'De la musique avant toute chose' is, in the first instance, a precept intended to prevent poetry from being either verbal painting or a consciously elaborated, heightened form of prose, both of which things it had tended to be in and before Verlaine's own lifetime.

The connection between poetry and painting had begun to grow close about 1830, when the Romantic predilection for *couleur locale* had necessitated a liberal use of colour in general. The innumerable representations of exotic scenes, beautiful landscapes, strange costumes which help to set the mood of Romantic escapism give rise to a descriptive technique which, with increasing mastery, reproduces the effect of brilliant and variegated painting. In particular, Hugo shows the utmost skill from *Les Orientales* onwards in creating the illusion of something physically visible to the reader. This tendency was reinforced in the later stages of Romanticism both by the insistence of upholders of the doctrine of *l'art pour l'art* that only beautiful forms were worthy of an artist's interest, and by the mid-century scepticism about the existence of anything outside the observable world of shapes and colours. A contemporary observer tells us that around 1840 'la Peinture détrôna la

Poésie',[1] and it is certain that for some thirty years, poetry and painting were more intimately related than ever before or since.

The manifestations of this convergence are multiple. The Bohemian artistic groups of the Romantic and post-Romantic era seem usually to have been compounded of equal proportions of writers and painters. Many of the writers of the time were either painters themselves or else closely associated with painters: Gautier and Fromentin were artists of talent, Hugo, Jules de Goncourt, Mérimée and Baudelaire were distinguished amateurs, the Goncourts, Baudelaire, Zola and Huysmans were all important critics and theorists of painting. Painters figure prominently in the fiction of the period, for instance in Balzac's *Le Chef-d'œuvre inconnu*, Mürger's *Scènes de la vie de Bohème*, the Goncourts' *Manette Salomon* and Zola's *L'Œuvre*. The Parnassians in general, sceptical about Romantic emotionalism, doubtful of the existence of any kind of spiritual ideal, found themselves with few poetic subjects except the evocation of visual beauty (and positivist philosophy), since that alone appeared to offer some guarantee of material reality. As a result the poetry of Leconte de Lisle and Hérédia contains a high proportion of descriptive writing, often of excellent quality. Théophile Gautier, who used to declare himself 'un homme pour qui le monde visible existe', is no doubt the most complete example of a poet using language for the purpose of recreating the sensations experienced before a picture, and Taine had good grounds for saying to him in 1863:

> C'est, je crois, que vous appelez poésie : peindre un clocher, un ciel, faire voir des choses enfin. Pour moi, ce n'est pas de la poésie, c'est de la peinture.[2]

There is a similar tendency in prose fiction, where the growth of Realist doctrines implied the depiction of scenes easily visualised by the reader (as we saw in commentary XV); and if the writer is concerned with stylistic elegance, the depiction often takes the form of a transposition on to an imaginary canvas. Gautier's tales and novels are full of such passages. Here is one in which he openly invites us to consider his description as a painting:

---

[1] Charles Asselineau, *Vie de Baudelaire*, quoted by Louis Hautecœur, *Littérature et Peinture en France* (Paris, Armand Colin; 1942), p. 94.
[2] Edmond and Jules de Goncourt, *Journal*, vol. II, p. 123.

Faites courir un brusque filet de jour sur la corniche et sur le bahut, piquez une paillette sur le ventre des pots d'étain; jaunissez un peu le christ, fouillez plus profondément les plis roides et droits des rideaux de serge, brunissez la pâleur modernement blafarde du vitrage, jetez au fond de la pièce la vieille Barbara armée de son balai, concentrez toute la clarté sur la tête, sur les mains de la jeune fille, et vous aurez une toile flamande du meilleur temps, que Terburg ou Gaspard Netscher ne refuserait pas de signer.[1]

The same method, employed more or less obviously and more or less consciously, can be seen in various formal descriptive passages in Balzac (for example, the artist's studio in *Le Chef-d'œuvre inconnu*), occasionally in Nerval (the palace in the *Histoire de la reine du matin*), in Flaubert (some scenes of *Madame Bovary*), the Goncourts (notably a number of transposed water-colours in *Germinie Lacerteux*) and Alphonse Daudet (whose novels are so constructed as to provide a maximum of descriptive set-pieces, with a minimal narrative framework). It is against this unending flow of description, with its implications of a solid material world devoid of any spiritual background, that Verlaine is reacting when he proclaims:

> ... nous voulons la Nuance encor,
> Pas la Couleur, rien que la nuance!

It is the exact opposite of Gautier's dictum in *L'Art* (1852):

> Peintre, fuis l'aquarelle,
> Et fixe la couleur
>   Trop frêle
> Au four de l'émailleur.[2]

The second *bête noire* which Verlaine attacks is rhetoric—everything which tends to make poetry into an oratorical and intellectual exercise. The Romantics, it is true, had tried to break with the classical concept of rigid formal diction in poetry, and Hugo, in his *Réponse à un acte d'accusation*, had declared:

> Guerre à la rhétorique et paix à la syntaxe![3]

---

[1] *La Toison d'or*, in *Fortunio et autres nouvelles* (Paris, Garnier; 1930), p. 202.
[2] *Émaux et Camées* (Paris, Charpentier et Fasquelle; 1892), p. 225.
[3] *Les Contemplations*, p. 20.

But in reality the Romantic revolution in poetry, if it overthrew the classical idea of an elevated poetic vocabulary, did little to touch the rhetorical basis of verse. It changed the rules, admittedly; the rhetoric became personal, emotive, torrential; but rhetoric it remained. One has only to think of Musset's declamatory tirades:

> Honte à toi, femme à l'œil sombre...,[1]

of the endless rolling phrases and pompous catalogues of Hugo,[2] even of the formal movements in Baudelaire, such as the denunciation of the *Femmes damnées*:

> Descendez, descendez, lamentables victimes,
> Descendez le chemin de l'enfer éternel...[3]

It is this continuing tendency to see poetry as the product of a controlled and codified manipulation of language which Verlaine is setting out to undermine when he says:

> Il faut aussi que tu n'ailles point
> Choisir tes mots sans quelque méprise,

when he proscribes

> la Pointe assassine,
> L'Esprit cruel et le Rire impur,

and when he urges:

> Prends l'éloquence et tords-lui son cou!

His own way of avoiding rhetoric is demonstrated here by the informality of the second person singular imperatives, by the casual omission of verbs, by imprecise turns of phrase ('c'est des beaux yeux derrière des voiles'), by familiar locutions ('tu feras bien, en train d'énergie'), by apparently artless repetitions (the unexpected recurrence of 'de la musique' in the eighth stanza) and by loose grammatical constructions ('si l'on n'y veille, elle ira jusqu'où?'). The result is a note of spontaneity and intimacy characteristic of almost all Verlaine's

---

[1] *Poésies*, p. 331.
[2] See for instance the passage quoted on p. 132.
[3] *Œuvres complètes*, p. 213.

poetry and as far removed as can well be imagined from the grand style
of much Romantic and Parnassian poetry.

It is likewise as a mark of disrespect for Parnassian ideas on poetic
composition as something accomplished in accordance with strict rules
and regulations, that Verlaine departs from the traditional laws of
prosody. If he advises the use of metres with an odd number of syllables
in each line, it is because the standard 'official' metres are mostly
even-numbered, and because the consistent use of, for instance, nine-
syllabled lines (as here) creates an impression of mild irregularity, of a
rhythm slightly syncopated and hence less obtrusive than the too-
familiar beat of the alexandrine. Again, his precepts run deliberately
counter to those of Gautier, who declared:

> Fi du rythme commode,
> Comme un soulier trop grand,
>   Du mode
> Que ton pied quitte ou prend.[1]

In the same way, if he waxes indignant about the exaggerated importance attached to rhyme, it is because Parnassian theory maintains that
strong, resonant rhymes, preferably *rimes riches*, are essential to the
formal beauty of poetry. Here one may suppose that Verlaine is replying
in particular to Théodore de Banville, who had written in his *Petit
Traité de poésie française* (1871) that 'la RIME... est l'unique harmonie des
vers et elle est tout le vers',[2] and that 'dans la Poésie Française, la Rime
est le moyen suprême d'expression et l'*Imagination de la Rime* est le
maître outil'.[3] Verlaine's preference for weak rhymes or even mere asso-
nance helps to prevent his poetry from having the stiff, contrived air of
much Parnassian verse, and it paves the way for the inauguration of the
Symbolist *vers libre*, with its optional rhymes and its indefinite number of
syllables. (Not that Verlaine approved of such revolutionary extremities.
Even Banville envisages the nine-syllabled line of *Art poétique*, with the
caesura after the fourth syllable, as a curious but perfectly legitimate
possibility, and the Symbolists could never induce Verlaine to lend his
name to their audacities.)

But while Verlaine's *Art poétique* is provoked by and directed at some

---

[1] *Émaux et Camées*, p. 223.
[2] *Petit Traité de poésie française* (Paris, Lemerre; 1891), p. 52.
[3] ibid., p. 268.

of the excesses of Parnassianism, it is far from being a purely negative document. 'De la musique avant toute chose' marks a radically new departure in French poetry, and one which was full of consequences for the future: the move from poetry as painting to poetry as music is almost as fundamental as the move from Classicism to Romanticism. Certain of the Romantics and Parnassians had shown an interest in music; it plays a large part in Balzac's *Massimilla Doni* and *Gambara*, in George Sand's *Consuelo* and in Nerval's *Sylvie*, Stendhal wrote lives of Rossini and Mozart, and Gautier was a music critic as well as an art critic. But for most of them the main attraction tended to be opera, where the purely musical experience was diluted by the theatrical element. Even George Sand, whose sensitivity to music was unusually high, reacted to it in such a personal and emotional way that the original aesthetic impression was almost invariably submerged by the waves of feeling which it aroused. It is only with Baudelaire (and possibly with Nerval) that one finds writers appreciating music for its own sake and in its own right, and it is significant that they were among the first people in France to recognise the greatness of Wagner, whose music was to mean so much to two generations of men of letters in France. From Baudelaire's time onwards, there is a growing acknowledgment of the fact that music as an art is far more than just an accompaniment to plays, songs or private musings, that it has its own powerful modes of expression, and that these, in certain respects, may even be superior to those of the other arts.

Verlaine, for instance, has clearly realised that music can never evoke visual impressions with any clarity (even if, for some people, sounds and colours are vaguely associated) and that poetry which creates vivid scenes and sights is always far removed from the condition of music; hence the substitution of nuances for colours. Similarly, however coherent the pattern of a piece of music may be, it can never translate the logical processes of the intellect; hence Verlaine's antipathy for the more intellectual forms of diction. What music can do, because it is non-representational, is to elicit a direct response of the hearer's whole being, without having to enlist incidental auxiliaries from the world around us (like the nominal subject of a painting). So when Verlaine tries to make poetry partake of the essence of music, he is (consciously or unconsciously) aiming at a purer form of art. The same ambition, sharpened by the prestige of Wagner's music and by Schopenhauer's contention that music stood at the top of the hierarchy of the arts, dominated much of the writing and theorising of the Symbolist school ten years after Verlaine's *Art poétique*—so much so that, as Paul Valéry later said,

Ce qui fut baptisé : *Symbolisme* se résume tout simplement dans l'intention commune à plusieurs familles de poètes (d'ailleurs ennemies entre elles) de « reprendre à la musique leur bien ».[1]

Divergences in the interpretation of this ambition were natural and numerous. Some poets followed Verlaine in creating melodious verse in which the logical and intellectual content was reduced to a minimum and in which the outside world was used simply as a means of expressing by analogy the poet's inner world (the first three lines of the last stanza are a good example of this kind of allusive imagery, in which the two terms of the comparison—'le vers' and 'la bonne aventure'—are equated, while the reason for the equation is left unspoken). Others, with Mallarmé chief among them, took a more complex and more abstract view of music as a system of interlocking relationships of sound, on which poetry could superimpose a system of relationships of sense and imagery. A few, led by René Ghil, attempted to construct a theory of 'instrumentism' which postulated rigorous correspondences between instrumental timbres, vowel sounds and colours. Almost all of them would have agreed with Verlaine in shunning clear, direct statement and proceeding instead by allusion, suggestion or symbol. Jules Laforgue is typical of his generation when he says:

Je rêve de la poésie qui ne dise rien, mais soit des bouts de rêverie, sans suite. Quand on veut dire, exposer, démontrer quelque chose, il y a la prose.[2]

There is no doubt that the change of emphasis from pictorial poetry to musical poetry corresponded to a rediscovery of the mysterious inner world of the soul as distinct from the outside world of appearances, which was all that the preceding generation could believe in, and that there was a good deal of truth (if somewhat belatedly) in the remark which Edmond de Goncourt recorded in his diary one Sunday in 1890:

[1] *Variété* (Paris, Nouvelle Revue Française; 1924), p. 97.
[2] *Œuvres complètes* (Paris, Mercure de France; 1925), vol. IV, p. 182.

Daudet dit aujourd'hui très justement que la littérature, après avoir subi l'influence de la peinture pendant ces dernières années, est aujourd'hui en train de subir l'influence de la musique, et de devenir cette chose à la fois sonore et vague, et non articulée qu'est la musique.[1]

Verlaine's *Art poétique* is one of the most significant landmarks in this change and one of the most interesting poetic documents of the second half of the century.

FURTHER READING

Louis HAUTECŒUR, *Littérature et Peinture en France* (Paris, Armand Colin; 1942).
Pierre MARTINO, *Parnasse et Symbolisme* (Paris, Armand Colin; 1925).

---

[1] *Journal*, vol. VIII, pp. 149–50.

XX

Anatole France

(1844–1924)

FROM *L'Anneau d'améthyste*

Le duc de Brécé recevait, ce jour-là, à Brécé, le général Cartier de Chalmot, l'abbé Guitrel et M. Lerond, substitut démissionnaire. Ils avaient visité les écuries, le chenil, la faisanderie et parlé cependant de l'Affaire.

Au déclin tranquille du jour, ils commençaient à traîner le pas sur la grande allée du parc. Devant eux, le château dressait, dans un ciel gris pommelé, sa façade lourde, chargée de frontons et surmontée de toits à l'impériale.

— Je le répète, dit M. de Brécé, l'agitation soulevée autour de cette affaire n'est et ne peut être qu'une manœuvre exécrable des ennemis de la France.

— Et de la religion, ajouta doucement M. l'abbé Guitrel, et de la religion. On ne saurait être un bon Français sans être un bon chrétien. Et nous voyons que le scandale est soulevé principalement par des libres penseurs et des francs-maçons, par des protestants.

— Et des Juifs, reprit M. de Brécé, des Juifs et des Allemands. Et quelle audace inouïe de mettre en question l'arrêt d'un Conseil de guerre! Car enfin il n'est pas admissible que sept officiers français se soient trompés.

— Non, assurément, ce n'est pas admissible, dit M. l'abbé Guitrel.

— En thèse générale, dit M. Lerond, une erreur judiciaire est la chose la plus invraisemblable. Je dirai même que c'est une chose impossible, tant la loi offre de garanties aux accusés. Je le dis aussi pour la justice militaire. Devant les Conseils de guerre, l'accusé, s'il ne rencontre pas toutes les garanties dans les formes un peu sommaires de la procédure, les retrouve dans le caractère des juges. A mon sens, c'est déjà un outrage à l'armée que le doute émis sur la légalité d'un arrêt rendu en Conseil de guerre.

— Vous avez parfaitement raison, dit M. de Brécé. D'ailleurs, peut-on admettre que sept officiers français se soient trompés? Peut-on l'admettre, général?

— Difficilement, répondit le général Cartier de Chalmot. Je l'admettrais, pour ma part, très difficilement.

— Le syndicat de trahison! s'écria M. de Brécé. C'est inouï!

La conversation, alentie, tomba. Le duc et le général virent des faisans dans une clairière et, pris du désir instinctif et profond de tuer, regrettèrent au-dedans d'eux-mêmes de n'avoir pas de fusil.

— Vous possédez les plus belles chasses de toute la région, dit le général au duc de Brécé.

Le duc de Brécé songeait.

— C'est égal, dit-il, les Juifs ne porteront pas bonheur à la France.

ANATOLE FRANCE, *L'Anneau d'améthyste*
(Paris, Calmann-Lévy; 1899), pp. 229–30

The Dreyfus case, which threw French public opinion into a seething turmoil for over five years, began in 1894 when the French counter-espionage services discovered that an unidentified French officer was passing information to the Prussian embassy in Paris. Suspicion very soon fell on a Captain Alfred Dreyfus, for no very good reason except that he was a Jew, and he was arrested and tried *in camera* before a court-martial which convicted him of treason, largely on the basis of evidence which was kept secret from the defence. He was sentenced to life imprisonment and transported to Devil's Island. It was not until 1896 that a new head of the counter-espionage services, Lt.-Col. Picquart, began to have doubts about Dreyfus's guilt and to suspect instead Major Esterhazy, an unprincipled, wild-living man who was deeply in debt. New investigations were started and questions were asked in the French Parliament, with the result that the military authorities, alarmed that their competence should be challenged, removed Picquart from his post. By 1897 some newspapers and politicians had, despite determined opposition, succeeded in creating a movement of opinion favourable to a reopening of the case, and Dreyfus's brother publicly denounced Esterhazy as the spy. Esterhazy himself then asked that he should be tried by court-martial so that he might clear his name. In January 1898 the court, after hearing the evidence in private, acquitted Esterhazy, but two days later Zola published in *L'Aurore* the famous *J'accuse!*, in which he alleged that the Government and various high-ranking officers were engaged in a conspiracy to suppress the truth and perpetuate an injustice. Thereafter events followed events with dramatic speed. A petition for the retrial of Dreyfus was signed by some 3,000 eminent people, leagues for the defence of civil liberties or on the other hand for the preservation of the honour of Army and fatherland were formed, Zola was convicted of libel and went into exile in England, anti-Semitic riots broke out all over France, the Government fell and Picquart was arrested. Then it was discovered that some of the evidence against Dreyfus had been forged by an officer named Henry, who committed suicide, while Esterhazy, the real spy, fled to Belgium. Eventually the Government submitted the case to the Court of Criminal Appeal to see if there were grounds for a retrial; the Court decided there were, and Dreyfus was brought back for a fresh court-martial at Rennes in August 1899. This time the verdict was the illogical but conciliatory one of 'guilty, with extenuating circumstances', after which the Government pardoned Dreyfus and the excitement subsided. It was not until 1906 that the Court of Appeal quashed the Rennes verdict and Dreyfus was finally pronounced innocent.

Until the time when the case became a political issue, Anatole France had not taken a very close interest in public affairs, but his scepticism about authority and his dislike of mob sentiments rapidly led him to join the unpopular party of those who were agitating for a retrial of Dreyfus. *L'Anneau d'améthyste*, the third volume of his satirical tetralogy *Histoire contemporaine*, is composed largely of fragments published as newspaper articles in 1897 and 1898, when the controversy was raging most furiously, and the chapter from which our extract is taken first appeared in November and December 1897, just before Esterhazy's court-martial and Zola's resounding protest. It gives France's sly and critical view of the forces which were combining to maintain the conviction of Dreyfus and ensure that the case should remain for ever closed.

The four participants in the conversation are all Right-wing and Catholic. The host, the duc de Brécé, is a rich, feudally-minded aristocrat, a former Monarchist deputy who could never understand what he was voting for but who made up for his lack of intelligence by the violence of his prejudices. One of his guests, General Cartier de Chalmot, is an elderly officer, full of confused honesty and unswerving loyalty to nebulous ideals, living in a world long past and unable to keep pace with modern life. The 'substitut démissionnaire' Lerond is a lawyer, who had resigned as deputy State prosecuting attorney in protest against the decrees limiting the activities of religious congregations in France, and the abbé Guitrel is a cunning and unscrupulous priest who is intriguing hard to be nominated Bishop of Tourcoing (the amethyst ring of the title is the Bishop's ring which he eventually wins). They are of course agreed in condemning Dreyfus's supporters as enemies of the Church, of the Army and of France. Brécé and Lerond are openly Monarchists, and the powerful, Right-wing legitimist opposition during the first thirty years of the Third Republic had among its main rallying-points the Army, the higher ranks of which still tended to be recruited from the old aristocracy, and the Church, which was in perpetual conflict with the Republic over education, religious Orders and the laicisation of the State. That is one reason why they are so fiercely anti-Dreyfus in their opinions, and it also helps to explain why Dreyfus's supporters thought the case had such far-reaching implications. After the collapse of the Second Empire the balance between a return to the monarchy and a new republic was very narrow indeed, and when the Republic eventually won the day, there hung over it a real and constant threat that the Monarchists, allied with other militant Right-wing groups, would try to overthrow it and set up their own *régime*. The abbé Guitrel, intent on power for himself and the Church, is represented as fanning the flames of his companions' resentment in order to increase their hatred of the anti-clerical forces—Jews, Protestants, freemasons and freethinkers—while the aged general sees simply that the good faith and justice of the Army are being impugned.

France is accurate enough in his depiction of the alignment of the anti-Dreyfusards, as they came to be called. The Monarchist *Action française*, led by Charles Maurras, was one of the most active bodies in trying to frustrate any revision of the Dreyfus trial. The close connections between the Church, the Army and the Monarchists led many Catholics to take a similar view, particularly as atheists like France and Zola were prominent among those pressing for a retrial and were aided by numerous Jews who understandably regarded the case as being above all a piece of anti-Jewish persecution. Anti-Semitism was already a powerful force in France before the Dreyfus case, partly as a result of a long-standing and virulent campaign begun by the journalist Édouard Drumont with his book *La France juive* in 1886, and partly because of the involvement of Jewish financiers in the Panama Canal scandals in 1892, which the Right wing exploited to discredit parliamentary republicanism. In addition, the general desire that the lost provinces of Alsace and Lorraine should eventually be wrested back from Prussia, if

necessary by force, meant that the Army at that time occupied a
position of special privilege and responsibility, and that anything which
might harm its prestige or its efficiency could easily be held to be a form
of treachery. That is why the duke and the general can be so adamant
in affirming that the seven officers who constituted the court at
Dreyfus's first trial could not possibly be mistaken.

Nor has France needed to exaggerate the fanaticism of his opponents'
views: it would indeed have been hard to surpass the violence of some
of the anti-Semitic newspapers. Even the more intelligent anti-
Dreyfusards expressed themselves with rare intemperance about their
adversaries (who gave as good as they got), and most of the arguments
which France here attributes to his fictitious characters can be found
almost word for word in Maurice Barrès's *Scènes et doctrines du
nationalisme*. The confidence in the judgment of the court-martial and
of the ministers who upheld it:

> Jusqu'à preuve du contraire, nous ne croirons pas que six ministres de la
> guerre et trois présidents du Conseil se soient trompés et nous aient
> trompés pendant six ans[1]

(which is exactly the same reason that the prince de Guermantes gives
for having been an anti-Dreyfusard, in Proust's *A la recherche du temps
perdu*:

> Je suis d'une famille de militaires, je ne voulais pas croire que des officiers
> français pussent se tromper.)[2]

The anti-Semitism: 'Que Dreyfus est capable de trahir, je le conclus
de sa race'.[3] The accusation that the Dreyfusards are in the pay of the
enemies of France (the notorious 'syndicate'):

> Les amis de Dreyfus, quelle preuve de la trahison! Et comment les sept
> képis[4] ne paraîtraient-ils pas tristes jusqu'au sombre quand, face à eux, le
> parti de l'étranger les somme de livrer à la politique des Juifs les chefs
> nationaux.[5]

[1] *Scènes et doctrines du nationalisme* (Paris, Juven; 1925), pp. 129–30.
[2] *A la recherche du temps perdu* (Paris, Pléiade; 1959), vol. II, p. 709.
[3] *Scènes et doctrines du nationalisme*, p. 152.
[4] The members of the court at the Rennes retrial.
[5] *Scènes et doctrines du nationalisme*, p. 160.

(This is again a view held by one of the fiercer anti-Dreyfusards in Proust's novel, M. de Cambremer, who

> considérait l'affaire Dreyfus comme une machine étrangère destinée à détruire le Service des Renseignements, à briser la discipline, à affaiblir l'armée, à diviser les Français, à préparer l'invasion.)[1]

The attacks on Protestants: '... des idées vaguement protestantes et quasi mystiques, où se refèrent les Dreyfusards'.[2]

But the nature of France's satire is just as revealing of the basic motives of the Dreyfusards. The *Histoire contemporaine* was begun before the Dreyfus case broke, and the characters in *L'Anneau d'améthyste* are the same as those in the two earlier volumes, so that the objects of France's sarcasm are singled out by old grievances rather than new events. But so telling are the events that the case becomes a powerful new stick with which to beat them and a new proof of how much they deserve the beating. In *Le Mannequin d'osier* the Church had been copiously ridiculed, the Army, in the person of the incompetent and old-fashioned Cartier de Chalmot, had been mocked, the aristocracy had been depicted as reactionary and dictatorial. France, himself one of the 'libres penseurs' whom the abbé Guitrel equates with the 'ennemis de la France', held strong anti-clerical opinions, and, like certain other supporters of Dreyfus, was inclined to see in the case a clerico-military plot, animated by anti-Semitism and designed to suppress independent opposition to Right-wing machinations. Zola is more open in his allegations in *J'accuse!*, where the Chief of the General Staff is said to have 'cédé à sa passion cléricale',[3] where the other generals are deemed to be equally liable to 'céder aux passions religieuses du milieu',[4] and where Dreyfus is described as the victim 'du milieu clérical où il se trouvait, de la chasse aux « sales juifs » qui déshonore notre époque'.[5] So one can see from France's chosen points of attack not only what lay behind the opposition to a reopening of the Dreyfus case, but also some of the half-hidden intentions, apart from the righting of an individual miscarriage of justice, which caused the Dreyfusards to attach such significance to the affair.

---

[1] *A la recherche du temps perdu*, vol. III, p. 235.
[2] *Scènes et doctrines du nationalisme*, p. 192.
[3] *La Vérité en marche* (Paris, Charpentier; 1901), p. 76.
[4] ibid., p. 78.
[5] ibid., p. 80.

What makes this passage so effective as propaganda is the consummate art with which France insinuates his points: the caricature is almost imperceptible, but a tiny change of perspective suffices to ridicule the whole opposition case. The setting of the ancient castle, the peaceful summer day, the atmosphere of leisured ease, the scrupulous politeness with which the characters are referred to, create an impression of remoteness from the contingencies of everyday life in which the brutal denunciations of the duke and his friends appear gratuitous, incongruous and slightly mad. Brécé, the most savage and most stupid among the four, speaks only in thunderous and dogmatic platitudes, and is incapable of altering his train of thought to take account of the subtler interruptions by Lerond and Guitrel; he just goes on repeating his assertions that seven officers cannot be wrong, and that the Jews will do France no good. The general, not very sure of what is going on, does no more than agree hastily when he is pressed for a contribution to the conversation, but the priest and the lawyer, more intelligent and more devious, encourage the duke in his fanaticism. Guitrel is too wily to commit himself completely (the adverb 'doucement' typifies his manner), but he seizes the chance to denigrate the opponents of the Church and quietly lends the duke the support of his spiritual authority (which no doubt accurately represents France's view of the role played by the Church in the affair). As for Lerond, his pompous circumlocutions inadvertently concede the case for a retrial when he talks of 'les formes un peu sommaires de la procédure'—one of the main Dreyfusard arguments was that the original conviction of Dreyfus was illegal because of the irregular way in which the court-martial had been conducted. Then Brécé repeats one of the favourite charges of the anti-Dreyfusards: that the whole of the agitation to reopen the case has been fomented by massive bribery and corruption from an obscure and sinister 'syndicat de trahison'; but the very fact that the duke simply utters the phrase parrot-fashion indicates how superficial the explanation is. Even more telling is the conclusion of the passage. The four friends, tiring of their discussion, are distracted by the flight of some pheasants, the general compliments the duke on the game on his estates, and the duke, whose mind has continued to work along its one track, abuses the Jews yet again. It is the unspoken connection between the 'désir instinctif et profond de tuer' nominally aroused by the pheasants and the duke's rabid hatred of Jews which reveals the irrational, senseless nature of anti-Semitism and which betrays the virulence of the passions lurking beneath the surface elegance of the conversation.

France's comments on the Dreyfus case in *L'Anneau d'améthyste* and in *M. Bergeret à Paris*, the concluding volume of the *Histoire contemporaine*, are combative and polemical. He was writing while the case was still a burning issue and he wished to throw his own strong views into the balance of public opinion. But passages like the one we have been considering are more than brilliant propaganda; they also serve to lay bare the reasons which made the Dreyfus case the occasion of such a profound cleavage in attitudes, ideas and emotions. On the one side there is an ideal of justice to the individual, mistrust of the influence of the Church, dislike of the establishment of birth and breeding, opposition to jingoism and militarism, and suspicion of Monarchist intrigues —views variously expressed in the works of writers like France himself, Émile Zola, Marcel Proust, Charles Péguy and Roger Martin du Gard. On the other side there is a certain conception of patriotism, a desire to maintain the principles of tradition and authority, loyalty to a class or a caste, an avowed or latent anti-Semitism and a fear that irresponsible agitation over what was at most an isolated injustice might weaken the whole nation in the face of Prussia. This is the line taken by people like Maurice Barrès, Charles Maurras, Jules Lemaître and Émile Faguet. The delicate but incisive mockery of the duc de Brécé and his friends helps one to understand why the Dreyfus case assumed such enormous proportions in the minds of a whole generation.

FURTHER READING

Guy CHAPMAN, *The Dreyfus Case* (London, Rupert Hart-Davis; 1955).

Cécile DELHORBE, *Les Écrivains et l'Affaire Dreyfus* (Neuchâtel and Paris, Attinger; 1932).

CHRONOLOGICAL TABLE

	EVENTS	LITERATURE
1802	Promulgation of Concordat	Chateaubriand: *Le Génie du christianisme*
1803	Bonaparte made Consul for life	
	Resumption of war with England	
1804	Napoleon proclaimed Emperor	
1805	Battles of Trafalgar and Austerlitz	
1807		Mme de Staël: *Corinne*
1810		Mme de Staël: *De l'Allemagne*
1812	Retreat from Moscow	
1814	Abdication of Napoleon	
	Restoration of Bourbons; Louis XVIII	
1815	Return of Napoleon	
	Waterloo	
1820		Lamartine: *Méditations poétiques*
1821	Death of Napoleon	
1823	War in Spain	Stendhal: *Racine et Shakespeare*
1824	Accession of Charles X	
1827		Hugo: *Préface de Cromwell*
1830	July Revolution	Hugo: *Hernani*
	Accession of Louis-Philippe	
1831		Stendhal: *Le Rouge et le Noir*
		Hugo: *Notre-Dame de Paris*
		Dumas: *Antony*
1834	Workers' riots in Paris and Lyons	Lamennais: *Paroles d'un croyant*
		Balzac: *Le Père Goriot*
		Vigny: *Chatterton*
1836		Musset: *La Confession d'un enfant du siècle*
1839		Blanc: *L'Organisation du travail*
1840	Return of Napoleon's ashes	Proudhon: *Qu'est-ce que la propriété?*
1842		Comte: *Cours de philosophie positive*
1845		Sand: *Le Meunier d'Angibault*
1847	Campaign of banquets against Guizot	
1848	February Revolution	Renan: *L'Avenir de la science* (not published until 1890)
	Abdication of Louis-Philippe	
	Election of Louis-Napoleon as President (December)	
1851	*Coup d'état*	
1852	Second Empire proclaimed	Gautier: *Émaux et Camées*
		Leconte de Lisle: *Poèmes antiques*
1854–5	Crimean War	Lévi: *Dogme de la haute magie*
1856		Hugo: *Les Contemplations*

EVENTS	LITERATURE
1857	Baudelaire: *Les Fleurs du mal*
	Flaubert: *Madame Bovary*
1859 War in Italy	
1860 Expedition to Syria	
1861	E. and J. de Goncourt: *Sœur Philomène*
1862	Hugo: *Les Misérables*
	Leconte de Lisle: *Poèmes barbares*
1863	Renan: *Vie de Jésus*
	Taine: *Histoire de la littérature anglaise*
1864	Fustel de Coulanges: *La Cité antique*
1865	Bernard: *Introduction à l'étude de la médecine expérimentale*
	Meilhac and Halévy: *La Belle Hélène*
1867	Taine: *Vie et opinions de M. Frédéric Thomas Graindorge*
1869 Liberalisation of Empire	Flaubert: *L'Éducation sentimentale*
1870 Franco-Prussian War	Taine: *De l'Intelligence*
1871 Armistice (January)	
Commune in Paris (March-May)	
1873 End of German occupation	
1874	Barbey d'Aurevilly: *Les Diaboliques*
	Verlaine: *Romances sans paroles*
1875 Constitution of Third Republic	
1877	Zola: *L'Assommoir*
	Daudet: *Le Nabab*
1880	Zola: *Le Roman expérimental*
1883	Renan: *Souvenirs d'enfance et de jeunesse*
1884	Huysmans: *A Rebours*
1885	Villiers de l'Isle-Adam: *Axël*
1889 Right-wing campaign in favour of General Boulanger	Bourget: *Le Disciple*
	Bergson: *Essai sur les données immédiates de la conscience*
1891	Huysmans: *Là-bas*
1892 Panama scandal	
1894 Dreyfus convicted	
1896	Zola: *La Débâcle*
	Barrès: *Les Déracinés*
1899 Dreyfus retried at Rennes	France: *L'Anneau d'améthyste*

Index